Stand-Up Stories

*Tales from Behind the Microphone During
Comedy's Golden Age*

Mike Vance

Stand-Up Stories

Library of Congress Cataloging-in-Publication Data

Names: Vance, Mike, 1959 – author
Title: Stand-Up Stories: Tales from Behind the Microphone During Comedy's
Golden Age
Identifiers: LCCN pending
ISBN 979-8-9879432-0-5 (hardback)
ISBN 979-8-9879432-1-2 (paperback)
ISBN 979-8-9879432-2-9 (ebook)
Subjects: LCSH: Performing Arts – Stand-Up Comedy

Printed in the United States of America

Contents

Contents

Dedicated to all the now ancient men and women who braved Friday night late show crowds and padded bar tabs, debased themselves in after hours clubs, lived on a diet of fast food and slept on highly questionable comedy condo sheets inexpertly fitted onto returned rental furniture – all to bring laughter to the deepest recesses of uncharted America.

Introduction

It's hard to fathom the magic of the stand-up comedy scene in the 1980s. The funniest young people in America were all getting in on the ground floor of a boom industry, working in great showrooms and horrid hovels to bring jokes to every corner of the country. Perhaps two to three hundred people were blessed with the talent, persistence and thick skin to make a living at it for over a decade. We were doing something special, and we were drawn to one another in what we failed to grasp in the moment would become a lifelong bond.

Repeated studies show that many people's biggest fear is speaking in front of a group of strangers. Now, imagine that those strangers, a few hundred of them, paid good money to hear you, and they are expecting you, on stage alone, to deliver a full house laugh every 15 seconds. Those who met that challenge very well, night after night, quickly developed a respect for each other. Working on the road, your fellow comedians were usually the only people you knew in the entire town. You performed, ate, drank and lived with each other. You traveled together between cities. They became your comedy brothers and sisters, sometimes close, and sometimes grudgingly accepted.

The first clubs devoted solely to stand-up comedy surfaced on the coasts in the late 1970s, and at the start of the next decade, fewer than a half dozen cities had full time clubs. Then, within two years, things exploded. The 1980s comedy boom was a time unlike anything since. Every city wanted a club, and people sometimes drove 100 miles or more to see the kind of stand-up in person that had previously only been available on the late night talk shows. It didn't even matter if they'd heard of the acts on stage or not.

Those first club owners very often cared deeply about the shows. Many of the owners, managers and booking agents became friends with the comedians who worked for them and made them money, and for a while, many of us were doing pretty well. Boy, did the comedy business get over that.

The local fame, for lack of a better word, of the comedians in a town that just opened its first comedy club is tough to imagine through the lens of today. By about 1983, comedy clubs were the rage nationwide. We were making appearances on all the local radio morning shows, and even some local TV. The best clubs were packed to the gills no matter who was headlining, and the audience was actually paying for tickets. They had a stake in the game, unlike the papered rooms that followed. Most of us even have stories about getting free merchandise at the local mall by promising to leave a store manager's name at the door. In the small pond where we played each week, whether Lubbock, Lexington or Laramie, we were genuine stars, if only in a generic sense.

Please understand. The vast majority of us never had any national notoriety at all. My longtime comedy pal Fred Greenlee suggested a good title for this book would be *Before We Were Nobody*. He's exactly right. It was the idea that you were "the comedian" that mattered. I lost count of how many times someone gushed at me about a TV appearance I never did. You learned that it was easier to thank them and walk away than correct and embarrass them.

Though there were certainly exceptions, the comedians of that era were mostly guys and gals in their 20s, and we were on top of the world. We also thought ourselves to be bulletproof, even more so than most 20-somethings. I've seen a comic fall off a table where he was dancing and another comic stitch his cut right there in the bar. I've seen a comic try to single-handedly steal a 600-pound wooden airplane from the roof of a travel agency. I've had a drunken sword fight, with real sabers, up and down a staircase while shouting lines from Errol Flynn movies. We would do most anything simply to make the people we considered our peers laugh. Good judgment away from the stage was rarely a thing among comedians of that era.

For many of these stories that follow, I was there, observing, if not actively taking part. The rest I heard straight from the horses' mouths. For all the young whippersnappers reading this book, I'll remind you that this entire time period took place before cell phones and personal computers, and in a few cases, that fact impacts the story. Barely removed from tin cans and string, we were reliant on pay phones, answering services and weird little devices that sent beeps into the receiver. That was cutting edge technology.

Today, thirty plus years removed from the 1980s, too many of the people in these stories are gone. Those who remain are wiser and older, fatter and slower. Dozens of the folks you'll meet within these pages now have decades of sobriety under their belts. In a handful of cases, some even maintain a veneer of respectability. I've taken the liberty of changing or omitting a handful of names to save those involved in those stories from any uncomfortable tap dancing around the kitchen table. If anyone does take offense, let me remind you that we were all very young, single and largely rendered stupid by our newfound, though likely fleeting, celebrity status. Plus, I can assure you that there are another three volumes worth of unused stories that struck me as only funny to irreverent comedians.

I've sprinkled in a little bit of explanation and backstory about the comedy business in those heady days of our misspent youths. Mostly, I hope the reader will get some laughs out of these sometimes bawdy tales because that is the sole purpose of the book. If they don't, it's their loss.

Forty years later the comics who made a living on the stages of the 80s still find no greater moments of laughter than when we are bullshitting with our peers from those days. The friendships are forever strong. Man, did we have fun.

Chapter One

The Beginning:
The Best Comedy Club in History

I followed Madame Cluck-Cluck; a middle-aged woman who made chicken noises to her grown son's piano accompaniment of Never on Sunday. Bawk bawk bawk bawk ba ba baawwwwk...

She was on first, I was on second. The first night of stand-up comedy ever held at the semi-famous Comedy Workshop in Houston, Texas. The club that would later be the starting point for comedians like Sam Kinison, Bill Hicks, Janeane Garafalo, Thea Vidale, and Brett Butler just to name a few. Others like Cheryl Holiday, T. Sean Shannon, Rushion McDonald, Dan Barton, Fred Greenlee and a dozen more went on to successful Hollywood careers in writing and producing. A few of us Workshop folks are still doing stand-up, either full time or when the opportunity suits. Comix Annex vets, the

Annex being the small room dedicated exclusively to stand-up a couple years later, had a crazy good reputation for over a decade. And it started with a woman making chicken noises. Go figure.

The Comedy Store, the Improv, Catch a Rising Star – those were the famous clubs where every top comedian wanted to showcase their act. What separated Houston's Comedy Workshop from those big West and East Coast comedy clubs of the era was simple: stage time. The tiny joint was packed for every single show, and once you became a regular, you could get ten or more minutes a night, seven nights a week. With other comics pressuring you to write new material, it was the best place to develop and improve an act that there ever was. Multiple comics like Andy Huggins and Joey Gaynor moved from Los Angeles to Houston in order to become Workshop regulars. They wanted to be able to get that 15 minutes seven nights a week. Other acts moved from Boston, Georgia, Austin, Tulsa, you name it. Famous touring acts stopped in after their shows at Houston theatres because of the club's reputation. It was the place to be.

Not only was I was on stage the very first stand-up comedy night in that building in February of 1977, I was also about the last guy to perform on stage when they shut the doors for the last time in January of 1990. I did literally thousands of sets in between. When I was not on the road, I was at the Workshop Annex. The place produced some famous comics, a few other people who were every bit as funny but never "made it", and it witnessed the proverbial butt-loads who weren't funny at all. The regulars around the joint have got to be one of the best bunch of characters ever studied. As big a fan of the Algonquin Roundtable as I am, the banter that flew at the Comedy Workshop on some nights was funnier than anything that Dorothy Parker and Alec Wolcott ever dreamt of saying.

· · ·

Just after the first of the year in 1977, when I was home from college in Austin for a weekend, the phone at my folks' house rang.

"Mike Vance? This is Lucien Cullen. I manage the Comedy Workshop."

Now, I had been doing some stand-up gigs around Houston and Austin. Mostly opening for bands and being the special guest occasionally at some disco. Easily the biggest one up to that moment had been opening for Kinky Friedman, a Houston native and Austin favorite who was then working without his band, the Texas Jewboys. Of course, these days people know Kinky as a big-time mystery writer and Texas gubernatorial candidate. But back then, I got paid a rich thirty-five dollars for three shows stretched over two nights. And I was glad to get it.

Meeting Kinky was a treat, though. The promoter took me back into his less than palatial dressing room at this big converted turn-of-the-century Polish club dance hall to introduce me. Having the star's dressing room at Fitzgerald's meant that you sat in the big storage area and looked at fewer mop buckets. Without getting up, Kinky extended the limp, finger-only handshake. Man, what a letdown. My first big star, and he's giving me this piece of shit Hollywood handshake?

Then he looked up at me and said, "Sorry, I didn't know whether to shake hands or lick the salt first. Tequila shot?"

Now that's how a music star should behave.

Like I said, the Kinkster is famous for other stuff now. I ran into him not long ago, and he said that he was enjoying writing and the monetary accompaniment. Back when he was a musician full-time, though, he managed to arrange one of the best brushes with celebrity that I ever had. And he did it all without his knowledge.

Kinky had a regular Sunday night gig every week at the Lone Star Café on Washington Square in New York City. After I opened for him the second time, he told me to drop by any Sunday I happened to be in New York. It just so happened that I made my first trip to New York City in 1978, and that was a treat in itself. A word of explanation.

Another pre-Workshop Houston comic, Steve Epstein, is to the best of my knowledge, the only person to have ever been both Ronald McDonald and the Burger King. Not the national one, mind you, just a regional clown. He would make appearances at the fast food stores and entertain adults and children. Often in ways that the owners had not envisioned.

Once a kid came up to him at Mickey D's and said, "My daddy says you're not really Ronald."

And Eppy answered, "Well, he's not really your daddy."

I'm pretty sure that marked the end of his Ronald gig.

But I digress more than normal. Epstein landed the coveted Burger King job and had to go to Burger King school, no shit, in Westbury, Long Island. He cut some great deal for a free hotel room, and I went with him, along with another comic, a woman named Randy Goodman. It was a cheap trip to the big Apple, and my first time there as an adult.

The best part perhaps was that every day we were there, a large collection of allegedly grown men was down the hall in a banquet room wearing cheap red beards, cheaper cologne and gold plastic crowns, practicing magic tricks, and singing, "I'm the magical mystical Burger King. I can do most anything!" It's a memory that, try as I might, will never be erased.

Naturally when Sunday afternoon rolled around, I took a train into the city, all by myself, and headed for the Lone Star Café. When I got to the door, I was told it was sold out, and that Kinky was not there anyway. Delbert McClinton was performing instead. This was unacceptable. Though I was only 19 years-old, I took the tried-and-true act-like-you-know-what-you're-doing approach. And I apparently managed to do a pretty convincing job because by the time I had finished explaining how Kinky and I were so close, I was sitting in the VIP balcony, free of charge, with Bette Midler, Neil Young,

John Belushi and a group of guys who had just finished shooting a yet-to-be-released movie called Animal House. I even got to have shot of tequila with the National Lampoon guys. I bought one for me and their whole table only to watch these Northern pansies try to sip theirs. Amateurs. Later, I accidentally walked into an unused kitchen in my search for the men's room and found Belushi and a friend laying out a highway stripe-sized line of cocaine. Still bent over the stainless steel table, they looked up.

"Not the bathroom, I'm guessing," I said.

They shook their heads and inclined toward the blow again.

A full evening of entertainment.

Anyway, back to 1977. I had this Lucien guy that I'd never heard of on the phone telling me that I had signed up for some stand-up night. I kept trying to tell him that I had never heard of his workshop and that I got paid to perform. I wasn't paying to take classes.

Finally, he explained that Workshop was just a name, and that a Rex Meredith had put my name down. Rex was a high school buddy of mine who had booked me on a few gigs. He was a singer, and he had started getting me some sets at places his band played. Rex was a terrific volunteer agent. In the age of disco, more than one venue was some glitter ball club where they stopped the records while I did fifteen minutes on the dance floor. And believe me, no one wants to listen to stand-up less than some half-drunk guy in an unbuttoned Quiana shirt who thinks he may be on the verge of getting laid. He wants the woman looking directly at his stick-on chest hair.

The Comedy Workshop had been doing original cabaret theatre and improvisation in Houston since December of 1976. By the next February, they had decided to do stand-up comedy on their dark nights of Monday and Tuesday. At the trial run that February, there were four of us. I drew the number two spot out of a smelly old prop hat.

. . .

My act seemed to go over well with the 30 or so people there. I was followed by the afore-mentioned Steve Epstein, a man who may be the most off-the-wall person I have ever met. He had also been doing stand-up around town. We were about the only two comics in Houston getting paid at that time. There was a guy named Dean Goss who owned his own dinner theatre and did stand-up before the shows started. We later worked that place for a few years.

Eppy had moved to Houston from Long Island when he was still in elementary school, but the New York accent remained. It is as strong today as it ever was even though he hasn't lived in New York since the 60's. To be precise, the accent is half Chico Marx most of the time. Eppy told me that in college, he also had an occasional helping of Amos and Andy. Even then, when he would figure out that he had just done something stupid, which was often, he would give a nice, slow, Chicoesque "Heeeeey, suuuuuure."

The last act was Lawrence Greenblatt, a very thin, distance runner/accountant-looking individual at the time. For a while, he appeared occasionally on the Howard Stern show, and for years afterwards, he was found on Melrose Avenue in L.A. holding some sort of wacky sign. When the verdict of the O.J. civil trial was announced, I saw Greenblatt strolling around in the background getting camera time.

Larry, who insisted on being called Lawrence then, did some schtick with carrots. Alan King and George Burns used a cigar for timing, so, since he was health conscience, he would eat carrots. Tell a joke, take a bite of carrot. Funniest thing he ever did, and he had dropped it from the act by the next week. Remembering to buy carrots was too large a burden.

Larry Greenblatt could hold his own as a source of stories. I recall a story that one time, he met this girl, a totally hot one. Way out of his dating league. In trying to pick her up, he apparently told her that he was a gourmet chef and would just love to cook lunch for her some-day. "Someday" arrived, but Larry had forgotten. About noon one day, he was awakened by this pretty girl banging on his apartment door, expecting her fancy French meal. A pillow-creased Greenblatt let her in, slapped together a peanut butter sandwich, set the plate down and said, "All right. Eat it and get out." Such a charmer.

Another time he bought a used Buick or Olds convertible. About a 1968 or so. He showed all of us at the club. Not a bad looking car. Larry left a good twenty minutes before I did that night. I finally took off for a downtown bar called La Carafe, and about a half mile down the street from the Workshop was Greenblatt's car stopped with the top stuck straight up in the air. He had tried to open the motorized top while he was cruising along about 35 or 40. It looked like a General Motors sailboat. I pulled up and asked if he needed any help.

"NO! Just go on."

I was only seventeen when the Workshop opened. Legal drinking age in Texas was eighteen back then, so I did what anyone else would do. I lied about my age. I turned eighteen shortly after that, but I kept lying about that for three or four years afterwards, just because I felt so foolish. Epstein was the one who called me on it years later.

"Sure, didn't you turn 23 last year, too?"

A few weeks after that first night, an even younger guy showed up. Two of them to be exact, Dwight and Bill, a comedy team from Stratford High School. Bill was Bill Hicks, who at the time was not quite sixteen. If I recall, they had to get a ride with someone to come perform. Bill was a shy kid then who didn't drink and had never remotely thought about doing drugs. Needless to say, he eventually got past that all that reticence. Not to brag, but I believe I hold the distinction of buying him his very first beer about two years later.

Hicks, of course, ended up doing a solo act and becoming internationally popular. But for a few years after he started showing up at the Workshop, Bill was cutting his own hair. I shit you not. He would show up with random chunks of hair missing just to make a joke about it on stage.

Bill's act in those first days was mostly painful musings of a high school kid with flashes of the hysterical, and he, like the rest of the top Workshop guys, learned quickly. In many ways, Hicks a year or two in was more purely funny than the social commentary he later relied on. A key portion of the act was him doing an impression of his dad, and he lived in mortal fear that his parents, who didn't even always know that he out doing stand-up in a night club, would show up in the audience. After Bill died sixteen years later, his mom became the most fierce guardian of his comedy persona.

Another of the very early guys within that first year was Bill Hinds, who draws the comic strips Tank McNamara and Cleats. Even though he usually did very well, Bill used to get wildly nervous about going onstage, which is a good guess as to why he stopped doing stand-up after a short time. But one night he had a classic ad-lib. At least I like to think it was an ad-lib, and he never repeated it. A joke had gotten a nice laugh. After it quieted, he said, "My hand is shaking I'm so nervous." Then he slipped it into his front pocket. "Well, I might as well put it to good use."

Robert Barber was there the second week they had stand-ups. He currently goes by Riley Barber, but he has been through O'Reilly Barber, O'Reilly Barbour, and God knows what else. He decided that he would change the name because people called him Bob Barker after the Price as Right host. Which would be irritating, don't get me wrong. But I met him as Bob, so that's what he remains in my mind.

Though I do introduce him as Riley to new folks. That name came from the mean street he grew up on in West U. Personally, I think he kept changing his name so often back then just so he could get a phone after the last one got cut off for non-payment. I can't recall which of our friends did it, but for a full year you found him in the directory under Kilgore Trout.

Another buddy of ours was working a club one time and asked the owner about some of the acts that had been there before. So, the guy starts walking down the back wall, pointing at all the framed headshots and giving a running commentary. This guy was great, this guy sucked, etc. When he got to a picture that said Riley Barber under it, the club owner said, "This guy was awful. One of the worst acts we ever had in here. A real pain in the ass." My friend held his tongue. The owner kept walking and about three frames down got to another picture of Barber, only this one's caption read O'Reilly Barbour. "Now this guy was really funny."

Barber loved being Irish. Who knows why? He is about 6'5" and, best we can tell, has no ankles. From the early days of the club, he developed the reputation for inadvertently knocking things over and breaking them because he didn't realize his own size and strength. He crossed his legs in Ron Crick's '54 Ford and kicked the car into reverse while driving down the freeway. He sat down in a club owner's boat in Florida and broke the seat. He murdered a tape player at Epstein's apartment. It became a running joke for the rest of us.

Once many years later, a bunch of us were hoisting a Christmas toast and Barber single handedly started a chain reaction of injury by accidentally elbowing Hicks or Andy Huggins in the eye. It started drinks falling like a Tik Tok dominoes video gone bad. The toast went something like," No man is poor who has friends. Goddammit, Barber!"

· · ·

Bill Silva was one of the other comics who stayed from that first year. Back then, Bill was working some sort of computer job and used to come to shows in a suit and tie. A cheap grey polyester suit and tie. He described himself as looking like the love child of Woody Allen and Yoda. Not far off, I suppose. Silva later became assistant manager at the club, and then worked as manager At Don Learned's Laff Spot comedy club after the Workshop closed.

Silva had been a computer programmer who quit his job to do comedy. He showed up in a suit, something that was not the norm at the Workshop. The only other guy who regularly wore business attire on stage was a middle-ager named O'Brien Stevens who opened his show with a threatening growl of "Let's hear it for the suit" in a tone that strongly suggested he'd be kicking your ass if you failed to applaud. I only figured out years later that his dad had been the local district attorney. Stevens, not funny, did not stay long.

Bill Silva did. He rather quickly started to show good skills as an emcee, so very frequently got booked in that role. Unlike most of the rest of us, he didn't seem to mind it too much, either.

From the start, we were a sociable and drinking crowd. After almost every show, a group of us would go hang somewhere. The most popular after show hangout back in those first years was a little bar on Market Square downtown called La Carafe. It is in a narrow building that happens to be the oldest commercial structure in Houston still on its original site. Silva, Epstein, another comic, Jimmy Pineapple, and I all ended up bartending there a few years later. Comics bartending. Big mistake. Although I must say we showed remarkable restraint in giving away only as much free beer as we did. On most nights, the customers still outdrank us by a slim margin. Other nights, oh well.

Just comics drinking could be a big mistake, or a series of big, but fun, mistakes. The Comedy Workshop's owner, Paul Menzel, bless him, liked a good drink of Dewar's himself. From very early on, we had employee prices. Which amounted to any drink for a buck. Plus, as often as not, manager or bartender willing, the employees "worked" late and drank until we were so inclined to leave. Some nights we inclined all the way up until sunrise and then went to breakfast. Lots of business folks stopping for a bite on their way to work were impressed with our social skills after we'd been drinking till the sun came up, I'm sure.

Ambus Braxton wasn't quite there at the beginning, but he came along pretty soon thereafter. He was the perfect bartender for the Comedy Workshop. Ambus was about 5'8" and sported a goatee for many years. He loved playing the angry Black man. Reality though is that Ambus was about the nicest guy walking. We all loved the guy. He had a great sense of humor, which is important for comics. And he could give a nice evil eye to those ingrates that stepped out of line. A nightly occurrence that. Oh yeah, and stay out of the waitress station.

Ambus stayed until the last light got put out, or auctioned off, in 1990. It was during his tenure that Mystery Bottle came to be. The bar at the Annex had a three-tiered rack of liquor bottles behind it. During one of those post-closing time soirees, someone came up with the plan to turn out the lights and spin a non-bartender around a few times behind the bar. Then you pointed them to the rack of liquor and, while the rest of us chanted "Mystery bottle. Mystery bottle", he put his hands on two bottles. Those two were mixed together and everyone took a shot. Sometimes we got a new taste treat. Sometimes we got banana rum and scotch.

The rules, written and unwritten, for the comics were the strictest of any club I ever heard about. There was no stealing. If you stole material, from within or anywhere else, you were tossed. The first offense usually cost you two weeks of not being allowed in the club. Since a budding comic had a pathological desire to be on stage, that was meaningful. Eventually you got a permanent ban. The pressure to write new and funny material made most everybody better. There were some damn funny bits going around back then. Since the place closed, I can guarantee you that most of us haven't worked nearly as hard on material. There is no impetus like pressure to make your peers laugh.

Man, oh man were there some unfunny guys, too. I have no idea the names of some of these schmos. And let me be the first to admit that we could be bitterly cruel to some of these people. You didn't want to come around with an arrogant attitude and then hop up on stage and be unfunny. Most of them were one and done. Some came back for a few weeks of open mic nights. Nobody starts off great, and it took working through a great deal of humility to find out if you really had a talent for writing and delivering jokes, which is a skill much different than getting laughs around the water cooler. Thankfully, most people recognized their limitations quickly.

New guys got about three to five minutes on stage. Though policies changed over time, there was always a fair amount of open mic time. Most of Sundays, if I recall. Monday, too, for a time. Once they had surpassed being a true open mic night newbie, but were not yet an official club regular, acts might be offered spots after midnight on a weekday. There were times that the Annex had so many acts scheduled even past 2 a.m. when the bar legally closed. They were playing to three or four people who'd just been cut off at the bar. You had to want it.

I remember this one guy who came around a couple of times. Big cocky Northeast type guy. He was on stage in the Cabaret one night doing an interminable five minutes. Lucien was still managing then, so he shined the flashlight on the back wall. The light. A subtle signal that your time is up. Say goodnight. The guy continued to bore and alienate the crowd. Lucien shined the light again until the guy looked straight back at him and nodded. Good, he saw it that time. Yet the guy kept going. Lucien shined the light directly at him. Right on his face. Mr. Confident just kept talking. Now he'd been up about ten or eleven minutes. Lucien walked to the edge of the stage and glared at the guy. He nodded over with this big "I'm killing 'em" smile and went right on talking. Lucien stalked to the back of the room, into the sound booth, and cut off the microphone. Our boy tapped the thing a couple of times, remarked how the mic must have gone out, and started another bit. By this time the audience has started to say, "I think they want you off." And "Hey, I think your time is up." He ignored them. Lucien cut the lights. No biggie, he had more "material". Lucien got a second flashlight from behind the bar and started crossing the beams on this guy's face. It looked like the opening night for a strip club. I think what finally did it was Lucien walking to the front of the club and saying, "Get off." So simple all along.

One more word about Lucien Cullen, who all of the comedians really liked. In the first months of stand-up at the Workshop, one of the most popular comics there was Ken, a guy from New York who did lame-ass impressions. I know because much of my act when I started were also impressions. He also did several bits that belonged to Billy Crystal, who was still a relative unknown back then. Eppy and I repeatedly told Lucien that the guy was stealing material.

"You're just jealous 'cause he's getting big laughs," was the reply.

Some months later, Paul Menzel brought Steve Moore, a fellow Italian hybrid, down for a look-see and to "give the comics some pointers". Steve Moore was a comic out of Minneapolis who was working lots of college gigs around the country. In the pre-comedy club days, that was the prime work. Even back then, Steve was lying about his age and the fact that he was from New Jersey. But more on that later. Though all of us came to love the guy, Moore showed up at the club with a clip board, an outlook skewed to think in terms of college gigs, and a large load of condescending paternalism.

One of the first acts he saw was this New York transplant who got a great response. Lucien was beaming next to the side of the stage and within ear shot of Epstein and me. Yes, that was one of his top acts.

Moore came racing up to Lucien, the manager, and screamed, "My God, how can you let this go on? Half that bastard's act is Billy Crystal's material!"

"Yeah, I kinda suspected that," was the response.

That was the proverbial beginning of the end for that thief's Workshop days. It was also the first of countless times that we would get to see Moore, a classic character, with his forehead veins popping out and white spit caught at the corners of his mouth. That visual is one of the most enduring for Workshop comics.

Many more stories about the good Houston comedians are coming later, but the fact is the vast majority of people who came to open mic night, egged on by their friends at the office, just plain sucked. There were exceptions, but earning your Stand-up comedy chops, and the acceptance of the club regulars, required perseverance and a thick skin.

We had some acts that were undoubtedly funnier to the regular comics at the club than to the public at large. There was one guy whose jokes were pitifully poor, but whose lack of segues made us drop to the floor with laughter. Whenever this open mic doofus would head to stage, the green room would empty. He thought he was doing great.

He would finish some joke about traffic. A few half-hearted smiles. Then silence. Then, "Women, you've seen 'em."

We would be pounding the walls.

As a rule, the regular comics never watched open mic acts. We stayed in the green room, telling stories until our own spots came up. It took a mention from one of us or a manager to get the regulars out into the showroom on open mic night, but once someone became a must watch, almost always for reasons other than they intended, we kept our eyes open for their time slot.

Nat Perkins was one who initially fit into the category of "instant" comic favorite. He became a pet project of most everyone. Nat was a big, tall somber looking guy who talked like Deputy Dog, only lower and slower. His whole bit was about how put upon he was. It included a tag line of "Sometimes I get very depressed..." There was a Dangerfield meets Gomer Pyle vibe to it. We loved him.

After a time, all the regulars started writing jokes especially for Nat. We were supplementing those he wrote for himself. One I recall was, "I went to the beach recently. I was clubbed and brutally beaten by a baby harp seal."

Nat became a regular, albeit not one of the top ones, and worked some regional road gigs for a year or two. Eventually, his comedy demise was him getting away from the somber persona that made him to begin with, but heavily character-driven acts are tough to sustain over time. The Houston comics loved Nat.

Stand-up comedy can be clean or filthy or a balanced mix of the two. I want to be clear that dirty is absolutely fine, if the jokes are funny. Richard Pryor, George Carlin, Redd Foxx – all acts filled with profanities, but all among the funniest Stand-ups of all time. Curse words are not a disqualifier for laughs. On the other hand, acts who rely on profanities merely for shock value or counting on the dirty word being the operative part of a punchline, are not funny. It's all about the joke. Sometimes the rhythm and timing and delivery of a line requires a good healthy F-bomb. But when that's all you've got, go back to your day job.

Then there are the comedians who just have a twisted, sick sense of humor. It's not for everyone, but it could certainly crack up the other comedians. As a general rule, Andy Hinson, with his Texas/hillbilly delivery, took the prize among Workshop comics.

There are so many of his lines that were delectably sick and funny. I can honestly say that more than a few have been stolen by other comedians, including some who probably have no idea about the true etymology of their lifted line.

Andy was the one who came up with "People say I have my father's eyes. I keep telling 'em, it was an open casket, anybody could have taken them."

One night a woman managed to get her child into the Annex without the person in the ticket booth realizing it. The club was strictly 21 and over. No comedian ever wanted to be self-conscious about some kid in the audience. Whoever was managing that night, probably the brilliant Jerry Young, tried in vain to get her to leave. She kept saying it was her choice to expose him to whatever content there was. Explanations and reason went unheeded. More than a couple of comics were a tad off their game with this 9-year old boy in the front row. There was only one thing for it - Andy Hinson.

Andy hit the stage with a couple of his usual deviant jokes. A few bon mots about fucking dogs until he was sure all the regular comics were seated along the back wall. Then he looked right at the woman and said, 'How much for the little boy?"

He may have wiggled his eyebrows and made a depraved noise or two. Sure enough, she quickly gathered up the youngster and started for the door. Everyone in the room, having observed the woman and the discomfort she was bringing, started dying laughing. And Andy kept his foot on the gas until she was totally out the door.

"He's cute. What do you say? I have money. It's cash."

Sometimes you just need some sketchy humor.

I guess show business has always attracted more than its share of lunatics. I know for a fact that stand-up comedy did. Some of them were harmless, just confused or especially needy people trying to find their place. Others were homicidal.

David West, for example was a roommate of Charles Montgomery, a Comedy Workshop regular. David had a girlfriend who hung around the Annex for a while in the very early 80s, Cynthia Ray. They both tried going on stage. Didn't really work out. Cindy flirted around with a couple of the comics. David got mad and threatened them. He once busted into the Workshop Cabaret Theatre piano player Pat Southard's house down the street and threatened him because Cynthia had run into the house to get away from David. Fortunately, it never escalated. Your typical nightclub behavior.

Until Cynthia decided that she wanted her parents' money, so she talked David into shooting them both while they slept. It took almost three years, but a beautiful undercover private investigator later lured David into bed (she denied that anything happened) and tape recorded him bragging about the murders. David and Cynthia went to prison, and hopefully are still there. As Steve Epstein used to say in his act, as they hauled Dave away he was yelling, "Okay, I killed them, but I banged the detective. Do you hear me? I fucked her!"

And Epstein had a vested interest, too. When Clifford Irving was writing a book about the case, Eppy could hardly wait to tell the world that he had once made out with Cynthia Ray. "Hey, she gave me tongue!"

Most folks that came through there weren't dangerous, just offbeat. There was one guy who called the Workshop and asked about open mic night. The person in the office told him to come by Monday at seven. It just so happened that Sonny (not his real name), manager to the stars, star of the managers, had closed the club the night before and, after a good deal of after hours drinking, had chosen that night to shampoo the carpet. Truth be told, that carpet was about fifteen years past the point that shampoo would have been helpful, but Sonny, the club manager, was in charge. At any rate, Sonny had all the furniture out on the sidewalk, and he had been up all night working. It was sunrise, the carpets were almost dry enough to put the tables and chairs back inside, when some guy in a tuxedo walked up and said, "I'm here to audition for open mic night." Now, the term "night" may have tipped off a lot of folks, but this gentleman was there in a tux at seven in the morning.

Sonny was wearing only running shorts. A good look for a sweaty 6'4", 270 guy with two pounds of hair on his back. With a straight face, Sonny said for the guy to come on in. He plopped down on a chair brought in from the sidewalk and proceeded to make the boy go through his whole ten minute act to silence in an empty wet club as morning rush hour traffic went past the open door. When it was over, Sonny says, "O.K., come back at seven tonight." The guy thanked him profusely and left, just damned thrilled to have passed the audition.

Sonny himself was one of the sweetest guys and biggest personalities ever. He looked like Avery Schreiber, but with his pants down. I say with his pants down because Sonny thought that nothing in the world was funnier than dropping trou. And who am I to argue? He was a terrific host, one of the best. He was born to play maitre'd. He loved being gracious to women and patronizing to the men just to the point that they didn't know for sure if they were being had. And if you stood facing him as he walked by, he'd flick you in the crotch. Yep, that was another of his favorite jokes- a hard thump to the Johnson.

I roomed with Sonny and Jimmy Pineapple for about a year. What an asylum that apartment was. Our leasing agent was a pretty blonde named Chris. Sonny used to go into the office and hide under her desk. Why many of us were never jailed on a regular basis, I have no idea. Weird coincidence. Some years later, Chris married my best high school friend, Pat McCarley. That was a fun story the first time Pat tried to introduce us.

"Yeah, man, I already know your fiancée. My roommate used to hide under her desk and try to look up her skirt."

But back to Sonny. He had a falling out with the Menzels and got fired from the Workshop. I got him a job in Tulsa, running the comedy club there. It used to make trips to that city a blast. Oklahoma must have just increased his fondness for pants dropping. Of course, it is a state where you often have to make your own fun. He picked me up in the airport one time and as we walked away from the gate, he loosened his pants so that they gradually fell of, as if by accident. Then he acted really embarrassed.

He did the same thing when he picked up Richard Lewis once. Richard went on the Letterman Show the next week going, "Dave, you know you get to a club in a new town, you don't know who's gonna pick you up at the airport. They've never seen you in person. Not real sure what you look like. There's a lot of looking...not in Tulsa. Just find the man with his pants down, and that's the manager."

Another time, during a January snowstorm in Tulsa, four of us had gone out after the show. As we left the bar, Sonny let the other two comics and me get ahead of him then started screaming. We turned around. Sonny had his pants and underwear at his ankles, his sweater and jacket pulled up around his neck, and his genitals tucked between his legs. He was standing in three degrees below zero weather repeatedly screaming, "It's gone! It's gone!"

Suddenly from around a corner steps a uniformed police officer who patrolled the outdoor shopping center where we were.

"What are you doing?" I believe was the question.

Sonny looked right at him and said, "My zipper broke."

Don't get me wrong, days at a time would pass when Sonny would wear pants, but there was one more good story. He was with Bill Silva playing golf one time on a deserted course on a weekday afternoon. To get a laugh, Sonny said he'd play the eighteenth hole naked. Fine and good until some old man who had been retrieving water balls climbed up out of the creek that crosses the fairway to see big Sonny walking toward the green buck naked holding his whole golf bag over his head. Oddly, the pro insisted that Sonny not return to that facility. Something about a collared shirt, apparently.

.   .   .

The nuts flicking thing got to be epidemic. Sonny loved to walk through a full Comix Annex and, without looking at you, thump the shit out of your package as he passed. Show's going on and suddenly for no discernible reason you hear some guy scream "oomph". One night he got four of us in a row while we were standing at the bar watching the show. Boom, boom, boom, boom. We doubled over with cramps like a Rockettes line after bad oysters.

He was a terrific manager. The complaint was that he gave away too much free booze. Probably true, but the recipients always came back and spent a whole lot more. And, of course, he didn't get along with Sharon Menzel. Frankly, it didn't help that one night she pulled into the parking lot about midnight, headed to her normal space that faced the dumpster, and saw Sonny's smiling face sticking up over the top. He was just standing there, giving a sly wave. Seems Sonny was getting a bit of extracurricular managerial bonus from some overly accommodating female patron whose head soon popped up from behind the dumpster, as well. Sharon failed to see the humor or the necessity of the situation.

After our Tulsa club went belly up, Sonny moved back to the Northeast and got married and had a son. He was Food and Beverage manager at a nice hotel somewhere in New England when he hurt his back. The hotel stiffed him on the workman's comp, and he ended up getting divorced. Today he's married to his high school sweetheart. Go Sonny. He's one of the nicest guys I ever knew, and we certainly shared some adventures.

One day, the Workshop office got a notice involving a tuxedo rental business selling off out of style tuxes. They notified every theatre in town, thinking they'd make good wardrobe or props. These things were dirt cheap. I'm talking under five bucks each complete with a pastel-colored ruffled shirt. Needless to say, roommates Sonny,

Pineapple and I drove over there and snapped up a half dozen of these God awful things.

We had not a clue what to do with them specifically, but wearing them someplace where we'd be obnoxious distractions was a given. To be honest, I'm not sure where all we ended up going, but I do know that we eventually ended up playing football in them on a major boulevard median through Memorial Park during afternoon rush hour. Oddly enough, that was another brainstorm which failed to get us a date.

Not all of Sonny's ideas were solid ones. For a while he drove a tiny white Honda Civic, about a 1978 model, back when those had to be the smallest cars sold in America. One afternoon with the three roomies and two girlfriends packed like bullfrogs into this thimble, Sonny decided to see what would happen if you tailed a police car for no reason. In case anyone is thinking about it, the cop eventually stops in front of you at a red light, gets out with a hand on his unholstered pistol and asks what the fuck your problem is.

Sonny's knack for being a gracious host got him a job at a new upscale disco located on the back side of Houston's famous Galleria. The place was called Celebration. It had been built as another disco called R. J. Maxwells' in the late 70s, a place where I once got paid to do a Ted Kennedy impersonation and debate a local DJ who was pretending to be Jimmy Carter.

In my humble opinion, the smartest thing Sonny ever did was give about fifteen comics special business cards which were good for two free drinks a night. Needless to say, we never stopped at two, and also needless to say we brought a raft of business in there besides ourselves. At a time when stand-up comics were folks that other folks wanted to be around, it was good publicity.

Sonny also made sure that when a concert was in town, he let the promoters know that the stars were welcome to party at Celebration following the show. That's how I almost ended up back in Tanya

Tucker's hotel room one night. It was in the bag, I tell you. Jimmy Pineapple and I were hanging out with Tanya, pounding drinks and laughing it up like old friends. She was kissing on me at the bar. She was wearing a fancy cowboy hat that she'd snatched off Jimmy's head, one that was gifted to him at a private gig. Then suddenly she's out the door with some beefcake assistant manager, still wearing Jimmy's fancy hat.

I also had a nice encounter with the mob at that club. No lie. I was standing at a urinal, a most vulnerable position, when some slick suit-wearing guy steps up next to me.

"Hey, I've seen your act. You're really funny. Those impressions crack me up. I'd like to send over a round of drinks."

After washing and drying our respective hands, he offered his. I don't recall the first name, but the last name was Marcello, and he paused before adding... from New Orleans.

My big-eyed look must have meant something to him because he smiled and added, "Yeah, that's my uncle."

I suppose connected fans aren't what they used to be. All I got was a couple of tequila shots, not a Sinatra-like swankienda in Palm Springs. I guess tequila shots are preferable to other shots associated with that family. Allegedly.

Sharon Menzel butted heads with several comedians at the Comedy Workshop. God rest her soul. The Annex had a bathroom hallway that was closed off from the little showroom. So naturally, that was the pickup spot for the comics. We would see a good-looking woman start for the bathroom, and we would grab a buddy and quickly happen to be having a conversation in front of the door when she opened it to come out. Then we hit on her before her date got suspicious. That's how I met my second wife. (Hey it was the 80's. The me decade. Blame Reagan)

Occasionally you wanted more privacy so you'd step into the

ladies room and lock the door. Your better class of women never went to the men's room for hygiene reasons. Although, if she did go to the men's room, chances were awfully good that she put out. Sharon Menzel had an uncanny knack for walking past just as some comic, usually Jimmy Pineapple, was stepping out of the ladies room with an impromptu date. She hated Jimmy.

To be fair, Sharon had to put up with some shit, too. The story going around was that she once pulled into the parking lot with her son, who was about six or eight at the time. He perked up, pointed at a Cutlass and said, "Look, there's daddy's girlfriend's car."

With all of the petty grievances back and forth, it was the Menzels, Paul and Sharon, who provided the launch pad for all of the first Houston comics. Dozens of people moved to Houston to take advantage of the stage time at their club. That is a debt that can never be adequately acknowledged. The Workshop and the Comix Annex changed all our lives for the better.

One last word: The Workshop became famous for slow pay or bouncing checks. Virtually every other club in the country paid at the end of the week in cash. The Workshop paid locals a week or two later in check. There was usually enough to cover about a third of the checks, so when the call went out that checks were written, there was a death-defying car chase of comics from around the city trying to get to the club and then to the drive-in bank. And when Menzel said, "Can you hold this for a few days?" that just meant drive faster.

Once when Jim Patterson went in to get a check that the Workshop had owed him for several days, Menzel held it in front of him, and in all seriousness asked, "What do you need the money for?"

"Because it's mine."

It actually got to the point where one teller that knew us would just shake her head and wave us through the line if there were insufficient funds.

I wrote a joke just for my friends: After the Workshop closed and became a dry cleaners, you could take shirts in there and the counter guy would say "Here's your shirt, don't wear it for two weeks." Old habits...

Chapter Two

Celebrities:
For Better or Worse

Like all of the 1980s road comics, I certainly worked with my fair share of comics who turned out to be big stars. Out of the major TV stars of the 90's with a background in stand-up, Tim Allen, Drew Carey, and Ray Romano are about the only ones who come to mind that I never worked with. It was such a small world, though that almost everyone else you ever saw on TV was someone with whom I shared a bill. Most of them came with stories. From celebrating my 22nd birthday with Robin Williams to rooming with Jerry Seinfeld for a week in Oklahoma, the comedians of the golden era were a very tight knit fraternity, if frats had female members, too.

The absolute nicest among them is Jay Leno. I knew him from when I was booking clubs in Oklahoma City and Tulsa, and we worked together more than a time or two. Unlike a few of the other guys, Jay always remembered you when you ran into him in L.A., too. Both when I lived out there and when I visited, Jay was always ready to hang out in the bar area of the Improv on Melrose in Hollywood. And that means hang out because Jay didn't really drink.

Even before Jay had all the money in his neighborhood, he loved cars and bikes. I think he had a relatively inexpensive collection started even when we were all working on the road. And Jay loved games. I remember working with him not too long after Atari or Intellivision had come out. He was travelling with an extra pair of suitcases full of this equipment. No exaggeration, this was before video games had been microchipped into laptops and hand-held devices. He had fifty pounds worth of this shit that he would hook up to the hotel room TV.

We went out after a show to get a bite to eat. After the meal, I was thinking sports bar which is my usual plan - cold beer and late ballgames. But Jay was on a tear.

"Let's go back to my hotel and play Intellivison" (or whichever one it was) "Why do you want to go watch a game when I have football that we can actually play. Or better yet this InterGalactic thing with jet fighters."

Jay was like a big enthusiastic kid with this stuff. He was having a blast. And that tied into his work ethic, too. The forty-five minute headline set is pretty standard. Not to Leno. He would routinely (no pun intended) do an hour and a half. He loved being on stage telling jokes. And, frankly, he was one of the few who could pull it off without losing the crowd.

I have seen a lot of guys go too long when they are having a killer set. The audience only has so much energy before they start to tire, no matter how well you're doing. And when you're closing, two other guys have been up before you ever get to them. Jay was very high energy on stage without being shrill or manic. In other words, not annoying, just damn funny.

Bill Silva worked with him for a week in Oklahoma City. When the clubs started to get in full swing, Jay was already a name because of all his Carson Show appearances. It was rare that the club owners didn't have Jay Leno staying in a hotel. But for some reason, he stayed at the condo this particular week with Silva. Perhaps because the club was new, so the three-bedroom townhouse being used for the comics' accommodations still had things like intact countertops, pliable carpet pile and working door knobs.

It could have been because the middle act was Michael Cain. Yeah, yeah, different guy. This one was Mike Cain from New York. A funny guy who had been around forever, including when Leno was working back East.

They had been out doing some sightseeing one afternoon in some big ass car Leno had rented. He was never one to sit still. On the way back to the condo, they stopped at a convenience store to get snacks. As they pulled into the apartment complex, Jay looks in the rear view and sees Cain just starting to take the first drink from a nice quart of cold milk. He hit the accelerator and swerved the car and soaked Mike Cain with milk. Then while Cain was swearing a blue streak, Leno was laughing so hard he ran the car over the curb, spilling even more milk.

He went on Letterman a few days after that gig and talked about doing the road with some of these young guys who have never been away from home. And they sit on the couch all day watching TV and eating Fritos and a half gallon of ice cream with a packet of Oreos crumbled up inside covered with chocolate syrup while they drink a quart of Coke. And then they can't figure out why their stomach "is a little upset". Not that Silva was young at the time, but we all knew where Jay got the menu plan.

Garry Shandling and I worked together at the Laff Stop in Houston. For the longest time after they opened, the first owner Howard Marcus refused to book any of the Workshop comics because he wanted to bring in "out of town talent". Fine and good, but the openers and middles he was getting from L.A. were sometimes much worse than he would have gotten in town. An agent out there was sending all of these people and taking a cut, so of course he's telling Howard to book from California.

I grew to like Howard a whole lot. After almost a year of all out of town comics, I was one of the very first local guys he started using. Then he opened his club in Austin, and I worked there, too. Howard was a great one for having business lunches at a topless club. And he picked up the tab. What a guy. Sadly, Howard had a stroke and died several years after the clubs opened. He was only in his forties. The theory going around was that he walked into the show room and actually saw one of those L.A. opening acts he booked.

Anyway, I was booked as an opener with Shandling. (I did both open and middle spots for Howard at the Houston club. Whatever he needed because it meant I could stay in town and still get paid.) I had seen Shandling on TV, but never met the guy before in my life. By the time I went on, he hadn't shown from the hotel. Nothing abnormal there.

I shook his hand and got an intro from him as the middle act was finishing up. Then I brought him on stage and started to head to the front bar.

"Hey, Mike, wait," Garry said from stage with that squinty face.

"Hang on, I want you to see some new stuff that I'm working on. Where were you going? Weren't you gonna stay in here and watch me? Mike Vance, ladies and gentlemen. Big round of applause. No seriously, I want you to watch the act."

So, I sat down by the side exit door and proceeded to let Shandling give me good natured shit for the next forty-five minutes.

Periodically he would look over and say something like," How did you like that one? I thought it was a little wordy. Do you need another beer? Yeah? Hey, bring my buddy Mike another beer."

I had a blast. Shandling was one of the funniest guys I ever knew. He had several bits that I can remember from back then, but one line I especially loved of his was "I always furnish my room with dollhouse furniture. Because it makes my dick look really big. 'Yeah Marge, it was bigger than the desk. I never saw anything like it.'"

We didn't hang out too terribly much away from the club, but we did have a good time visiting all week. I was a little disappointed when I ran into him at the Comedy Store in Los Angeles about a month later, and he gave me the old who are you, oh yeah, good to see you, excuse me, I got to go.

There were some comics who you could meet over and over and they genuinely didn't remember you. Yakov Smirnoff falls into that category. I had met him a dozen different times over the years. He was one of the comics who lived at "the house" which Mitzi Shore, the owner of the Store, rented to about five very lucky insider comics.

Some years after the heyday of the house, when Ollie Joe Prater, Mike Binder, Argus Hamilton, and some others lived there, my buddy Jimmy Pineapple moved into the basement room. I had gone to L.A. for a visit, and when Jimmy picked me up at the airport, we went straight to the club. Jimmy had a spot in the Main Room that night, which is the biggest room at the Store.

The Comedy Store is in the building on Sunset Boulevard that used to be Ciro's in the Hollywood glamour days. Flynn and Bogart used to hang out there, need we ever say more. Mitzi had gotten it in a divorce from her husband, and comic, Sammy Shore. She turned it into one of the most famous comedy clubs in the nation. She had it painted black all over to put folks in that laughing mood, I suppose. Still, the Store and the Improv were the only two places to work out at the start of the 1980s in Los Angeles.

While we were visiting with various folks in the club, we ran into Yakov. Jimmy reintroduced me and told him that I would be staying at the house for a few days. Fine with him.

David Crosby was there that night. He was somewhat of a regular at the Store back then. That was during an "on" drinking period. Since I have no other specific memories of that evening, it must have been a successful one.

We got back to the house and went to sleep. About nine the next morning the first hint of dehydration started to rear its ugly mane, so I went upstairs to the kitchen for a glass of water. I was standing there in my underwear putting ice into a glass when Yakov came to the edge of the kitchen, saw me, and froze. He slowly picked up a spoon, spatula, or some other equally effective weapon from the counter. I was hung-over, so I just stood there staring at him. Slowly he stuck his hand out and said, "I am Yakov Smirnoff."

I shook his hand and say, "I'm Jimmy's friend Mike, and I'm going back to bed."

"Oh yes! Yes! Jimmy's friend."

I can only guess that Yakov figured some felon in his briefs had broken into the house to get a drink of water. Thank God comics are largely pacifists.

Many comics went out of their way to help an act they liked. Three L.A. headliners who come to mind for me were Argus Hamilton, Vic Dunlop and especially Ritch Shydner. One night, after I had moved to Los Angeles for the second time, Ron Robertson and I were watching TV at our apartment in the Marina. By that time, mid-1983, we were both making decent money touring the country at the new wave of comedy clubs, but we were still not solidly in at either of the Hollywood clubs. The phone rang, and it was Ritch asking where we'd been the last week. He had arranged showcase spots for us at the Improv, and we needed to hustle our asses up to Melrose because we went on around 10. We did. He not only put in a good word, but was proactive in booking spots and making sure Budd Friedman, the famous club owner, watched us. Now, that's a great guy.

I think every comedian worth his or her tequila salt can still name those who provided good advice or dropped a good word with a club owner. Many times, it was done anonymously. I know in later years,

I'd mention good acts I'd worked with to certain club owner pals. Sometimes it was as serendipitous as who was in the office when you called a new place for a booking. It was not at all uncommon for the comedians to drop by the club to kibbitz during the day, and if an act called in, the owner would ask if we'd seen them. Though there were some exceptions, most road comics took care of their own.

Every once in a while, you hear one of those terrific live mic stories. I had the good fortune of being involved in one of those myself.

A pal of mine, Paul Provenza, who had the lead role in *Northern Exposure*'s last days, was playing at the Laff Stop in Houston. I was off on the opening Tuesday, so Ron Robertson and I stopped by to visit. The other two guys on the bill were Captain Rowdy as the opener and Lowell Sanders as the middle act. Lowell had a sister in Houston who had brought about 70 folks from her work, so the house was packed.

Because it was so crowded, we had to scrounge for a quiet place to swap the latest stories. We decided on the sound booth, a glassed-in area at a back corner of the show room. Paul sat on a stool, I leaned against the door frame and Ron leaned on the sound board with his back to the stage where Rowdy was doing his act.

I've noted, Paul and I always had uncannily similar taste in waitresses, so that's where the conversation started. Paul told of a conquest or two, and I was just about to share a wonderful tale, no pun intended. Fortunately, Ron interrupted.

"No. You got to hear this one. I'm on stage in La Jolla (or wherever) when this long-legged broad comes in with a date."

Ron was reflecting the standard feigned sensitivity found among men in those days.

"She sits right up front. She's got on this short, short skirt. And she's got thighs like a small forward."

That reminds me of the greatest sports related-description for a pretty woman I ever heard. It happened when Rob Bartlett, hysterical man, and I were working together somewhere or another. This lovely young lady passes causing me to say, "That is fine. She's got thighs like Rodney McCray."

Without missing a beat, Bartlett adds, "And titties like Hawthorne Wingo."

Sports and women often went together in our conversations. Jimmy Pineapple once said of my then stormy love life, "Vance has been thrown out more times than Kenny Singleton." Feel free to insert your own slow-footed ballplayer. But I digress, as usual.

In the sound booth, Ron continued. "About ten minutes into the act, she uncrosses her legs, and this woman ain't wearing panties. I'm seeing everything this bitch has to offer. And she's just looking me right in the eye. The loser she's with doesn't have a clue..."

The door to the sound booth was suddenly thrown open, and an out of breath waitress ran in.

"The mic is on!" she yelled.

Apparently, Ron had moved his big butt against the sound board and the slide control that worked the booth mic went up to a position just perfect for letting the entire club hear our little chat. We looked out and a roomful of two hundred patrons were pounding the tables in laughter. Some were literally lying on the floor doubled over. Best of all, Rowdy was off the stage, standing under a speaker, pointing up.

When our little gab session came to a screeching halt, Rowdy let the laughter continue on its own for a couple of beats then said, "So what'd the bitch do then, Ron?"

Robertson turned as crimson as Bear Bryant's neck while Provenza and I hit the floor laughing. I was in so much pain that I crawled out of the sound booth on my knees.

Richard Lewis has long been one of my favorite comics. When Ron Robertson and I were booking the Oklahoma rooms, I made sure to put myself on the bill with him a couple of times. I was somehow oddly pleased to find that he is pretty much the same tortured manic guy offstage that he plays onstage.

As an illustration, a bunch of us were hanging out at the front bar of the Improv on Melrose one night when Richard showed up for his set. It just so happened that Leno had stopped in looking for his buddy, Kevin Rooney. Every time Richard would pace frantically through the room, from bar to bathroom to showroom, Jay would make it a point to get in his face with a "Hey, Richard. How ya doin'?"

Richard would wave him off. "Get out of my way."

Jay would laugh and laugh. Obviously enjoying this little game immensely.

"Hey, Richard. What's up? Where you been working?"

"Fuck you, Jay. Leave me alone."

Jay kept yukking it up and saying, "He's been doing this 20 years, and he still gets this crazy. He's out of his mind"

This went on for a good twenty minutes until Richard hit the stage. He had a great set, as he always did. After the applause died down, he walked through the doorway into the bar, looked surprised to see Leno, extended his hand and muttered, "Hey, Jay. How have you been?"

Every comic at the bar fell out. That's just Richard. Or was then. I haven't seen him since he quit drinking, but I'm sure he's still hysterical. I don't guess it's changed his sense of humor.

Anyway, back to Tulsa. My buddy Gene McGuire of Dallas was the opener that week. We really hadn't seen much of Richard during the day. He was working on some project and putting in a lot of hotel room writing time. But at night, he would hang with us for a few minutes at Pete Mesquite's, the after show bar of choice there in the shopping center where the club was located.

One particular night, a very sleazy, sexy little blonde latched on to Richard after the show. The sort of bleached blonde you'd normally expect to see weeping in the background while they roll the rock star's body out of the hotel room. And I think that's the exact mental picture Richard was getting, too.

While Gene and I stood on one side of the big square shaped bar, Richard and his wannabe girlfriend du jour visited around the corner, several stools away. The show he put on just for us was pure genius.

We sat there and watched Richard Lewis, oozing charm. Tossing back his head as he laughed politely. Buying the drinks with the savoir fare of a Ronald Coleman. Suddenly he excused himself and walked down to me and Gene.

"Jesus. This girl is great looking, but how sleazy does she have to be to just come up to me and drag me out for drinks. I mean, I like sleazy, but this one may have actually been shooting up in the bathroom three minutes ago. I think of the possible things she might be carrying. What should I do?"

Armed with a non-committal answer from us, he moseyed back over to the blonde. More laughter, more knowing smiles, another round of drinks, then the "just one minute finger" waggled, and Richard is back next to us.

"Oh, my God! She's started telling me everything she wants to do to me. We're in Tulsa, for Chrissake. Who knew women here had ever even read about those things? But it's like running a gamut of disease. I should have had my dick laminated. But look at that body. Oh, shit. What would you guys do?"

"Her," was our rather obvious answer. And Richard was back down to the woman. We laughed so hard. He must have made five trips over to give us the update and question routine. Though the actual dialogue is my own re-creation, you get the gist. It was a terrific show after the show. To be honest, I don't recall if he left with her or not. I mean, for the sake of the story, who cares?

Besides a fair number of the people I worked with over the years gaining a modicum of celebrity, a few even ended up with my ex-girl-friends. Rich Jeni and I first worked together in San Antonio in the early 80's. Good enough guy, very New Yorkish, funny act, and huge woman hound. Precisely what you're looking for in the acts you get booked with. I don't remember that he had major success in the booty department that week, but it probably wasn't for lack of trying. We had a blast that week.

An actress who lived with me for a while, Kris McGaha, later moved out to L.A. and was Rich's girlfriend for a long time.

One of the best stories about meeting women even more shallow than we were came from Jeni. He was in Pittsburgh, I think it was, and he and the club owner picked up these two women who had been at the show. It should be noted here that there were several club owners around the country who lived vicariously through the comedians and what they saw as their girl-chasing exploits. The flip side of that was one West Coast owner I can think of, who strictly forbade comics from speaking to the waitresses at his two clubs. We came to find out that the policy stemmed from his hen-pecked home life and sheer jealousy.

But back to Rich Jeni and the club owner who wanted to be one of the guys. They went out for drinks and eventually back to Rich's hotel room. He was just starting to get some good TV shots by that time, so he rated a mini suite. They turned out the lights, and Rich got into bed with one of the ladies while the club owner was on the couch with the other one. When all the moaning subsided, the owner's voice in the dark says, "Why don't we switch?" The girl in bed with Rich said, "Oh I don't think so. I have a boyfriend, and we're really serious."

The last time I saw Rich was in the early 90s at Catch a Rising Star in New York. I was standing against a wall when he came in. He walked up and said hello, and literally as they're introducing him, looked at me and said, "Did you ever work Myrtle Beach?"

"Yeah."

"The owner's wife came to the condo and fucked all three of us. Gotta go." And he walked on stage. You got to love a guy that can fit a good, ribald road story into less than ten seconds. Rest in peace, my brother.

When comedy clubs first started to boom around the country in the early 80's, there were a very limited number of comics good enough to be middle acts and headliners. Consequently, you tended to run into the same guys fairly often. Of course, it was largely coincidental who club owners booked together, and as mentioned earlier, there were some people who I never did meet. Others I seemed to work with once every few months.

One guy I worked with several times was Vince Champ. Vince was a nice guy/dull act type. He was early twenties, good looking, and deep voiced. He went out of his way to always be the articulate, non-threatening California Black man. But Vince was genuinely friendly, and I always had a decent time sharing a condo with him on the road.

We had a very memorable week together in Milwaukee. A nice club had opened up in the suburbs north of downtown. I was booked there the first week of August in 1986. I know this because my wife at the time was scheduled to have a C-section the next week and give birth to what would soon be my daughter. We had scheduled everything so that I would work right up until the birth date and then have six weeks off. You have to do that when you are self-employed and not covered by insurance. (I finally paid off my daughter's birth six years after I had divorced that wife.)

Milwaukee was to be the very last stop before the blessed event. I made certain when I booked it that there was nothing squirrelly in the condo set up. I stressed my situation to the owner when we set up the date. My wife is about to pop momentarily, I have to be available at all times. No problem, he promised. He lied.

The problems became evident as soon as I had my luggage in the car. The club was owned by two brothers who had made some money in the construction business or whatever and wanted to get in on the stand-up comedy boom. They liked comedy, and they opened a very nice, big club. The brother that picked me up seemed like the dominant type-A guy. With A standing for asshole. I assumed that he was in charge.

Almost before we paid the airport parking, he started bitching to me in an angry tone about how comics had trashed his stuff. Ranting about how comics were worthless scum. He told me that he had bought an old car for the comics to use and that someone had wrecked it on their last night and left it in the alley behind the club without telling him. (What was he thinking giving a car to comics?) And then he mentioned that someone had run up a big phone bill so he had the phone taken out of the apartment.

Whoa! Stop the car. No phone in the apartment. My wife was due to have a baby. I had to have a phone or you can take my happy butt right back to the airport.

He changed his tune entirely. Turned on a dime. He understood. He and his wife lived right downstairs. I could use his phone anytime I wanted. I could give out that number to my wife. He or his wife would be more than happy to take me anywhere I needed to go. Against my better judgement, and because I desperately needed the money, we kept driving toward the apartment.

When we arrived, he showed me around. Vince was already there. The owner raved about the nice big waterbeds we had to sleep on. (I don't like waterbeds.) He showed both Vince and I where his apartment was and reiterated to come by anytime.

We didn't have much time before the show, so I showered and headed downstairs to use their phone. No one home. The next morning came the big strike two. Vince and I were both up by the crack of eleven and hungry. This was typically grocery store time for comics. You always go stock up on sodas and sandwich fixins to save yourself some money the rest of the week. One or two little problems. It was pouring down rain, and we had no car. Looking out the window, we couldn't see anything that remotely looked like a shopping center. There was no phone or phone book. And, of course, again, no one was home in the owner's apartment.

Finally, about three-thirty in the afternoon, the trophy wife of the club owner showed up. She had no idea about any promises that her husband made. No, we are not allowed in her apartment to use the phone. No, she doesn't want to drive us anywhere. No, she doesn't know where her husband is. Good afternoon.

About fifteen minutes later, someone was banging on our door. I mean pounding. Vince opened the door to a very large, very wet man with a very intimidating look on his face. It seemed this was the other brother. He just got a phone call that we had been downstairs harassing his sister-in-law. Apparently, he was there to beat the shit out of us. Who knew how big he was? His older brother was all of 5'4".

It turned out that the big guy was the single and partying one of the two. I don't think he had been single long because he was living in an office at the club. But after we explained the situation, he took us to the store and then took us out beer drinking most every night after the shows.

Why did I bring up anything about Vince Champ? Well, in 1997, I was sitting with a friend in a sports bar, and on one of the TV screens a big picture of Vince pops up.

"Hey, I know that guy! Turn up the sound."

As it happens, a show called American Justice was breaking the story on a serial rapist who had been attacking women at college campuses across the country. Same M.O. of finding them alone, often in a music practice room or study lounge. After much investigation and collection of physical evidence, authorities traced the pattern to Vince Champ's stand-up comedy shows on the same college campuses or other campuses within easy driving distance. He was going to prison for life. Holy shit! This wasn't hitting on club waitresses, this was out and out brutal, serial assault! This was a string of felonies of the worst kind. Clearly, I didn't know old Vince as well as I thought. The news spread like wildfire among the comedian world. We were beyond shocked. At least I know he didn't drive anywhere the week we were in Milwaukee.

I've never been one who was too impressed by meeting famous people. Hell, most of them are lots more famous in their own minds anyway. But blame that on *Entertainment Tonight* and all the spin offs that followed. There are a handful of folks who I would have dearly loved to sit down and have a beer with; Groucho, Paul Newman, Gregory Peck, Jonathan Winters. That's always been my gauge of fame, by the way. Would I like to buy them a beer? Most of the ones I'd really like to meet were dead before I was born, like Bogart, Gable and Errol Flynn.

It's inevitable when you start making money in show business that you'll have your share of brushes with greatness. Some of them have been just passing moments that you can hang onto for life. Sometimes you end up being buddies for a night with someone way over your head.

Every once in a while, you run into someone totally out of the blue, too. Those quick encounters can be fun. One time I was in Cleveland, Ohio working at Hilarities, a terrific club that used to be in the Warehouse District. We stayed and worked right downtown. I've walked to many a baseball game at the old Municipal Stadium and a couple at the Jake.

There used to be a mounted cop who occasionally worked security at the comedy club. He also worked the Indians games at Municipal. If you brought his horse a treat, he'd wave for the gate attendant to let you in free. This was in the days when the Tribe drew a good seven, eight thousand people on most nights. We'd walk to the ball-park and watch the first three innings then go back to the club about three blocks away and do a show. If it went extra innings, you could sneak back and catch the end. I snatched a grounds crew raincoat from there one time. It was just laying across a chair in an empty section. Now, why wouldn't anyone want a yellow rain slicker that said INDIANS across the back? Point is - it's mine now. And let me add, that the same jacket saying GUARDIANS probably has a lower street value.

At any rate, there I was in Cleveland in the middle of winter. I had bills to pay, so I was walking around downtown looking for a post office. I finally spotted it and was in the crosswalk heading to the other side of the street. Strolling the opposite way were three older guys in long overcoats. Just as we pass, I look over and see that the little guy in the middle is Sammy Davis, Jr.

Without thinking, I blurt out the first thing that comes into my head, which happened to be, "Sammy! How's it going?" Like we were old pals.

Now, while I would have loved to hang with the Rat Pack, meeting Sammy Davis, Jr. was never necessarily high on my agenda. But he just looked at me without breaking stride, held up his first two fingers, and said, "Peace, man". The perfect Sammy encounter.

Ron Robertson used the "how's it going" line once. He was playing golf in L.A. and, like most of us, was over in the rough looking for his ball. All of a sudden he sees a golf cart speeding through the rough, heading towards him alongside the parallel fairway. As it gets closer, he realizes it's Charles Bronson.

Like I said, you blurt it out without a thought.

"Chuck, how's it going?" Ron says.

Pedal to the floor, Bronson squints back and says through gritted teeth, "Like shit."

                                    .   .   .

Ron Robertson had another embarrassing brush with fame, though he likely didn't know it at the time. He was wandering through the pool area of the Sheraton Town Lake in Austin, trying to look cool while he checked out the women. One incredibly white skinny woman was sunning herself, no doubt slathered with a three-digit SPF.

Ron looked at the closest male by-stander he could find, some guy with an unruly, bleached mop of hair and a dark beard, and nodding to the pale chick asked, "Is this bitch dead, or what?"

He got a slight laugh and a deadpanned English accented "Right."

I think it was later that Ron found out he'd been talking to and about Dave Stewart and Annie Lennox of the Eurythmics.

One of those celebrity beer moments happened in Blacksburg, Virginia, of all unlikely places, especially considering that it was a day Carl Faulkenberry and I had booked ourselves into Augusta, Georgia for Masters week. One of the main reasons I started working Rick Hogan's rooms in the first place was an eye toward going to the Masters. I knew full well that tickets to the event were impossible to come by, but I had been told that on Sunday afternoon, the locals start leaving to go to parties where they watched the finale on TV, so they can see all the action at once. That's when an outsider could score a pass.

Eventually, in 1985, I made it inside the sacred gates of Augusta National. Just like the locals said, we got there about noon and started telling our pitiful golf story to all who walked out. It took about half an hour for Carl and I to score badges for free. I paid twenty bucks for one for Patsy, a cute schoolteacher from South Georgia who had come up to hang out with me for a few days.

The three of us were now at Augusta National on Sunday afternoon. We walked up this shell drive. More like skipped probably. We were so thrilled. We passed the press tent and another hospitality type tent and then crested the top of the hill. There on the left was that stately clubhouse that we'd been seeing all our lives. Farther down in front of that, Amen Corner swept toward the pines and azaleas. And right in front of us, on the first tee, was Jack Nicklaus. That was one goose bump damn moment right there. The only other times I ever got that feeling just from being in a place was my first time in Wrigley Field and every time at Monticello. It was awesome.

That was the year after my favorite golfer, fellow Texas Longhorn Ben Crenshaw had won his first Masters. I was hoping to see him do well. No such luck. That final afternoon, after we were thoroughly entertained by Lee Trevino for a few holes around Amen Corner, we grabbed a spot by number sixteen and watched them come through. We saw some putts that broke damn near around the world on those bent grass greens. We saw Ray Floyd put one in the water to lose the lead. Saw Seve Ballesteros miss a chance. It was one of those sports moments I'll never forget. But in the end, it was cold, boring-as-hell, slow-playing Bernhard Langer who won it. Bastard.

But getting to that paradise took on a little twist. We were going to go down there a couple of days early because on our last visit, our local Augusta pals assured us that they could get us on the course for practice rounds. Well, we showed up only to find that there was no place for us to stay. The nice condo that the club owned had been co-opted by someone deemed more important than us. Of course, being comics, club owners thought everyone was more important than us. It could have been a bag boy from the A&P for all we knew.

Grudgingly, they promised to honor our contracts and let us stay in the living room of the manager's one bed room apartment once the shows started. Damn nice of the bastards. So, for two nights, Carl and I had to find a place to stay. That obviously didn't include anywhere near sold out Augusta, Georgia during Master's week.

As long as we were in the neighborhood, by Texas standards, we thought we'd go do some politicking with the wonderful ladies in Richmond, Virginia, April Pasquerella and Sandy DiPerna. So, we drove up to hang out with them. They were also nice enough to let us use the couches in the comics' apartment. It seems odd saying that now since I've grown so accustomed to sleeping on beds these last several years of adulthood.

Frankie Bastille was headlining the Richmond Comedy Club that week. Another of the legendary party boys of the 1980's. Frankie could drink right along with us, but he also added some of the harder chemicals that Carl and I never dabbled in. To put it another way, the vast majority of the 80's road comics partied like rock stars, but some, like Bastille, were the Stones, while others of us were merely Ace of Base. Neither Carl nor I had ever met Frankie in person, but to say his reputation preceded him seems insufficient.

The three of us got into discussions about Tom Waits after we had shut down the local bars on that non-show night. And to show you what a sweet and generous guy Frankie could be, the next morning there was a Tom Waits cassette for each one of us laying on the counter along with a nice note. Where he managed to find these Tom Waits tapes in the middle of the night in Midlothian, Virginia, I will never know. God forbid he got up before noon to say goodbye, but that was a hell of kind gesture to a couple of guys he had previously known only by reputation.

One little aside story about Bastille was when he worked with my buddy, Rick Tempesta, in Charleston. Bastille always cultivated this ultimate bad boy image. He reveled in it. He went out of his way to make that bad impression on everyone. Frankie sported a soul patch back when only Dizzy Gillespie and Leon Redbone knew what the hell one was. Because of things like that, he was usually able to pick up a certain sort of women. One particular night after the show in Charleston, Frankie brought a woman back to the house where everyone stayed. Rick and the forgotten opener were already home, watching TV. The best the opening act kid could manage was a sad and jealous look at the party couple as they headed toward the bedrooms.

Instead of taking the girl all the way down the hall to the headliner's master bedroom in the back, Frankie entered the door to the opening act's room just off the den. He quickly shot a smile at the other guys and ducked inside, locking the door. From what Rick told me, the opener had this whipped dog look on his face. Not only was he not getting laid on what was probably one of his first road appearances, but now somebody else was about to knock some off in his bed. How disappointing and rude.

They sat there tortured through the usual moans and grunts, thinking the worst of Bastille for taunting them. Then they thought they clearly heard Frankie say "go ahead". A moment of silence and "Do it". The bed squeaks started again, and there between the grunts and groans was a soft barking noise. Then "louder".

"Aarf."

"Louder."

"Aarf! Aarf!"

Frankie was having the young lady put on a show solely for the benefit of his two fellow comics who weren't getting any. Such a thoughtful guy.

That's the Frankie Bastille that hung out with Carl and me in Richmond before we journeyed with April and Sandy to Blacksburg, Virginia the next day for the grand opening of the Blacksburg Comedy Club, their newest operation. It was located in the Hilton there, if I recall. Some nice chain hotel, at any rate. And we even got to save some money on rooms thanks to the generosity of the very lovely Miss April.

We went and watched the grand opening show. Probably did guest sets. I don't recall for sure. But I do recollect that the party place in town happened to be the disco nightclub there in the hotel. Carl and I went there to pound some drinks after the comedy show. It was so packed that you couldn't move through there. In fact, some drunk woman got pissed at Carl because she thought he rubbed against her tits on purpose. Jeez, lady, you damn near had to share clothing to squeeze through by the bar.

Not being big disco hounds, Carl and I found our way to a quiet back room and grabbed a table. I think it was us and one drunk couple in which the guy thought he had culled a potential filly from the herd. We had just gotten our beers when out of the blue, Dick Gregory came walking in with two older women who were dressed like they just left church. What a non sequitur.

Gregory had been a hero especially to Carl since he was a kid. Carl's dad worked for the Episcopal Church and had been very active in the Civil Rights movement during the sixties. So having a Civil Rights icon walk in out of thin air was something else.

We walked over, apologizing from the start about disturbing them. Introducing ourselves as fellow comedians, we thanked him for his groundbreaking work in comedy and in establishing a foothold for Civil Rights in this country. Then we went back, sat down and tried not to stare.

Gregory and his friends only sat there for a few minutes before they got up to head out the back entrance that led to the lobby elevators. On his way, he stopped by our table and shook our hands a second time. He apologized that he didn't have the time to sit and talk with us, explaining that he had lectured at the university that evening and needed to walk his friends out and then get up to bed. Finally, he wished us good luck in our careers with a warm sincerity.

Carl and I were thrilled, to say the least. Dick Gregory had taken the time to go out of his way, albeit only a few feet, to be gracious to us. It's always wonderful to see someone famous be nice to strangers. You hear too many stories of the other kind. Hell, I'm telling some of them here.

We were still basking in the glow of the fame that might have rubbed off on us when the waitress showed up with another round. Before we could reach for our money, she said, "These are paid for."

Her voice dropped to a whisper in a certain manner I've heard all too often in the South as she added, "That older Black man bought them for you." Apparently, she expected us to be grateful for not turning us in.

Bob Saget, star of *Full House* and *Funniest Videos* and who knows what else, was always a heck of a nice guy to me and everyone else. Act-wise, he relied on a stream of consciousness delivery that often eschewed actual jokes for sick and random comments like "I have the body of an eight-year-old boy and the mind of a German Shepherd, and they're both in the trunk of my car if you'd like to see them." I always kind of liked it in a weird way, especially when he followed it up with a deliberately lame Beatles song parody.

I worked with Saget at the Laff Stop in Houston one week in what must have been early 1982 because I was married to wife numero uno at the time. I've often dropped down a notch on the bill to stay in Houston and work since it allows you to play a club more often during the year. So, I was opening and a Canadian actor/comic named Michael Rapport was middling. Saget, who was not yet any sort of TV star, was closing the show.

The first night of the week, a Tuesday, the crowd was so small that we worked in the front lounge which only held about 70 people at best. That night it was half full, or half empty depending on, you know... Saget had gotten about ten minutes into his act when one guy among the 30 shouted out some woman's name. I'm talking about a random heckle along the lines of "Mrs. Higginbotham!"

Saget stopped and looked at him. He yelled again, "128th Street".

It turned out this guy in a tiny crowd in Houston had gone to elementary school with Bob Saget in Philadelphia. Playing the percentages, Bob did the next five minutes about people from the old neighborhood.

That week my then wife, Melissa, and I took Saget and Rapport out to Cadillac Bar, back then a very good Mexican restaurant. Bob took a chip and dipped it cautiously into the red salsa. He then flailed around and drank an entire glass of water.

When the waiter came over to see if the Heimlich was necessary, Bob said, "Do you have anything milder?"

With a perfect deadpan look and a slight Mexican accent, the waiter answered, "We haaavvve ketchup."

The first time I worked Kansas City was at Stanford's on St. Patrick's Day of some year in the mid-80s. Sinbad, who was later on *A Different World* and had a few good movie roles, was a fairly new comic and was the co-opener that week. He was mainly there so he could have a place to stay and pick up a little money between other gigs. The show that first night was a crazy zoo. Some guy passed out at a front table after heckling for most of Sinbad's act, and the room was so packed that they left him there rather than try to make everyone stand up while they carried him out. I had a great, if rowdy, set, and a good chunk of it making fun of the dude snoring at table 2.

Later that week, Prince was in town, playing at whatever the big arena venue was, and Sinbad and I decided that we needed to meet Apollonia. We procured a clipboard and some scribbled on pieces of paper, and we strolled into the arena through a service door like we owned the joint, looking at the crews setting up, making check marks on the paper and asking various people where Prince and Apollonia were. We pulled the act off for a while. Eventually some guy said, "you just missed them, I think they headed back to the hotel." We hustled across the street to the hotel, punched the button for the appropriate floor, and made it damn near three steps off the elevator before the bodyguards turned us around. The old clipboard gag had reached its limit of effectiveness. We never met Prince or Apollonia. At least I didn't. Sinbad might have years later. But I will always associate that story with him, and will always appreciate the value of a clipboard and an attitude.

Not every road comic got along with each other, to be sure. Jenny Jones, before she had her decade-long TV show, opened a week in Oklahoma City with me as middle act and the hysterical and under-rated George Miller as headliner. David Letterman often said that his good pal, George Miller, was his favorite comic. The housing set up had George in one condo, and Jenny and I sharing another.

To say that we did not hit it off was an understatement. Some friends had warned me that she was difficult, not something that benefitted an opening act, for sure. It didn't help that I, like most comedians, am an inveterate and cocky smartass. It was much worse when I was in my 20s. The newly installed, middle-aged club manager there in OKC was totally smitten with her, drooling and fawning all week, and she seemed to encourage it. For the record, he was a complete jackass who did not last long in the job. In fact, the entire club got run into the ground after the original team had made it one of the best comedy rooms in America, but that's another story.

I remember her being on some odd diet that required her to boil water with lemon every night before bed but allowed her to eat Fudgsicles or something. My uninvited analysis of that health scheme did not go over well.

Mostly we stayed out of each other's way. I had plenty of friends to hang out with in OKC since I had been one of the original founders of the club before the lucrative partnership fell apart. George and I went to lunch most every day, even though he was not the most naturally social and outgoing guy. He was famous for his cramped little apartment across the street from the Comedy Store.

What he and I both enjoyed the most about Jenny was that the week started with her saying she was soon to do a *Tonight Show* slot. That was, of course, the holy grail of TV at the time, and it went through Jim McCawley, the talent coordinator for Johnny Carson. When George and I asked Jenny for details about her upcoming spot, she told us that she had auditioned for McCawley more than once, and he told her she had seven jokes that were ready for the show. Since an average Carson Show spot probably had 18 to 20 jokes, that's like me saying I was about to buy a new Ferrari... as soon as I had the money.

I had also gotten showcases for McCawley a couple of times the previous year, and he was extremely nice to me, for some reason. Last

I heard was that I needed about four more jokes to fill out the set he envisioned. That sounded like a cavernous divide in some ways. When George Miller and I watched Jenny, though, almost none of her laughs came from anything remotely resembling clean material. I recollect her big closer being a lewd prop piece with dolls.

The entire week, standing in the back of the club with George while I was waiting to go on, we watched Jenny's act. And without fail, when she would pull out her Barbie and Ken dolls and demonstrate various sex acts, George would lean a bit closer and drawl, "Do you think that was one of the seven?"

Carl Faulkenberry was just starting in radio, long before he got into comedy, and he was working for an AM station in New Orleans. It just so happened that the Super Bowl was there that year, and Carl scored credentials. A couple of nights before the game, he's at the Superdome press lounge, most likely trying to scam free food. The place was dead. There were a few ancient scribes scattered about, all silently reading competitors' papers. The door opened and Bill Murray walked in with a woman and another guy.

This was the late 70s when *Saturday Night Live* was new. Not one of the old writers even looked up, but Carl brightened and walked over to say hello. Murray was as gracious as could be, and the two were soon engaged in a lively badinage. (I bet a guy I could get that word in the book)

Before long, Carl was giving Bill Murray some unsolicited advice on how to make SNL a better show. Welcome conversation, I'm sure. He was saying that they needed better and more diverse musical guests.

"Like who?" Murray asked.

Carl reeled a couple of names off. The third or fourth one was Little River Band.

Murray went into this immediate attack of fake rage.

"Little River Band! The Little River Band?" He's screaming and running around the room.

He stepped over to one of the old writers who was buried in newsprint and pulled down the top of the paper.

"Excuse me, sir, but have you ever heard of The Little River Band?"

"No," the man said firmly as he returned to his reading.

Bill Murray looked at Carl and gives a smug Oliver Hardy nod. Carl stepped right back over to the same old guy.

"Excuse me, sir, but have you ever heard of Bill Murray?"

"Look, quit bothering me," the writer answered. "I don't know any of those crazy new music acts."

About the third time I ever went up at the Comedy Store in L.A. was set up by a couple of friends as a showcase for Mitzi, the owner. I was trying to get made a "regular" so I could call in for spots every week. The showcase acts went up fairly early in the evening, just before the prime acts. You got eight minutes if I recall.

On this night in 1981 or so, I hit the stage and got off to a good start. About three minutes into the act, I did a Ronald Reagan joke to a nice response. In fact, the laughs grew into applause and went on too long for the joke. I was trying to figure out why when, out of the corner of my eye, I see some guy standing at the corner of the stage. I looked down, and there was Flip Wilson.

Now, Flip Wilson, thanks to his albums, had been my favorite comic when I was in elementary school. I never missed an episode of his TV show. I even won the sixth grade talent show with a series of impressions that climaxed with me in a wig doing his character, Geraldine Jones. Big laughs, trust me. So here was this boyhood idol whom I was seeing for the first time in the flesh, and he's six feet away and talking to me.

The first thing out of Flip Wilson's mouth was, "I voted for Reagan."

"Yeah, a lot of people seemed to want a president whose favorite book is Hop on Pop," I answered.

We exchanged a couple more lines on the subject before Flip walked away toward the back of the room.

"That's pretty bad when celebrities are coming in off the street to heckle." I said.

I started to segue back into my act when Flip returned. This time he stepped on the corner of someone's chair, hopped over the drink rail and got on stage with me. The audience died laughing.

"I didn't come in to heckle," he said. "I came in to talk about my wife."

I believe that Flip was going through a divorce at the time. At least that's a safe bet. What I do know for sure is that he proceeded to do about a five minute improvised comedy duo routine with me. I have a sneaking suspicion that he dropped in a couple of one-liners he'd been working on, too. But we got huge laughs. Me and my new partner, Flip. When he left, I'd been on stage for about twelve minutes.

"Flip Wilson, ladies and gentlemen." I tried to make it seem like the most natural thing on earth. "I just hope that all those laughs count toward my audition."

Mitzi or someone let me stay up for another four minutes before I got the light. When I walked off to a huge ovation, Argus Hamilton, one of the top comics at the Store, ran up to me to tell me how great I'd done and how he was so glad that it was me who had been forced to improv with Flip Wilson and not him. Argus was incredibly gracious.

Flip also came over and shook my hand, saying something like "I knew you could handle it, or I wouldn't have gotten up there."

"Let me know when you're ready to go on the road," I told him.

Then I walked, on air almost, over to Mitzi's table. Argus came with me and put in a very good word. And Mitzi looked at me, and in her whiny voice said, "I really couldn't tell because Flip Wilson was up there. Come back next week."

One of the least favorite people I ever worked with was Andrew "Dice" Clay. First off, let me just opine that anyone who gives themselves a nickname is a fucking idiot. Secondly, not funny in my opinion. Thirdly, his reputation was that he actually went to the trouble to steal some of the awful material he used to do. Are you following me?

I first met him when we were booked together in Dallas at the old Comedy Corner on Greenville Ave. at Park Lane. It had been a disco and was all tricked out to look like the inside of an ice cave, a geographic feature that abounds in the Dallas area. He's headlining and I was middling for the week. He was doing some sort of all chicken diet, if I recall. Cooking up whole chickens by the pan full all week.

I was booking the Oklahoma City room back then, in 1981 or so. And Clay was relentlessly begging for a booking there the whole week. I kept telling him that the club was new and was flagrantly violating the then-state law in rampantly Baptist Oklahoma that there was no liquor by the drink. We wanted clean shows. Needless to say, his was not even close. Not to mention the lack of humor part.

In an uncharacteristic attack of niceness, I finally gave in and told him that if he could work cleaner than normal, he could have a middle spot for two weeks.

He leaned back on the couch at the condo, waved his cigarette, and said, "Dice don't middle".

Immediately, I mimicked his little wave and replied, "Then Dice don't work".

He promptly went back to L.A. and badmouthed me and my booking partner, Ron Robertson, to Mitzi Shore on a daily basis, from what I heard. I was working the Comedy & Magic in Hermosa

Beach, and occasionally at the Improv, but it probably did hurt Ron some at the Store.

Clay told me all about the movie he was writing for himself while we were in Dallas those two weeks. His role model was Sly Stallone. He planned the same career path. Just to make sure, he gave himself a nickname - Dice. It sounded macho.

Once he was near Bruce Baum in one of the Comedy Stores in L.A. Bruce called him Andrew, which is how he had always been known to people.

Clay looked at Baum and says, "You can call me Dice."

Just before he walked away, Bruce looked back at him and said, "No Andy, I don't think I can."

Once Ron Robertson and I were working in Palm Springs at a club that my old high school pal, Rex Meredith, was booking. Rex had gotten out of music after some throat problems affected his singing voice, and he was doing comedy. He had gotten himself a sweet house emcee gig in Palm Springs at a nice room run by a total lunatic.

Toni Cosentino, a cute petite blonde woman, was an agent in L.A. Very nice lady, and easy to deal with for bookings. She booked the Dallas room where I'd worked with Clay, as a matter of fact. So, it wasn't surprising that when a private party gig in Palm Springs came up that week, she gave it to Robertson and me and to Andrew Clay.

It was in the home of some high-roller out there and would be lousy with Hollywood celebs. One of the guests was Larry Gelbart, creator of *M*A*S*H* on TV, so Toni played up the exposure angle along with the small money involved. Clay was to do a set early, then Ron and I would go over after our last show and entertain some more.

We drove up in front of this sleek, long and low, modern desert house. Valet took the car. I remarked to Ron that it didn't look very crowded, but we figured the valets are keeping the cars tastefully parked out back.

Once inside, we started to wonder if they're also keeping the guests out back, too, because there's no one there. About 20 people were scattered around this palatial house (which has its own built-in stage, by the way). The owner came up to us half angry and half apologetic. According to what he told us, Clay showed up and was so filthy and insulting, unfunny and base that most of the guests, including Larry Gelbart, had left the party.

We would not be going on at all, but we were welcome to stay and drink. He slipped us a little cash for our trouble, and Ron and I proceeded to get commode hugging on his best Scotch.

Only when we got back to L.A. did I find out the whole story. From what I was told, Clay had borrowed Toni's car to get to this gig in Palm Springs. Graciously, she said okay. Clay went to her house, got the car, and he and his girlfriend (whom he introduced to everyone as "Dollface") drove to the show. Toni told me the end of the tale. According to her, coming back after ruining the party, Clay noticed that the car was almost on empty. In fact, he ran out of gas three blocks from Toni's house. So, what did he do? He dropped the keys in her mailbox and went home without ever even bothering to tell her where her out of gas car was located. Then he ducked her calls for a few days. You know, having been such a hit at the party and all.

One note about Toni. She once delivered one of the great lines of all time. She was describing the woman who was manager of the Comedy Corner in Dallas, to an interested, horny comic. When asked about Joyce's body, Toni said, "Well, they're not big tits, but they're long."

I was working up in Dallas another time when I went over to the club early. I should mention that the Comedy Corner was always a fantastic gig for several reasons. Wonderful audiences and several very good friends among those local comics, people like John McDowell, Gene McGuire, Bill Engvall, Dave Little, Bill Farmer, and not to mention the great club manager, Kevin. The first owners were very nice folks. I had favorite places to go eat, drink and buy books. It was sweet.

The Corner was also one of the very few clubs that had a regular house emcee. First it was Engvall, who went on to Hollywood success, and then Gene McGuire. The other two house emcees who immediately come to mind were Dennis Philippi at Sir-Laffs-a-Lot in Memphis and Spud McConnell at the Grin Room in Baton Rouge. All were extremely funny dudes. To be house emcee, with some audience members who came back every week or so, you had to do a fair amount of talking to the crowd, use your material rather sparingly, and write jokes that went with the requisite announcements. Your job was to warm up the crowd, and these guys got that job done.

There was a place called Judge Roy Bean's across the parking lot from Dallas' Comedy Corner that made some nice chili burgers. I was going to grab myself one before the show. As I started to walk over there, a cab pulled up in front of the comedy club. Some guy with a guitar started to get out. I'm thinking to myself, "Oh great, some hack guitar act. I'm gonna have to suffer through this shit tonight".

But when the would-be musician turns around, it was a friend of mine from San Francisco named Doctor Gonzo. A very funny guitar act. No hack at all. He was on tour with Huey Lewis and the News. The band was doing a private debutante party at the Anatole Hotel that night for some mogul's daughter, and Gonzo had the night off. He was hoping to audition for a booking at the club.

I set him up with a hearty recommendation and a guest spot, and then we got that burger together. After the show, the two of us went to the Anatole to see the private show that Huey Lewis was doing. This was during their "Sports" tour. They were the biggest band in America that summer. One can only imagine what kind of coin the high roller had laid down for his daughter's shindig.

The backstage area was an unused kitchen, and we could step over to one side and damn near be on stage with the band. Gonzo introduced me all around, and it wasn't long before the two of us and Huey Lewis were shooting the shit about all manner of show business topics. Somehow, I expressed a lustful opinion of Latoya Jackson, and you can almost still see the slack-jawed expression on my face when Huey said, "Hey, you want to go out with her? I can give her a call." Given that I'm still waiting, I can only assume in hind sight, the Huester was joshing.

That was the night I first learned, as one is tattooed with knowledge deep down in their soul, how many, many women act around rock stars. I'd certainly seen a few comedy groupies, and country & western mega-fans, too. Rock & roll was a different animal, as I observed at the Anatole.

From our backstage vantage point, we could see a bevy of hot women watching and dancing. They outnumbered guys at the party at least two to one, probably a much better ratio than that. And each one of those women were glassy eyed and damn near salivating to what I could only figure were subliminal messages in the songs. Not long before the band was finished with their one set, the road manager came up to Gonzo and asked if he and his friend, aka me, wanted to do the round up. That consisted of walking through the audience and inviting about 20 women to the band's party suite upstairs.

The party upstairs was most everything you see in a movie scene. Huey excused himself and went on to his room, but the rest of the band was basking in what was likely their nightly delight. We drank free booze, ate hors d'oeuvres and watched as the woman circled the band members like horny sharks. Twice one walked up to Gonzo and me and asked what we played.

"We're professional comedians," we said.

Sometimes, they managed to say "oh" before they walked away.

One of the memorably fun evenings was hanging out with the Boston bon vivant Lenny Clarke, a man who later got his own eponymous sit-com. I was headlining Hilarities in the old Warehouse area of Downtown Cleveland, and Lenny was on the road opening for Dolly Parton, one of my all-time favorite performers. Lenny had called the club and left a message that he was coming by after his set. The Houston and Boston acts held each other in high esteem. I was looking forward to it.

Hilarities was one of the biggest rooms on the comedy circuit. More than 400 people inside what still looked like an old warehouse. In addition to the giant showroom, there was a sizable front holding area and bar. Nick and Carlene Kostis owned the place, and they made it a great place to work. They also had a club in Cuyahoga Falls, and I headlined both twice a year. Later they opened a couple of places I worked in Florida, too.

In the late 80s, the two Ohio clubs were packing them in, and this night was no exception. Being such a huge room on a single level, Nick had built a taller stage than the step or two up that was found in most comedy clubs. This one had to be at least three feet high, maybe more. Seated in the front row, at a table right next to the stage, was a young couple that would have qualified as yuppie in those years. Both very attractive folks who were clearly having a good time.

The crowd was hot, and about 20 minutes or so into what was a very fun set, the woman part of this couple propped her feet up on the stage. The edge of the stage was damn near at the height of her head, and her short skirt hiked up accordingly. I could see everything she had to offer, and both she and her boyfriend knew it. They just smiled, and I kept going on getting laughs. After 10 minutes of this, I couldn't hold back any longer. I started making jokes about it, and the audience was whooping it up, even though they certainly didn't have my bird's eye view. I've always been known for my work improvising with the crowd, and this was a gold mine. The laughs were getting louder and longer, and finally, the woman kicked off one high heeled shoe, flipping it up onto the stage. Without missing a beat, I scooped it up, poured Miller Lite into it and drank. The joint came unglued. People were on their feet screaming approval.

Nick and Carlene, who had been back in the office, came busting into the showroom with fear on their faces. He told me later that they had never heard such a loud noise and thought a hockey fight had broken out. The crowd was so great that Lenny Clarke, who showed up during my set, went on and did about 15 minutes after me even though he wasn't getting paid and had already done a set for a packed arena full of people.

Now, I have to tell you what Lenny was wearing. It was an all-white suit that was a cross between a cruise ship captain and a Star Trek dress uniform. The jacket was an Eisenhower cut with white epaulets on the shoulders, and when I say all-white, I'm talking Utah Republicans in a blizzard. Not a drop of color to be seen.

After the show was over, we took a cab down to the Flats. At that point, it was, shall we say, a neighborhood in transition. There were enough cool dive bars to make it a destination for partiers, but over half the drinkers you saw were hard core, blue collar guys who worked the docks or the boats on Lake Erie. It was eclectic.

Lenny and I found a hopping joint with an Italian sausage sandwich cart out front. I grabbed us a couple of sausage dogs while Lenny went to the bar. There was only one open table, all the way in the back corner, so I grabbed it. Lenny, in all his gleaming glory was shimmying his way through the crowd with a full pitcher in one hand and two icy mugs in the other when a big stevedore-looking fellow accosts him. Lenny's a big dude, but this local was his equal, and he stepped menacingly in front of Lenny.

"Nice suit," he said very slowly and disparagingly.

Lenny, hands very full and trying not to spill, looked right back at him and said, "Hey, thanks for saying so. I really appreciate it. I was worried that the epaulets were too much, so that means a lot."

Then, with the guy's jaw on his chin wondering what just happened, Lenny continued to our table. We laughed it up until closing time, and still not ready to stop drinking, we adjourned to

Lenny's hotel suite downtown. It was very fancy, but more importantly, it had a mini-bar. We quickly availed ourselves of its contents and continued our possibly profane storytelling. Lenny showed me the French doors that opened onto the hotel atrium, and we left them open for the view. In fact, we decided to serenade the other guests with a few Frank Sinatra tunes delivered a cappella. Evidently, we thought more of our 3 a.m. singing than some of the other folks since we got a phone call from the front desk politely asking Mr. Clarke to close his balcony doors.

We did, but come to find out that occasionally, drunks are loud. Even with the doors closed, we got a second phone call about an hour later stressing that we really needed to hold it down. The third scolding, not long before dawn, came in person when the desk clerk knocked on the door to say that Mr. Clarke's guest would need to leave the hotel. What the hell, by that time, the mini-bar was pretty well picked over anyway.

Chapter Three

Comics and Sports:
Enough Wannabe to Go Around

There are a huge number of comedians who wish they could have been sports stars, and conversely, at least some professional athletes think that it's pretty cool to have funny guys hanging around. All in all, it has made for some terrific moments.

Following sports takes up a huge chunk of time among a significant chunk of comics, too. We had time on our hands, and we loved our teams and hated our rivals. A good portion of those could be classified, like myself, as mildly obsessive. Billy Crystal and his fucking Yankees. At least he grew up there, and came by it honestly.

He told a story about playing in a celebrity game at Dodger Stadium when he was starring in the very underrated TV series *Soap*. He played short and not braggingly admitted that he made a couple of good stops out there and picked up a nice clean hit or two. Afterwards a Dodger scout sought him out, shook his hand and was all compliments.

"Hey, you showed some really good stuff out there. Obviously you've played some ball. How old are you?"

Crystal was beside himself.

"I'm twenty-seven."

"Ah. Nice meeting you," and the guy walked off.

Pro sports are a much younger man's game than pro comedy.

Jeff Foxworthy is a die had Braves fan. He used to go watch them in spring training just like I'd go watch the Astros. We got to do a spring training game, and I did get to drag him to an Astros game at the Dome years ago. I know he's from Georgia, but during the 1990s, those Braves of his were almost as obnoxious as those Yankees. And Tom Glavine would never be in the Hall of Fame if they called his pitches off the plate.

Speaking of the Yankees, Adam Leslie, another NYC native and diehard Yankee fan, also happened to be among the biggest gamblers I've ever met in my life. He would spend all of his time off at the track or at OTB or at a jai alai fronton someplace. He did take my Los Angeles roommate Ron Robertson and I to see some jai alai in Florida and gave us a betting tip that paid off. He said to read the program and check out the Basque players, which includes many of them. Find a Basque guy who's been doing badly, and then bet on him. Adam swore that his countrymen would tank so the guy didn't get sent back home. We won twice that day.

What money Adam didn't blow on greyhounds or horses, he partied away. His big finish was a Wizard of Oz take off where he wore an orange traffic cone on his head as the Wicked Witch. Legend has it that one night he had done so much blow that he kept having to wipe his nose during the bit, and the cone kept falling off. Quite the twisted sight gag for the other comics.

I was working the Comic Strip in Ft. Lauderdale one time that

Adam was in town mainly to spend his earnings at the track, and just happened to be booked on the show at nights. That also happened to be the same week that he turned me onto sushi for the very first time in my life. That, my friend, was a wonderful gift.

This week at the Strip fell during Class A ball season back when the Yanks had a facility there in Ft. Lauderdale. We had been out to catch a minor league game earlier in the week. Apparently, the big club had some shindig going on because a bunch of retired stars were in town for something.

Adam came back to the house where we were staying on a simultaneous emotional high and low. He would go to the track for the early races and then rush back to do his set. The format at the Strip was three, sometimes four comics who would rotate and get paid the same money. Usually owner Richie Tienken booked good acts, so folks got a hell of a show.

This particular evening, Adam had been walking out when he spotted Yogi Berra, Whitey Ford, Billy Martin and Mickey Mantle all lined up against a wall. This was total kid-in-a-candy-store moment for Adam. He walked up and asked if the four of them, his boyhood heroes, could please sign his Racing Form. He went down the line as each one signed until he got to Mantle who just looked at him and said, "Get the fuck away from me."

I guess we all know that the Mick had his good days and his bad ones. And standing there with dropped jaw after your boyhood idol just told you to fuck off, that one also turned out to be a bad day for Adam Leslie.

———

I've done several celebrity golf tournaments over the years. I had plenty of very funny sports-related material in my act, I was a very good joke writer who could add some customized laugh lines, and I was on the lower end of the spectrum when it came to being likely to make a complete ass of myself. Working these tournaments meant that I do a set at the banquet and round out the field of golf celebrities. The guys who didn't pay full price to play would get stuck with me.

What it's also meant is that I got into situations with people who I otherwise wouldn't be hanging out with.

I was in El Paso for one event in 1986. This one benefitted the Cancer Treatment Center and was hosted that year by Jim McMahon, whose Chicago Bears team had just won the Super Bowl. The tournament organizers had seen me at the grand opening of the Comic Strip and paid for me to come back out to play golf. What a blast. At one point I was coming back from free golf on a courtesy van with Johnny Unitas, U.S. Senator Harrison Schmidt and me. Just the three of us. Nice long drive and a lively conversation, and I just keep thinking, "Man, they are going to turn around just about any minute and say ' what the hell are you doing here?'"

It was at that tourney's show and gala later that night that I got involved in one of those newspaper making gaffe stories.

The show was a private event at Bart Reed's afore-mentioned Comic Strip club. It was a sparkling, great room for those first years. Ollie Joe Prater was headlining the room that week. I was just there for the golf. Sure enough, when they told Ollie that he'd have part of the night off, he insisted, being the ham he was, that he get to do his full 45 minute set for the golf celebs. And he had to close the show.

Fine with me. Less work. So I went up and did fifteen minutes of sports material then repaired to the back of the room where Bears kicker, Kevin Butler, a good guy, waved me over to their table. It's Butler, McMahon, coach Johnny Roland, and a couple of the other Bears who had come in to play golf. Butler and Roland seemed like a couple of good guys, but most of the rest were being slightly obnoxious pricks, to float an unbiased opinion. Significantly, there was also a reporter from the El Paso newspaper who was out to do a story on football star Jim McMahon.

McMahon, wearing the trademark sunglasses indoors, was holding court and having a few beers. Jim started getting a little rowdy and his attention span was getting a little short. About five minutes into Ollie's act, McMahon, who was pretty drunk by then I'm guessing, started saying to everyone else at the table something like "this guy is awful. How much would you give me to go piss on the mic stand?" Class guy, that Jim. No takers stepped forward, by the way.

What did happen though, was that the next morning's edition of the *El Paso Sun* had a big story on McMahon's night out that included the "urinating on the microphone stand" idea. When I stumbled down to catch the last shuttle bus to the golf course, Butler and Unitas were already on it, reading the article and laughing heartily.

We waited on McMahon, the last golfer unaccounted for. When he finally dragged himself onto the bus, looking a little worse for wear, Butler handed him the paper already folded open to the article about him. It was great fun to see all-time legend Johnny Unitas rag Jim McMahon all the way to the golf course about how any bonehead could sit there and get drunk, stupid and obnoxious with a reporter at the table.

The best one of those tournaments I ever played in, by far, was Bobby Mitchell's Hall of Fame tournament in the Washington, D.C. area. I lucked into that because a good friend of mine, Rick Delisi, was working as marketing director at the resort in Leesburg, Virginia where it was played. My job would be to fly free, play golf for two days, eat and drink for free, do a 30 minute set, and pick up a check. That didn't suck.

One interesting note about Delisi. He was once a contestant on Wheel of Fortune. After the show, in which he pocketed some cash but was not the big winner, he called Jim Patterson who was then his roomie. His first words were, "Hey, you remember how we always talk about if we ever get a little extra money, we'll buy all this booze and drugs and women and have a huge party for all of our friends?"

"Yeah," Jim said expectantly.

"Well, I just blew $250 on an E."

Back in Virginia, every one of the celebrity golfers in this event were NFL Hall of Famers, except for two special guests from the NBA, Bill Russell and Oscar Robertson. The first guy I met when I got there was Tom Fears from the old Rams. What a wonderful guy. In the hospitality room, I got to hear Chuck Bednarik do a get-off-my-lawn rant about how these softies in the NFL today only have to play one side of the ball, a diatribe complete with him showing off his gnarled fingers from his playing days. High-falutin' company for a die-hard sports fan like me.

We had a couple of hours blocked out the first full day for a practice round just for the celebs, and that included me. Rick told me to go down to the starter about noon and he'd have my golf bag sent up. When I got down there, I looked up and saw Jim Brown, Willie Lanier, and Kenny Houston on the first tee. I couldn't believe it. The starter said, "You'll be with the next group. I'll have your bag loaded on that cart over there."

I walked to the cart, met two of the members of the foursome - Ace Parker who played for the New York Football Yankees in the 1920s, and Packers great Jim Taylor, who was slathering sun block on himself like he was about to swim the English Channel. At one point I thought I was about to play golf with Gertrude Ederle.

Then I heard a voice behind me.

"I hope you don't mind bad driving."

The man extended his hand.

"I'm your cart partner, Don Maynard."

Oh, my God. I'm playing golf from the same cart as Don Maynard. The guy I used to pretend to be when I was throwing a football around my backyard. The classic end of the game scenario. Namath fades back. He looks up field. I throw the ball high in the air toward the other side of the yard. And Don Maynard runs under it! I fall to the ground for no apparent reason. Touchdown Jets!

The round turned out to be terrific. Maynard couldn't have been nicer. We complained about women and generally knocked the ball around in a general bogey golf sort of way. The best part was watching Don Maynard snipe at Jim Taylor for hitting three balls off every tee. And hear Taylor complain in return about Maynard using his ball retriever at every water hazard we encountered. There's something about knowing that an NFL Hall of Famer looks for somebody else's lost golf balls that I find comforting.

The banquet was that night about eight, followed by a tee time of roughly first light the next morning. Everyone went into the huge banquet hall, then the Hall of Famers were introduced one at a time as they walked through doors with a pretty model escorting them.

I was seated at Oscar Robertson's table. Unfortunately, he didn't talk to any of us pedestrians. His absolute goddess of a daughter happened to be going to school in DC, so she was his "date", and they spent all evening catching up. The nerve.

Well, I'm here to tell you that the intros went on forever. People's stomachs were growling all over the room. It sounded like backstage at *The Lion King*. Then after we ate, and, more importantly, before me, Bobby Mitchell did his annual roasting of his fellow Hall members. There were 30 or 40 of them. It was a very nice thing...in theory...if you didn't happen to be the comic who had to follow it.

At some point, as the number of people who were leaving because they teed off in six hours climbed past the 200 mark, the tournament director motioned me over and told me to cut my act to 20 minutes. Half an hour later, I got cut to 15 minutes.

Finally, after all the announcements, plus another reminder that tee time was 7:30 sharp, Bobby Mitchell introduced me. By that time, Marion Motley had been done with dinner and in bed for three hours.

A few folks had stayed to hear me. And they were very nice. Sonny Jurgenson and Bill Russell were right up front. They laughed harder than anyone. Bill Russell was without a doubt one of the best laughers I've ever had in any audience. Too bad he was not willing to travel.

I did a few jokes about sports, ad-libbed a few more about the celebs still in the room, including one about being stuck in the rough behind a small growth of trees that turned out to be Russell's clubs, then Rick and I strolled to the bar. Ah ha! So that's where everybody went.

The highlight of the evening for me was yet to come. Rick and I eventually found ourselves hanging out with John Riggins. I had lucked into some Redskin tickets a couple of years prior to that when they just happened to induct Riggins into the RFK stadium ring of honor, or whatever it's called. He followed Joe Theismann, who got a lukewarm round of applause, likely more than he deserved. Then they introduced Riggo, who bolted from the locker room in helmet, uniform and full pads and raced onto the field before he bear hugged Joe Gibbs. I told him how much I had enjoyed the moment, even though I'm not a Skins fan.

But what I really wanted to thank Riggins for was for being the star of one of my favorite White House stories. He confirmed it and added a few details.

After one of the Redskins Super Bowl victories, some Reagan staffer invited Riggo to a White House reception. He admitted to Rick and me that he'd been nervous as hell. So, he started drinking. Apparently, the White House has an open bar. Who knew? One of the other guests that evening was brand new Supreme Court Justice Sandra Day O'Connor, who Riggins didn't find to be that much of a charmer.

That's probably why he walked up to her, slapped her lightly on the shoulder, and said the immortal words, "Loosen up, Sandy baby." Now that's funny. He told us that the Secret Service gentlemen who escorted him to a waiting taxi not long after that, did not share my sentiment.

Then when Riggins found out what I did for a living, he bought us another round of drinks and started asking me all sorts of questions about working in front of a crowd. He had gotten into doing a part in a play and thought the whole concept of being on stage was brutal. I told him I'd be inclined to take it over getting body slammed by Jack Hamm.

We were having a fine time until the very young and beautiful girl that was sitting with Riggins became bored with the conversation and said she was going to her room. He downed his drink, shook our hands, and ran after her. I couldn't blame him. Bottom line here is that I'd be glad to go drinking with John Riggins any time.

Super Bowl in 1984, Raiders and Redskins, it was colder than shit in Houston that day. I had just moved back there from Los Angeles. That was when Andy Huggins, Jimmy Pineapple and I rented a nice two-story townhouse together in a very fashionable neighborhood on the west side of town. Still not sure what that rental agent was thinking.

We had a ton of good times at that place. I specifically recall watching a kick ass college hoops game between Indiana and Illinois, and I remember a Mondale party we hosted to watch a presidential debate in '84 where four people showed up. That should have told us something about the upcoming election, but we still floated the keg and finished a bottle of Crown. Oh yeah, and broke a cheap coffee table.

But that Super Bowl week, Kevin Nealon was in town. I had worked with him a few times before, so I invited him to come over for some homemade chili and the game on Sunday. That Saturday night, our heat went out. It was probably in the high 40s in the living room.

It was advisable to eat the chili fast. He and I and one other out of town comic sat on the couch wearing heavy coats. About every ten minutes, without fail, a deadpanned Nealon would look over and say, "Thanks, Mike. This is really nice."

Carl Faulkenberry and I used to go to Florida for baseball spring training every year. Carl is one of my closest pals ever, and we both live and breathe sports much of the time. We managed to pull it off for twelve straight seasons. When we first started going, it was to small ballparks with a real down home feel. I think the White Sox were still playing in a high school field. You got very close to the players and could talk baseball with them if you wanted. Nowadays the parks are bigger and more expensive with much less access. Like many things, progress has ruined it to a large extent.

Chris Dipetta, from Atlanta, was the one who booked us in one of our first spring training dates. We were playing the Ramada Inn in Sarasota directly across from the airport. We drove down there in mid-March from a week-long gig in Atlanta. There was one night off in between.

The trouble was that the day off, a Monday, was the night of the NCAA basketball final. Georgetown and Villanova that year. There was no way that two sports fans like Carl and me were going to miss that. So, we formulated a plan to drive until game time and then find a bar to watch the game. After it was over, we'd go on to Sarasota and check into the hotel. Simple enough.

When it was getting close to tip-off, we were around Gainesville, Florida. So, we headed toward the campus knowing there was bound to be a suitable bar nearby. We ended up across the street from the University of Florida in a place called the Salty Dog Saloon. We had a sandwich and started drinking beer which we found out was only eighty-five cents a can.

It soon became apparent that we were the only ones in the joint who were rooting for Villanova except for one professor who was originally from Philly. The rest of the place was filled with front running college boys who were for Georgetown because they were favored to win. We started betting beers.

Not long before midnight, we staggered out of the Salty Dog Saloon and very stupidly decided that we could still drive to Sarasota. By then it had also started to rain, one of those Gulf Coast downpours that one usually has to go to South Asia to enjoy. One of the troubles was that we were full of victory beer. Not only should we not have been driving, but we also had to pull over every forty miles or so to pee.

We had already stopped behind a shopping center, behind a hotel dumpster and on a dark stretch of road before we got to Tampa. As anyone who has ever urinated outdoors can tell you, a big city is the worst place to need to pull over. Give me a blanket of brilliant stars to whiz under any day.

We had been looking for another suitable spot for some time, and the rain was a blinding downpour. Finally, on a stretch of elevated road, we spotted a large area blocked off with cones away from the main lanes. We whipped in and whipped out. As we were getting drenched but relieved, we looked up and realized that we were right in downtown Tampa. The skyline was close enough to touch. Ah, what classy guys we are.

It was 2:30 in the morning by the time we pulled into Sarasota. We found the Ramada and were thrilled to pull under the canopy out front. Finally, hotel rooms and sleep.

Well, in the words of Howard Cosell, it was not to be. The desk clerk informed us that the hotel was full, so we would be staying in a nearby apartment that they had rented for the comics. Unfortunately, she had no idea where the key was. After a look or two at our scowling drunk faces, she decided on waking up the night manager who was off premises. It took another half hour for him to show up and give us the key. We were sneaking up on 3:30 A.M. when we located this swankienda in a complex behind the hotel that might have been up to standard in the late Forties. Maybe.

But, the key fit the lock, and there were beds inside, so at that point, it served our purposes. We opened the door and groped for a light switch. Click. Nothing. No lights. It was still storming outside, so we used the lightning and dim street glow to stumble into the kitchen. It turned out the kitchen light was the only one that worked in the entire place. A solid 60 watts to cover a two-bedroom hell hole.

By the time we rolled out the next morning and looked around, we were hoping for dark. In the living room next to the lonely couch was a table that held what Carl dubbed the world's tallest lamp. A table top thing that stood taller than he did. Needless to say, it had no bulb.

There was a woman named Marie who had somehow been put in charge of the comedy show at the hotel there. Judging by her disposition, she'd last had sex during the Hoover Administration. Bad complexion, bad breath, and a whiskey/cigarette voice that would have made Selma Diamond say "Lighten up".

As has been my experience from time to time, Marie was one of those people with whom I butted heads from the start. Maybe because I had the audacity to mention that we'd like to stay somewhere with lights.

I made the trip to Florida for Spring Training for eleven years straight after that. I took the best bookings I could get to finance the trip, but to put it plainly, Florida has way more than its share of shit gigs. Carl often went with me. I mean, what could possibly be better than doing comedy at nights in a club that gives you free drinks and sitting in the sun watching baseball during the day. In the end, you leave with a slight profit. That's heaven, boy.

With a dozen consecutive years of memory, they get a little jumbled up. But another terrific one was the NCAA basketball final of the very next year. It usually happened while we were down there, so it, too, became a ritual.

In 1986, a high school buddy of Carl's joined us for some fun in Florida. He was a sportscaster in Indianapolis and an all-around terrific guy named Dick Rea. He would make a few more of the Spring trips with us in later years.

But that year, the one forever marked as when Carl and I stole the wedding cake, was Louisville and Duke in the hoops finals. Since it always fell on a Monday, we generally didn't have shows those nights. So, we would find a place and settle in for some serious game watching.

That Monday afternoon in 1986 we had been to the beach at Clearwater. Some state park with decent sand and only a moderate crowd. We dredged up a nerf football from someplace and were running pass patterns. I had been down by Carl while Dick took off on what our physical abilities would allow was a slow post.

Carl heaved the ball, wet and heavy, just over Dick's shoulder. It bounced off his fingertips and smacked an older woman right in the back of the head. She had been kneeling at the water's edge picking up shells or something when this nerf football caught her. We rushed over. The nose piece of her glasses had made a small cut on the bridge of her nose. A trickle of blood was starting to appear. We fussed over her and apologized, especially Dick.

As she was assuring us that she was fine, her grown son walked up to find her mom surrounded by three men and blood running down her cheek. Carl and I quickly slipped off while Dick absorbed a rasher of choice words before he joined our retreat. Sorrr-eeee.

So, after injuring an old lady, we went back to the hotel, showered, and set off to find the perfect bar. We chose it based largely on the fact that Dick needed to pee. Traffic was at a standstill, there was a bar and restaurant, so this must be the place.

It was incredible luck. It was called Schooner's, owned by a guy from the Midwest who recognized jovial beer drinkers when he saw them. We had three huge tenderloins and fries. By tip-off, we had laid a great drinking base.

Like the year before, we were totally outnumbered by fans of the other team. Naturally, being real men, not some sort of panty wearing girlie types, we were solidly for Louisville. I should note that I hate Duke for several reasons: The game with Kentucky in 1978; the game with Kentucky in 1992; they show up in the Final Four too often; Coach K always looked like he just swallowed a turd; they're in a state which elected Jesse Helms over and freakin' over; and it's where Nixon went to law school. In short, somebody's got to pay.

We nestled in at the center of the bar and were soon surrounded by loud Duke fans. As was becoming the norm, we were the only ones rooting for Louisville. Just about the time the Dukies had determined that we were obnoxious in a fun, harmless way, the door opened, and a guy in a wheelchair rolled in. He was likely in his sixties and was unmistakably the curmudgeonly type. He pushed people out of the way until he was right next to us. Dropped a couple of semi-mean spirited comments. And we instantly became his best buddies.

He was from Indiana or Illinois or someplace up there, and more importantly, he was a fourth Cardinals fan. Everyone in the bar knew the guy, so protected by him and fortified by a few pitchers, we got louder. All in good fun, mind you. We were making everyone laugh. We're comics for crying out loud.

Sometime toward the end of the first half, after a little Louisville burst, our new pal started leading us in the first chant of "ACC Sucks!" It wouldn't be the last. Once again, we ended up winning more beer than we could drink. I walked across the street to a pay phone and called my dad back in Houston. Of course, he had just watched the game and was thrilled that a team from his native Kentucky had won. He was expecting my call. I miss those talks.

Not that this has to do with anything, but as I was writing these last few paragraphs, as Duke and another team I can't stand were about to tip off on TV, I kept hearing a noise and some chirping in the big hibiscus bushes outside my office window. I got up and opened the blinds. I swear to you that a beautiful red male cardinal was about a foot from my face, just chattering away. Pretty cool coincidence.

The most memorable incident of that spring happened a day or two after Dick went back to Indianapolis. Carl and I had a few more days of work the next week at a very fancy Mexican restaurant complex near the Clearwater airport. They had a comedy club in a room upstairs over the lush gardens and patios and comfortable dining rooms. We were playing there through Saturday before we drove back to Houston.

The week was fine. Shows were fun. Nice crowds in the little room upstairs. We finished up the late show on Saturday and grabbed a couple of beers, hovering around the manager, waiting to hear the magic words. Finally, after fifteen minutes or so, we went up and asked about settling up.

"What do you mean," he said.

"Getting paid."

Blank stare.

"We're going to take off, and we need to get our money for the week." We told him.

"But I don't pay you until after the show tomorrow." He kept a pretty straight face. He wasn't smiling. Oh shit, he was serious.

We explained, quite calmly at first, that we were booked through Saturday, not through Sunday. We pointed out that we had to drive all the way back to Houston and repack before we headed to wherever we might be working on Monday. We couldn't stay for this show they'd obviously added without telling us. We demanded our pay, in full, right then.

He swore up and down that they'd always had a Sunday show. Other comics later told us otherwise which just confirms that even part-time comedy club managers who really work for a restaurant turn into liars. He stood his ground and refused to pay us the full amount we had been promised. We were getting shorted almost $100 each because of this imaginary Sunday show he wanted to add. The only concession that he'd make was, and here was his fatal mistake, to give us an open tab at the downstairs bar for the two hours before closing time.

Well, do I need to say it? Carl and I proceeded to pour as much beer down our throats as we could, chased with a shot or two or three or.... All the while, we're rehashing this unexpected and unwarranted cut in pay. And we're getting madder and madder. Finally, about one in the morning, we reached the "fuck this place" breaking point.

We got up, tipped the bartender, bad-mouthed the club manager, and headed toward the door.

It just so happened that a large wedding reception was breaking up about the same time. In fact, right by the front door was a totally unattended rolling cart, the sort you usually saw in high school audio video rooms. This one held three large sections of very fancy wedding cake. It had been disassembled, probably to go home with the bride's parents.

Don't get ahead of me. We're not thugs or unsentimental cretins. We only stole one of the three sections. Using our drunk logic, we figured that would be plenty to bring down the wrath of the father who'd dropped a few thousand bucks just moments before. And bring it down right on the head of the manager who'd screwed us out of our money. Sort of making our own karma, if you like.

I went outside and brought my car up to the front entrance. Right on cue, here comes Carl, gangly legs going all directions, running across a (I swear to you) swaying rope bridge over sunken gardens and carrying a beautiful round tier of wedding cake about two and a half feet across. He tossed it into the back seat and jumped in as I sped out of the parking lot like Starsky and/or Hutch. He kept looking behind us to make sure we weren't being followed.

We made it almost a half mile before we passed another bar and decided we still had time for a nightcap.

You might be wondering what one does with an entire tier of wedding cake. Well, at two in the morning, after drinking for a few hours, you eat it. We got back to the hotel and strolled right through the lobby with the thing. Took it on up to the room to chow down. Not exactly the late night run to Waffle House or Krystal that you'd expect in the South, but it would do.

Of course, we had no utensils and no napkins, so we had to eat it with our hands. That wasn't a pretty picture. Especially since Carl was pacing around on the phone having a fight with his girlfriend. I did find an unlocked linen closet down the hall and made off with about thirty-five towels to clean up our messy room. When we woke up the next morning and surveyed the carnage, we packed awfully damn quick and promptly left the state.

One post script to this story. In December 2000, Jim Patterson went over to visit Carl, who was then living in the St. Pete area. They were sitting around one night drinking with a few other old friends and swapping stories. Suddenly Jim started urging Carl to tell the wedding cake story. Carl shakes his head, shrugs his shoulders, and denies remembering that one.

Jim tried to prompt him. "You know, when you and Vance stole the wedding cake."

Carl kicked him under the table.

"Come on," Jim continued. "I love that story. It's hysterical. When the club screwed you on the money."

It wasn't until later that Carl could explain to Jim that one of the guys at the table that night was the one who had booked us into the Mexican restaurant gig. Nice going, buddy.

That agent was Bob Shumaker who has booked the Coconuts clubs in Florida for years. Some of the gigs left a little to be desired, but Bob was always a great guy to me.

He told me a story one time about he and three friends going out to dinner at the fanciest steak house in Tampa. One of those joints with a really nice reputation in the region. If Bob had ever taken me to dinner there, I might know the name.

Well, after dinner, they decided to walk up to the cigar bar and lounge area. They were sitting there, sipping on Bourbon and Cokes, when they spotted one of those bottles of liquor that sit on its own fancy pedestal. Little pin light aglow underneath it. Obviously very special.

Bob inquired about it. The bartender told him that it's the best bourbon they have. Real designer stuff. The smoothest they'll ever taste. So, Bob orders a shot for each of them. As the bartender watches, all four guys dump the shots into their Cokes.

"Umm, tasty." Bob told him. Or something like that.

When the bill came, Bob found out that those shots of special bourbon cost about sixty dollars apiece. Trying hard to maintain his dignity, he paid the bill and slinked out. It's best to put an episode like that behind him. Lesson learned.

But the pain wasn't over. About a year later, Bob had an occasion to celebrate and found himself back at the fancy steakhouse again. After dinner, his party went to the bar for a couple more drinks. While they were sitting there, trying to be inconspicuous, the patron right next to Bob pointed to the fancy bottle behind the bar which was still there, sitting on its own special pedestal.

"What's in that bottle?" He asked.

"That's our best bourbon. Costs sixty dollars a shot," the bartender (a different one) answered. "Funny story. About a year ago, these four morons come in and each order a shot of it. Then they pour them into Cokes. Can you believe that? Wasting sixty dollar shots in Coke."

He and the patron laughed and shook their heads knowingly. Somehow, a year later, Bob had managed to be humiliated a second time. His apparent fate to be endlessly shamed before the best-heeled diners in Tampa Bay.

Carl and I were also involved in a scheme to go out drinking with the legendary broadcaster, Harry Caray. The Cubs were in town to play the Astros, and we wanted to go have a cold one, or four, with the greatest baseball fan of all times. I happened to know that the Cubbies stayed at the Stouffer's Hotel in Houston's Greenway Plaza at that time, so, fully expecting to wade through waist deep shit to get a hold of him, but knowing we had to start somewhere, I called the hotel switchboard.

"Harry Caray's room, please."

Ring. Ring.

"Hullo," answered the incredibly familiar raspy voice on the other end.

Holy shit, they put us right through. This was the last thing we were prepared for.

"Hi, Harry. My name is Mike Vance, and I'm with Carl Faulken-berry. We're comedians here in town, and we're good friends of John Fox."

Fox had been in the booth with Harry and told us what a great guy he was.

"John Fox? I love John Fox. You must be great guys, too. What can I do for you?"

'Well, we just wanted to take you out for a beer after the game. We were hoping you could come over to the Comedy Workshop where we'll be playing, and we could go from there."

"Sure, sounds great. Give me directions."

And just like that, I was giving directions to Harry Caray. I finished, and suddenly there was a long pause.

"Wait a minute. We have a night game!"

"That's okay, Harry. The place is opened late."

"Well, give me the directions again. I just threw them away."

As one poetic fan in Chicago said on the day Harry died: "You loved him because he was a knucklehead just like all the rest of us."

Well, we were so stoked that we blew off our sets that night and went to the ballgame instead. There was no way we were going to let this opportunity slip away. We wrote a note, complete with yet another set of directions, and handed it to the press box guard who swore he would deliver it to Harry. Yeah right.

After the game, we scurried down to the players' entrance to make sure we didn't get shut out.

Carl and I stood there like a couple of groupies watching the Astros get in their cars. Catcher Alan Ashby had personalized plates that read "E2". I always thought that referred to the fact that he bought a Pontiac Fiero.

Finally, Steve Stone came out, Harry's color guy. We ran up to him, and said that we were comedians looking for Harry. Stone told us that Harry would be coming out a different exit, and that we should walk around to the other side of the Dome. Being the gullibly sophisticated gents that we were, we believed him.

We were over a quarter of the way around this massive round ballpark before it dawned on me that there was no other exit from the floor level. Cussing Steve Stone, we wheeled about and started hoofing it back to the loading dock. Suddenly I stopped in my tracks.

"Fergie Jenkins!"

We were passing two guys whom I recognized as Jenkins and Cubs catcher, Jody Davis.

"Can I have your autograph?"

"You got a pen?"

For once in my life, I did. And it just so happened that Gulf Oil Company had been good enough to sponsor a giveaway that night commemorating Nolan Ryan passing Walter Johnson for the all-time strikeout record. I thrust the ball at Fergie who took a few minutes to check it out. When he had signed, Jody Davis reached over and took it.

On instinct alone, I snatched the thing out of Jody's hand and said, "Sorry Jody. Hall of Famers only."

As I started thinking about how I was about to be punched out by a big league catcher, Fergie Jenkins and Carl Faulkenberry hit the ground laughing. I mean Fergie was doubled over. Given the circumstances, all Jody Davis could do was shrug.

We never did meet up with Harry. We went back to the comedy club, but he never showed. There are however, three postscripts to this story.

One is that a couple of years later, Carl was in Chicago working a room downtown and had the occasion to sit down for drinks with Steve Stone. Stonie admitted that he probably had sent us on a wild goose chase that earlier night, but according to Carl, he turned out to be a hell of a guy after all.

The best part came a few years after that. Carl had gone back to his high school reunion in Lafayette, Indiana. Though he had lived most of his life in Louisiana, his dad had been working up north during those years, and Carl became a stand out guard on the high school basketball team. He also told me years later that he was thumbing through his yearbook and was shocked to discover that he had graduated with some nerdy band guy who grew up to be Axl Rose.

Anyway, some guy at the reunion was talking to Carl and said, "Hey, the weirdest thing happened about five years ago. I was watching a Cub game on WGN. I think they were in Houston or someplace. Anyway, Harry Caray said that you and some other comedian were there at the game, and I'll bet he went on for the whole half inning about what terrific and totally funny guys you two were. It was really something. I couldn't believe that you knew Harry Caray"

I'd give anything to hear that recording.

One final coda to this story. Three decades later, I told the tale in front of my chapter of the Society for American Baseball Research. At the next month's meeting, one of my friends in the chapter handed me a manilla envelope. It was a nice 8x10 of Jody Davis inscribed: "To Mike, You're not in the Hall of Fame, either. Jody Davis."

The Houston comics were all huge Astros fans above most anything else sports related. We went to a ton of games. Ron Robertson had some kick ass company season tickets in the early 80s, and I had season tickets myself off and on starting in 1986. We also had plenty of ticket connections. That meant many good stories for Houston comics at the old Astrodome.

One of the signature moments of the Astros franchise was when Mike Scott threw a no-hitter against the Giants to clinch the NL West in 1986. I had tickets in my season ticket package, but ended up getting booked at the Knoxville Funny Bone. That was an eventful week. I was working with Leo Nino, a funny guy who became a good pal that week. He used to crack me up when we did improv by introducing himself as Dexter Mathoraphan.

For some reason, Leo was on a kick that week of asking women to show us their tits. It was absolutely astounding how many did it, some in the middle of nightclubs. Really nice ones, too. I love this country. One important side note: don't try it at Safeway.

The Mike Scott game was an afternoon game. It wasn't on regular TV, so I went down to the bar where we had been hanging out every night after the shows and sat in a back room by myself drinking iced tea and yelling for the Astros. Toward the end of the game, a handful of locals came in to watch it. That night at the club, I paid $100 to buy up all the surplus cheap champagne and plastic glasses left over from the previous New Year's Eve show. They poured a glass for every single person in the sold out room, and during my act, we all raised a toast to the Astros. For the record, I hate champagne, so I drank Miller Lite.

Pat Shannon, brother of genius comedians T Sean and Charlie, was at the game that day. I should mention that Pat had a reputation of being fairly obnoxious from time to time. He had once been ragging on Tommy Lasorda from a seat behind the visitors' dugout. At one point during the game, Lasorda came out to cuss at whoever was heckling him. When he stuck his head up over the dugout, Pat spit tobacco juice on him from two rows back. Lasorda went ballistic, as you might guess, and true to what I'd expect from Tommy, had the wrong guy thrown out.

I'm not sure what Pat was doing that no hitter day, but it got him tossed in Astro jail. Like most stadiums, they had a holding cell in the bowels of the joint for unruly fans. So as a huge crowd cheered the Astros second ever trip to the post season, Pat Shannon cooled his heels under the stands.

At one point, a veteran Houston Police Officer who lived on the same block as the Shannons happened to stroll by. This was a guy who Pat had known all his life, and it smelled like opportunity.

"Excuse me, Officer Johnson. Hey, it's me, Pat Shannon from across the street."

Pat was all sweetness and light.

"What are you doing in here, Patrick?"

"It's all a big misunderstanding, sir. Could you please get them to let me out of here?"

"Sorry, son."

"But you've known me my whole life. They blamed me for something that someone else did. I just want to go back and watch the game."

"Well, you should have thought about that."

"Oh yeah! Well, why don't you go home and fuck that fat wife of yours!"

There are two other little Mike Scott related stories. A whole bunch of us went out to a game a couple of years later. Scotty was pitching and took a no-hitter into the seventh. I know there were twelve comedians in a block of seats. It was a Sunday afternoon game and happened to be miniature bat day, so we were totally surrounded by screaming Little Leaguers who were armed. My dad went with us and must have bought the whole section four rounds of beer. He was having a great time.

Joe Restivo was there that day along with several other guys who happened to be in town working one of what at that peak time must have one of nine Houston comedy clubs. One of the guys was some opening act from Louisiana who was seeing his first major league ballgame. From time to time, he would turn around and ask if all baseball games were this boring because nobody ever got a hit. He was dead serious.

For some reason, Faulkenberry hated Mike Scott. Just to be contrary, I assume. But when Scotty got out of the top of the seventh, Carl cussed him and got up to leave. Three of us were wrestling with him in the aisle trying to make him stay and watch. He busted loose and sprinted to his car. He said that when Ken Oberkfell of the Braves broke up the no-no with one out in the ninth, he almost drove back just so he could taunt us all.

John McDowell, a genius joke writer from Texarkana, once ran into Mike Scott in an airport late in his career. Scott's, not McDowell's. At the time, Johnny Mac had Scott on his rotisserie baseball team, a league that I was also in. So, when he saw Mike Scott traveling without the team, he strolled right up and introduced himself. You need to picture this balding guy with the world's biggest chin (he called it the kickstand of love) and a heavy East Texas twang.

"Mike, John McDowell. I'm a comedian from Dallas and a big Stros fan. Hey, look, buddy, I got you on my rotisserie team this year, and wanted to say that you're doing a heck of a job. But if you ever get in a situation where you have a big lead and Mike Piazza comes up, groove one will you? I got him, too."

Jimmy Pineapple and I used to go to tons of Astros games in the Dome, and there was a spot on the field level, past all the seats, where you could walk around and stand above the corner outfielders with a heavy wire mesh in front of you. Our big rival then was the Dodgers. We hated the Dodgers. Since we had seats down the third base line, left field was a damn convenient spot to heckle. We would go stand behind Dusty Baker in left field and rag on him mercilessly. We'd bad mouth the Dodgers in general, Dusty's fielding, Lasorda's mother, you name it. Eventually he would flip us off behind his back. And we would roar approval and applaud and cheer. By the time we brought Carl Faulkenberry around to show him one time, it had gotten to the point where we could just use verbal shorthand. We'd go to our spot and start yelling "It's us Dusty. You know what we're here for. You know what we want." And Dusty would flip us off behind his back. Sometimes we'd yell "Dusty, we can do this the hard way or the easy way." and he'd flip us off. Often you could see him laughing.

Once we were in LA and figured out how to get behind Dusty out in left field at Dodger Stadium. We started screaming, "Dusty! It's us." and you saw him straighten up and whip around. There we were waving. And he just shook his head and laughed. I don't remember if he flipped us off that time or not. I was thrilled when the Astros brought him in to manage. What a wonderful guy.

George Kanter is a comic from Phoenix. Very nice guy who had these athletic good looks and salt and pepper hair. He was a huge a huge sports fan who somehow made friends with LPGA golfer Jan Stephenson back when she was a seriously incredible babe.

He was also very good buddies with Terry Mulholland, the left-hander who pitched for damn near every major league team twice. I think he's still out there somewhere, and Terry has to be like 68 by now. So, when we were in Chicago and the Phillies came to town, the team du jour for Mulholland at the time, George got us primo seats for free.

Not only that, but through a very sophisticated Wrigley Field security system which I think, no lie, involved a hole punch and the ticket stub, we had access to the private family and friends area outside the Phillies clubhouse. In fact, it looked to be almost all family the day we were there. Terry's dad was there also, and after we all visited for a bit, George and I waited in a closed off area of the concourse while Terry showered.

We watched all the Phils come out dressed to go out to dinner. Little kids, obviously belonging to the families of teammates would go up and ask for autographs. Finally, Len Dykstra came strolling out in some velour sweat suit and a ball cap. Right in front of us, a little boy, about eight years old, went up with a pen and some paper and asked for an autograph.

The always worthless punk Dykstra literally slapped the stuff out of his hand and said, "Fuck you."

Sometimes your perception of these guys is wrong. In that case, it was dead solid perfect.

Jim Patterson and I had booked ourselves at the two Funny Bones in Chicago in the late 80s specifically so we could go see a series with the Astros at Wrigley. We got up there two days early to catch all three games. The first one turned out to be the second night game in the history of that ballpark. They hadn't known when the lights would be ready, and after a rain out with the Mets, we lucked out. Our seats that night were in the front row of the upper deck between home and first. None better. The row houses behind the fences were lit up like a Hollywood movie set version of Wrigley. It was incredible.

After the game, we went downtown near the hotel we had gotten for Monday and Tuesday might. Hit a couple of clubs. We were standing in a bar when Jim suddenly looked toward the door and said, "There's Walling and Agosto."

I thought he meant some guys who looked like Denny Walling and Juan Agosto, two Astros players. We all used to make those look alike jokes. But no, he meant the real Walling and Agosto.

We sat there and talked to them and had beer for quite some time. Walling and I even exchanged phone numbers because he was going to come see my show the next Saturday out at the Comedy Showcase not far from his house in Houston. The Stros had a Saturday day game, so it was perfect. When we went back to the hotel, I couldn't have been happier because I finally had a buddy who played for the Astros, and that meant free tickets and hanging with the ball players.

I kid you not, Denny Walling got traded to the Cardinals less than a week later.

I must have really pissed him off.

John Farneti, who was then a part time comedian and full time attorney, also happens to be a huge sports fan. He and his buddy, Tom Terrando, both of whom grew up in North Central Illinois, have long collected vintage jerseys and caps. Tom even turned the big room in the upstairs of one of his houses into a miniature indoor baseball field complete with wallpaper of fans.

They were thrilled when a chance came up to go visit with a favorite son of the hometown. Russ Meyer had pitched for several National League teams back in the 1950s, most notable being the perennial World Series bound Brooklyn Dodgers. They called him the Mad Monk because he had a volatile temper. Once with the Phillies he threw his spikes at the ceiling of the shower room, and they stuck there. In spite of being a bench jockey and pissing off most everyone around him, he won 94 games in the bigs, including 17 in 1949 and 15 in 1953.

More importantly for us, he was the bench coach for the Yankees when Buck Showalter was there in the early 90s. And since he had been a childhood pal of both Terrando's and Farneti's moms, they wangled a spate of free tickets for two games when the Yanks came to the old ballpark in Arlington to play the Rangers. I got invited along, as did Farneti's little brother, Geno. Even better, the big lawyers popped for the rooms.

We checked into some suite hotel near the ballpark where the Yanks would be staying. Assuming that big money ballplayers get big money rooms, we opted for the concierge level, accessible only to high rollers like us, and the New York Yankees. We made sure to secure rooms just down the way from the always open concierge hospitality room. Even though I am a lifelong Red Sox fan and rabid Yankee hater, this was going to be fun. It helped that this was during a time when the Blue Jays ruled the AL East, and the Yankees finished fourth.

As it turned out, only Showalter had a concierge level room. But I did see Don Mattingly had the room directly across the big atrium from me, and one floor down. I saw him twice when we both happened to be coming or going at the same time.

The high point was a lunch with Russ. A great treat to listen to this salty 70-year old guy talk about the old days. It was also cool as shit to hear him completely bad mouth Tim Leary. He went on at vituperative length about how they just wanted Leary to throw the ball and not nibble around the plate like a pussy. It was also interesting to note that when he kept saying "we", he meant the New York Fucking Yankees.

We also worked in a side trip over to Dallas and played catch on the Grassy Knoll. That got us some looks. While on the block, we went through the museum in the Book Depository. It's amazing how close you are to where JFK's motorcade rolled by at 8 mph. There is no way that Oswalt could miss. How anyone could see that and think there was a conspiracy is beyond me. Talking about the closeness of the window, Geno said, "The real conspiracy is that it wasn't a shooting, it was a strangulation."

We went to the game that night and managed to get a quick hello in to Russ before the first pitch. It turned out to be an extra inning affair in a pouring rain. We bailed and went back to the hotel bar. The theory was that we'd just hang out with the players when they came back. The trouble was that the game lasted for ever because of a rain delay, and the bar closed at midnight. We got kicked out before the team returned.

Plan B was that we left a message for Russ to come hang with us in the hospitality suite. We brought a bunch of beer down there. It was almost as good. That is except for the fact that a 70 year old guy wasn't up to partying till dawn with four idiots like us.

What did happen was that again, for the sixth or seventh time that week, when I walked down to my room, Mattingly was coming back from the ice machine. He looked at me kind of funny and did the old chin nod thing. About thirty minutes later, I was walking back to the suite and saw him looking out his window. He spotted me and jerked the curtains shut. In other words, we never did get to party with the Yankees, but Don Mattingly did think that I was some sort of creepy stalker.

There is one piece of video that I'd love to have. A whole bunch of us went to a Stros game one weekday afternoon. As was the norm for the Dome on those occasions, we had a large area to ourselves down the left field line. I can't recall everyone who was there, but I do know that at least three Shannon brothers were present and Riley Barber. Midway through the ball game a pop up landed right in front of us in foul territory.

Andy Van Slyke was playing left, and he picked it up and tossed it to Barber who had run down to the front row. It hit him right in the hands and bounced back on the field. Van Slyke shook his head and picked it up again and tossed it to Barber. This time Barber looked like Jerry Lewis as he juggled it then dropped it behind him where a little kid scooped it up and ran back up the aisle.

The coolest part was that the announcers in the booth were yukking it up at the ineptitude. I know that because Charlie Shannon had been taping the game, and I got to see it once. It would have been much more than once except that Charlie had a habit of misplacing things. I don't think he lost them, they just got put into piles and became impossible to find. I can only hope that the tape of Barber's big league moment might still resurface.

Riley was not the only comic who let a souvenir ball get away. At the All Star Workout Day in 1986, Jim Patterson let a ball that Charlie Hough tossed to him sit on top of his head until some kid behind him snatched it. The thing was stationery atop Patterson's cap while he tried to reach it. Of course, Jim had the good excuse of being rather drunk at the time.

Back then, the All Star Home Run Derby was nowhere near the spectacle it is today. They held it during the day. We got four tickets. It was me, Patterson, Cliff Moore and Rick DeLisi. We must have gotten there about ten in the morning to make sure we got the prime seats in the outfield that we wanted: Left center field in the front row of the bleachers. We were going to catch ourselves some home run balls.

Soon after we were seated, the whole section around us filled in with about four million kids. There we were, an island of beer drinking grownups in the front row. We had fun bantering with various players while they shagged flies, including Hough, who was then in his mid-seventies, I think.

The obvious by-product of all that beer was a trip to the bathroom. And in the middle of the Derby, no less. Being serious baseball fans, DeLisi and I waited until a lefty was up, so we wouldn't miss out on our chance to catch history. Then we dashed for the men's room which was up about forty rows and then another 100 yards away.

We were both breathing a sigh of relief at the urinal trough when we heard one of the biggest yells ever. It seems that with all our clever planning, we both managed to miss the longest home run in the history of the Astrodome. Daryl Strawberry crushed one that hit a speaker hanging from the roof in right center and was still going up. Somehow, I don't think we could have experienced history any other way.

We didn't just watch sports. We also played. For several years, the Workshop comics had the most undisciplined softball team in Houston. Most other teams took us in stride, but there were a few who thought our antics were insulting. I don't know what they cared, they usually beat us.

I sometimes played outfield and sometimes played second base, my old baseball position. One night I made some flip-up sunglasses with a Groucho nose attached. Everybody thought it was tremendously funny. Late in the game I nestled under a towering pop-up, flipped the glasses down and the dark lenses made me totally lose the ball which dropped almost on top of the bag. Guess that trick would work better if it's not a night game.

Riley Barber was the most uncoordinated man on Earth. I mean the man had no ankles, just leg then foot. We put him at catcher. I kid you not, one day there was a pop-up at the plate. Barber circled under it about six times before he tripped over his feet and fell flat on his face. The ball landed on the back of his head.

Without a doubt, though, the funniest episode ever was at the very end of a game that we were finally going to win. Ron Robertson, who played minor league ball, was on the mound. With a rare comedian victory one out away, Ron induced a lazy fly to left center, right at the sure-handed Jimmy Pineapple. Pina had recently bought a wide-brimmed plantation style hat, and he was wearing it in the outfield. Since the ball was right to him, he decided to do one of his patented between the leg catches to wrap up the win, only with the flourish of catching it in his hat. He pulled the thing off, reached around his back and thrust it between his legs as he had done with his glove a hundred times before. The ball slammed directly into his nads. Jimmy dropped to the ground one way. The ball went another way. And we were all laughing so hard that the batter circled the bases. Classic.

Bill Silva, Conrad Lawrence and I started the first all comedians golf tournament. It was held at H&H Ranch north of Houston. A few in other cities followed our lead with Michael Finney's Arizona shindig being the best known. Ours though was not for charity. It was a Sunday and Monday thing exclusively where comedian and comedy club owners and managers could meet up, party and play bad golf.

From about 1985 to 1988, it was a highlight of the year for dozens of comics and owners. Someday I'll share some of those hijinks.

As fun as the Houston tournaments were, though, the single biggest moment I recall from any of these took place at Bruno Schrippa's inaugural comedy golf tournament in Syracuse. It was a one day affair with a fairly small turnout being the first year. Bruno booked me at his club Wise Guys on the back end of it. My great pal Ron Robertson was there, too. Otherwise, it was largely acts from the Northeast and Midwest. I knew several of them, but some were strangers. I think Ron knew even fewer of them.

Ron would be the first to tell you that he could sometimes be rather standoffish with strangers, so when some guy in shorts and black socks came up to us and introduced himself as we were strapping our golf bags to our cart, he gave him short shrift, as they say. After a few basic exchanges, Ron finally looked at him and said something along the lines of, "Look, pal. Nothing personal, but my friend bus is already full." As soon as it was out of his mouth and the guy was walking away without further comment, Ron looked at me and said, 'That was someone I needed to know, wasn't it?"

"Yep. That was the manager of the New York Improv."

As stressed elsewhere, comedians are not early risers. The first tee time for us was early afternoon, and the course there at venerable Drumlins Country Club had been pretty busy that morning. As Bruno had about 30 or 40 comedy golfers gathered on the first tee for a ceremonial opening, a steady stream of those early golfers were coming up the parallel fairway on 18.

After a few words of pomp, Bruno declared the first Wise Guys Golf Tournament open. With all of us watching, he pulled back his driver and unleashed the biggest slice I've ever seen on a golf course. Though struck solidly, the ball took off at damn near a right angle. Coming up the 18th was a cart with a big, middle-aged dude in the passenger seat. As golfers are prone to do, he was riding loose and comfortable with the outside leg hanging out at an angle. Bruno's tee shot hit the guy square in the nutsack on the fly.

Every last one of us screamed with laughter. We couldn't stop. Many of us had to lie down on the grass because we could no longer stand up. The sheer absurdity of it, and the visual and the noise. It was so bang-bang. Tee shot, muffled scream from a guy on the next fairway, and that was followed by said guy tumbling from his golf cart holding his groin like the famous George C. Scott short film on *The Simpsons*.

It took a solid ten minutes for us to wipe our tears and shake the stitches out of our respective sides. Those of us who didn't tee off for another 15 or 20 minutes walked back to the pro shop for spare golf balls. Unexpectedly, we found the offended and wounded golfer in there raising holy hell with the club pro.

"It hit me right in the balls!" this guy is hollering. "And then they all just laughed! It's not funny!"

One of us managed to choke out, "Sorry, sir, but yes it was." With that, we all started howling with laughter all over again. In fact, I was laughing out loud just typing this.

Several of the Houston guys also put together three all sports comedy shows toward the end of the Workshop time. The Players to be Named Later, as we billed ourselves, were Carl Faulkenberry, Jim Patterson, Riley Barber, Andy Huggins, John Farneti and myself. We wrote some very funny and timely sketches, if I do say so.

In a rare stroke of marketing genius, we invited a different local sports media personality to every show to host a fake Sports Center "broadcast". The guys ate it up, and not coincidentally, mentioned us frequently on the air. That's also when a handful of us hooked up with Craig Roberts from the local NBC affiliate. It turned out to be a great collaboration since I personally ended up doing sports comedy shows with Craig on two different television stations.

There were some memorable bits that we did in those things. Barber and I played two 90-year old New York boxers who swung at each other and complained about our ailments. Carl played Bobby Knight at a press conference introducing the new female assistant coach he had been forced to hire. The coach was portrayed by the moustache toting Andy Huggins wearing a red dress. I did Gary Cooper as George Steinbrenner giving a bitter and caustic farewell as he was suspended by Major League Baseball.

The one moment from those shows that none of us will ever forget took place during the last one. We were about five minutes to curtain at Stages, an Equity theatre where we had gone since the Workshop had closed down several months before. All of a sudden, Barber was no place to be seen. He had given a reason only to Huggins, and when I heard it, I went fucking ballistic. As the curtain was about to rise, the boy had left the building to go move his laundry from the washer to the dryer.

Dick Rea, my Indianapolis sports casting buddy, was a nice connection to get into a few sports events for a while. I remember one time that Carl was going to be in the area and planned to hook up with Dick, who had to cover a college basketball game between Indiana and Notre Dame. The idea was for Carl to meet him at Market Square Arena, but for some reason, the two never hooked up before Dick had to go take his place on press row.

Being of the mind that if you act like you belong someplace, people are not that inclined to bother you, Carl walked through the loading dock of the Arena. He kept turning corners, wandering down hallways until he found a tunnel to the floor. Why stop there, right? He spotted an empty folding chair under one of the baskets and plopped his ass down in it.

Meanwhile, Dick Rea is sitting courtside, wondering what happened to his buddy, Carl. He figured it out when the opening tip got loose, and Carl tossed the ball back to the ref.

I was working in Indy one summer when Larry Bird was hosting a charity basketball event called Larry's Game. He had invited various friends and teammates of his to come play, but the top of the list, aside from Larry himself, was Isaiah Thomas and this Michael Jordan fellow. Without thinking twice, Dick got me a credential to come haul cable behind the camera guy, a job that has since disappeared in the days of wireless everything. Technically I was a producer, the TV and movie catchall.

I sat in a press area under the basket and enjoyed watching these NBA guys have some fun. When it was over, it was time for us to do our interviews. Bird wasn't doing one on ones that night. Instead, everyone had to come into the locker room as a group. My credential didn't get me in there, so I waited by the door and listened.

That's was when Bird was coming back from an ankle injury, and the main story was if he'd be ready to play the next season. What I heard, and what Dick confirmed, was Bird being a complete prick. He dodged questions about his ankle, as if that wasn't what everyone wanted to know. The interview ended when someone asked something along the lines of: "Where would you say the ankle is right now? 80%? 70?"

Bird went into a profanity laced tirade about that being a "stupid fucking question", and that was the end of the interview. Bird most definitely lived up to his reputation.

Michael Jordan was next. He came over to where we had set up, in an area just inside the walkway to the court. He was supremely professional, not friendly or outgoing, but when the Sun Gun on the camera came on, the famous Michael smile flashed and the answers were warm and genuine. When we were done, he asked if we got what we needed, and he was gone.

Isaiah could not have been looser. He was jacking with us before we started, joked with us during the interview and acted almost like he was wondering where we were all going drinking afterwards.

I know everyone has good nights and bad nights, and that those things come out into interaction with the public, but I saw three different approaches to an interview that night. It was a lesson I would go on to learn many times over in my various media jobs around sports.

One last favorite moment from the Astrodome. For some reason, Jimmy Pineapple liked the Cubs. It was likely because all their games were on WGN in the afternoons. Or it could have been simply that Wrigley Field was such a very cool place to go. I do know that it spread across most of his family in New Roads, Louisiana, though. His sister, Mary, was a freaking fanatic about them.

She and I went to a Cubs game at the Dome one afternoon that was, as usual with Dome day games, sparsely attended. We had great seats behind first base. At one point in the game, we thought we spotted Carl Faulkenberry sprawled across three seats in the loge section, as was his custom. I walked all the way up there to check.

As I was waving to Mary from two decks up and saying it was some other guy with equally lazy ballgame posture, Ryne Sandberg, the object of all her lust, smoked a line foul that caromed off the back of the seat next to her, the seat I had been sitting in.

When I got back down there, Mary was slapping at me for being gone and not catching the Sandberg ball for her. I did feel compelled to point out that I'd be leaving the ballyard on a stretcher right then if I hadn't been fortunate enough to get up when I did.

Mary had gotten tickets for her and her husband and Jimmy and me one time. They weren't bad seats, in the mezzanine behind third. We were meeting there.

Now one thing that my dad instilled into my brain at a tender age was that you were never late to a ball game. Jimmy agreed. So, as we kept waiting at the West Gate behind the plate for Mary to show her happy ass up, we were getting more and more agitated. Finally, it was game time, and no Mary. In these pre-cell phone days, that also meant no phone calls.

As we stood there, two very attractive ladies walked up and asked if we needed tickets. Now technically, we had committed to pay Mary for two of hers, but these girls were cute. What would you do?

The upshot of the deal was that when Mary arrived and couldn't find us, she and her husband, Fred, went on in. She spotted us a couple of innings later. It wasn't that tough since we were the guys with two hot babes in the first row behind the Cubs on deck circle. She might have been a little pissed, but we had a good time visiting with Shawon Dunstan anyway.

But the real story about Jimmy at a Cubs-Astros game was yet another night. A few of us were there in our preferred area of the field boxes behind the visitors' dugout. We were probably about 20 or 25 rows up. We had been drinking beer and generally cracking jokes for the whole section. The Cubs were out in front by a couple of runs.

For some reason, I seem to recall that the reliever was George Frazier, the guy who holds the distinction of having been the losing pitcher in three games of the 1981 Series when the Yanks coughed it up to the Dodgers. Just for the record, the night of Game Six of that Series, the one that caused the famous Steinbrenner apology to Yankees fans for his team's sucky play, I was in New York taping a Showtime special. When we walked out of the theatre, the gutters were literally filled with Yankees caps. Sweet.

Frazier pitched for the Cubs in 84-86, and was every bit as effective. This particular day, he proceeded to give up hit after hit to the Astros. The lead vanished, and then the good guys went ahead by two. I know that one of the hits was a sweet double by Jose Cruz which brought me and most normal fans to my feet. It also made Jimmy snap.

As all the Astros fans around him starting sending taunts in his Cub cheering direction, he started loudly joking back at them and calling for a pitching change. When Cruz doubled, Jimmy screamed, "That's it! Where the fuck is Frey?" Then he jumped from his seat and took off down the aisle. If nobody else would, he was going to make a pitching change.

About halfway to the dugout, with the whole section pointing and laughing, Jimmy looked back with an expression that said something like "If you guys don't stop me, I'm going to have to jump over the dugout and will be going to jail. I'm committed to the joke, help me out."

We chased down the aisle after him, and in high physical Buster Keaton style, pulled at his ankles to stop him from going over onto the field. A few Cub players looked up to see what the deal was, and the entire section applauded. Most importantly, we saved ourselves some bail money.

Chapter Four

The Road:
Sleazeballs and Huge Amounts of Fun

Club owners could be great people or real assholes. Not surprisingly, the big, wonderful clubs had owners who liked the comedians and appreciated that good acts were talented individuals who wrote their own funny material and delivered it with a special style. At the other end of the comedy rainbow were owners looking to make a fast buck and who cared about nothing else. They had a background with music clubs and would happily go back to booking cover bands in a heartbeat, except that comics were usually cheaper. Some of these club owners genuinely took pleasure in abusing their performers, and their cocktail waitresses.

I found one owner in Longview, Texas who had a regular scam going. Each week he made the comic put down a credit card to secure the hotel room, then he would reimburse them on payday. This was nowhere near the industry standard. Comics often showed up in a town with little cash and credit cards maxed.

Adding to the problem in Longview was that this slimy prick didn't bother paying for the tax which amounted to another thirty bucks a room each week. And since payday was Saturday night, he was nowhere to be found until the club opened again on Wednesday.

That same club had a bartender who was quite friendly all week. Not bad looking either. "Here, let's do a shooter," she'd say. When I'd get off stage, she had a tequila shot ready for me, and she was nice enough to join me so I didn't drink alone. All good until time to close out at week's end when I found that she had been putting her drinks on my tab.

And that absolutely pales next to a criminal low-life who owned a few clubs in Ohio for a while in the early eighties. Cincinnati, Columbus, maybe another one like Toledo. He had a high profile partner in the venture that had played for the Bengals. Though, I don't think the football star figured into the criminal portion of the business in any way.

Well, this owner and his hired goon managers, used to bring comics into the office at the end of the week for payday. The way comedy clubs worked, you did the paperwork, then cashed your check out of the bar receipts. And here's this pond scum owner looking at you saying, "How much white and how much green?" In other words, we want you to take some of your pay for the week in cocaine. The more the better since we're dealers.

I know at least one comic who got roughed up a little bit when he said what most of them said. That "all green" would be just dandy, thank you. As opposed to explaining to the Citibank Visa people that you couldn't pay them that month, but you could give them a really good buzz.

.   .   .

Howard Marcus' wonderful Laff Stop club in Houston had lots of silent partners roaming around, but it was always my understanding that there was one major backer. Whoever the guy was, he supplied one of my favorite funny club owner stories.

The way we comics heard the tale was this: The gentleman was up in years. Inevitably he passed on. The family gathered for the reading of the will at the attorney's office, just like in the movies. They went through all the family possessions to the various children, and then they got to "my interest in the Laff Stop Comedy Club"

A buzz starts in the room. "Laff Stop? What? Dad owned a comedy club? This is terrific. We didn't even know he owned this. Wow!"

"The Laff Stop goes to (made-up name) Betty."

"Who's Betty?"

A very attractive blonde woman in her forties raises a hand and says something along the lines of "That would be me. I was your father's mistress".

What a great scene out of real life. Talk about stuff that Dad forgot to mention.

Agents in the stand-up business work often for the clubs, not the comics. They may book ten or more rooms. At their peaks, a handful booked the proverbial shitload of one-nighters around their given region.

One of the earliest and, in my opinion, absolutely sleaziest was Jerry Stanley who booked a ton of one nighters in New York and New Jersey. My introduction to Jerry should have told me everything I needed to know, but in the comedy biz, I guess you just grow used to sleaze, lies and incompetence.

Through great recommendations from other agents and comics, plus a follow-up on the proverbial "send me a tape", I had finally gotten booked into the Richmond Comedy Club in Virginia. It was small, but generally thought of as one of the hottest rooms in the country. It was booked by Sandy DiPerna and April Pasquerella, wonderfully nice people.

A few years after this little incident, I became brief but good pals with April. She was much fun. Another one of many I'd like to see again. Sandy turned out to be a completely terrific person, too.

Anyway, the first time I was ever booked to work for them I took the precaution of calling a couple of weeks out just to double check on everything before I made my plane reservations. I got Sandy on the phone and was told that I wasn't booked there.

"What? We confirmed this three months ago." I was pissed.

"You called and cancelled," she said rather coldly.

"I did not. I've been looking forward to coming there. I want my date." More pissed.

"Well, Jerry Stanley called and said that you'd tried to get a hold of us, but couldn't. So, you cancelled with him. He's already booked Sam Greenfield in that week."

"Who the fuck is Jerry Stanley? I didn't call anyone." Now I was supremely pissed.

It seems that this dickhead was also the manager for Sam Green-field. So, when Sam's booking for that week fell through, he looked at the calendars for clubs with which he had a relationship, didn't recog-nize my name, and called Richmond with a "Mike couldn't reach you, but he had to cancel" tale. By the time I found out, promo had been printed with Sam's name instead of mine. And I was screwed.

I called and railed at Jerry's secretary to no avail.

The stupid irony of the situation is that I later did gigs for Jerry and ultimately let myself get screwed over by him a second time. Yeah, I know...shame on me.

Because Jerry now knew my name, I was able to use *him* was my thinking. When I would go to New York, I'd call Jerry and pick up three or four of his one-nighters to defer some cost while I tried to get spots at the big clubs in Manhattan. It was a good system, and a popular one.

I found out two things. First that Jerry hadn't changed, and second, that he was taking more than we were getting.

Ron Robertson and I made a great trip to New York one time. Back in those days, Ron was selling fertilizer. And I don't mean that euphemistically. He was a marketing rep for some national fertilizer and peat moss company. His territory included the western half of the United States. So, naturally, ahem, he managed to pull off a trip to New York City on the expense account.

We got a room at the Algonquin being the literary geniuses that we were. And for spending money, we had booked about ten days' worth of Jerry Stanley's one nighters. They paid $55 a person back then, if I recall. Same rate no matter who you were on many of them.

Our first night in town, we went to Catch a Rising Star, the top comedy club in town in the early 80s with apologies to Richie Tienken and Bob Wax over at the Comic Strip. The Improv had faded a tad by then from what it had been at one time. We're in the front bar at Catch, hanging out with guys we knew in New York, when Jerry Stanley walked in.

My first clue that I was about to get greased up again was when one of the comics standing near me said, "Jerry Stanley? I haven't seen him in town in twelve years."

Jerry lived over in Jersey.

Not that we were all that important, but at the time we were booking the club in Oklahoma City which happened to be one of the hottest in the country. Since Jerry also managed several comics that we used, he didn't want to piss us off.

"Hey, Mike Vance," Jerry says. "I was just in the neighborhood. You should have told me you were in town. I could have got you some dates."

It was so outrageously lame that I actually laughed out loud.

"Jerry, this is Ron Robertson, my booking partner in the OKC club. We're in town because you gave us each over a week's worth of dates. Don't pull this shit on me."

"What? My assistant must have screwed up. I know I don't have you down."

"Jerry, I talked to you personally. Do not screw me on this."

"Oh, man," he said in his best concerned voice. "Maybe I can find something for you."

The end result, and by that I mean felt on my end, was that Ron and I split a spot or two and did two others where we each got the whole $55. Woo-hoo.

One of the split spots was at the Eastside Comedy Club on Long Island. That was a very hot room back then. We chatted with Billy Joel, a big comedy fan who lived close to there. And I was introduced to a young comic who Richie Tienken at the Strip was managing. This kid named Eddie Murphy.

Murphy wasn't too friendly since he was surrounded by his buddies. Oddly enough, Tienken brought him out to LA not long after that and happened to walk into the Improv when I was standing in the front bar. Eddie really wanted to chat then. Talked about the Showtime comedy competitions we had both been in the year before. My guess was he spoke because he didn't know anyone else in the room that night. But we had a good chat.

Another person hanging at the Eastside that night was a comic who is now a successful writer. That's sort of an irony since I'm convinced that was the night he saw a bit of mine about electric football that suddenly appeared in his act after I left town. Writer, huh?

Odd thing about that electric football bit. It has caused more controversy than any other I've ever done. Something very similar was also done by Larry Miller and Bob Worley. All three of us were doing it at the same time in different parts of the country without the other person knowing it. Makes sense when you think about it, because every boy of a certain age range probably had one of those classic turds of a toy. Larry told me a few years later that he had dropped his after only a short time. A guy from Lubbock who saw me do it at the club there also ripped it off from me almost word for word, though he claimed for years that he never saw me. Odd since I recall meeting him in the club.

And one time, a funny comic named Fred Wolf approached me at the Laff Stop in Houston and accused me of stealing the bit from Bob Worley. We talked it out, and he realized that I had it at the same time. Simultaneous creation does occur. But much more often it's plain theft, too.

And just so you know, not all comics steal material. In fact, if you're funny, you usually go out of the way to make sure you sound different. Otherwise, you're going nowhere. Your jokes are how you make a living, and stealing them is no different than breaking into someone's home and taking shit.

Anyway, that night at the Eastside Comedy Club, there were a lot of comedians hanging around, and one of the most embarrassing moments for anyone I've ever known took place right there in front of them.

Robertson was introduced by the emcee, and as he walked up the three steps to the stage, he tripped and fell right on his face. Spilled his drink and put his nose right into the carpet. Well naturally, I bust out laughing uncontrollably. Could not stop howling.

The sad part was that everyone else in the room was silent because they thought it was a planned prat fall, and that the guys from Texas were low-brow, Jerry-Lewis loving rubes. The emcee just shot him a disgusted look and left the stage. Poor Ron started his act with an apology and continued with a face as red as a beet.

That same trip the two of us and David Sayh went to the Boss' hometown of Asbury Park, NJ to do a one nighter. David Sayh was a nice guy, solid act who is the all-time poster boy that you toss out when someone tells you how "exposure" at a given event will turn your career around. David did the Carson show over 50 times. Fifty. And no one except the most die-hard comedy students have a clue who he is. No offense, David. Love you, man.

He was also one of the bigger booty hounds I've ever met. I mean not just someone who'd go off with any woman who passed by, but someone who'd really work hard at it. I had him booked with me in Oklahoma City one time. (We rescued a little terrier that week and tried to make him the "condo dog")

One night early that week, the comics and staff finished the show and adjourned to the bar across the mall for more drinking and some appetizers. We'd been there about twenty minutes when the manager walked over to our table and asked one of us to go to the phone and handle a problem with one of our comics.

John Hildenbrand, the Joker's GM, picked it up.

"John. David Sayh. I'm locked in the club."

You see, we had designed Joker's with a sky box style green room for the comics. It was in the back of the showroom and featured a large plate glass window with blinds that prevented the audience from seeing in. David had met a girl from the audience, culled her from the pack, and taken her into the green room to close the deal.

He was still trying to convince her to go back to the condo when John closed out the last waitress, turned off all the lights, and locked the front door. David and his would-be date were plunged into total blackness in an unfamiliar nightclub.

Somehow, he managed to feel his way into the office, turn on a desk lamp, and find the number of the bar across the way. (The first thing real comics learn in a new town is what bar you hang out in after the show.) When we all walked back to the club to let him out, we saw David and his date peeping out the mini-blinds at the front door. I don't think he ever scored that night.

David Sayh was also the guy who was working in Birmingham with me one night. The old Birmingham Comedy Club was a terrific room. It was in an off brand motel on the second floor. The comics rooms were just down the outside balcony around the corner.

A friendly but new-to-comedy magician was the opener that week. His name escapes me, but I'll go with Jim. We worked together in Columbia once, too. Nice guy.

Well, Jim had mustered all of his material to put together his fifteen minutes for the opening act. Second show on a sold out Saturday, Jim did his show to a good response. I followed with my half-hour. Jim returned to the stage, made a couple of announcements, and introduced David Sayh. Applause died into silence. No David.

"Ladies and gentlemen, David Sayh!" he tried again. Nothing. David was nowhere in sight.

The owner called David's room as Jim struggled to hold the attention of the audience. No answer. Jim was given the "stretch" signal and promptly broke into a sweat.

On a hunch, no pun intended, I walked down to David's room and knocked loudly on the door. He finally answered in his underwear, a woman visible under the sheets behind.

"David, you're on."

"Okay, I'll be right there.

"No. He's introduced you three times at least. He has no more act."

The crowd finally saw their headliner run through the back door and onto the stage still tucking in his shirt and zipping up his pants. He did the whole show unaware that his hair was sticking up on one side. One of the great entrances in show biz.

So that's David Sayh, long time veteran New York funny man, who was trusted enough to pick up Jerry's agent fee from the Asbury Park room that night. The owner paid each of us and handed David an unsealed envelope for Jerry's take for the month. Unsealed is just begging to be looked at, and we obliged. While we were doing the show for $55 a night, Jerry's take was around $600 for the month if I recall. He was getting about 50% commission and booking scores of one-nighters a week. What a dick.

. . .

There was a comedy team working in Manhattan back then named Alto and Mantia. Bobby and Buddy. A very slick act that had been together for years. Bobby was as laid back as Buddy could be tightly wound. They were a hoot to hang out with.

They had a high stakes poker game that Ron Robertson and I sat in on one night. At least, high stakes to me. Dollars and fives and tens which meant that the pot could get up into the hundreds pretty fast. Mike Cain, Mark Schiff, and Steve Mittleman were some of the other regulars. All extremely funny guys who were nothing but serious during this game. Talking too much would net you a nasty look and a "shut up".

The night we were there Schiff was the big winner. He took his cash to his room and passed out literally on top of it. Personally, I'm still convinced he was only pretending to be passed out so the game would end and the rest of us would leave his apartment.

Alto and Mantia took Ron and I to the trotters at the Meadowlands one night we were up there. I hit a trifecta with a semi-long shot in the last race. Buddy had been betting $100 and more on some races. Too rich for my blood. But I had been up enough to box three horses in the tenth.

I didn't know much about horse racing, but looking at the racing form, it seemed to me that one 20 to 1 shot was way better than those odds. So, I took two favorites and him. There was a photo finish. Everyone stood up to leave, throwing their tickets on the floor.

"Hang on," I said.

Buddy wheeled around and glared at me.

"Don't fucking tell me you had that eight horse."

I just grinned.

I collected over $650, by far my biggest haul before or since. And Buddy refused to talk to me the whole way back to Manhattan.

Ron and I went back to the hotel on the way. It seemed two young ladies whom we had met the night before at a one-nighter in

New City, NY were going to meet us at the bar in the Algonquin at midnight. We never expected they'd show up, but sure enough there they were. Go figure. Buddy and Bobby went on to Catch.

Finally, we got them on the elevator to go up to the room. For ten days running, we'd tumbled in drunk, bleary-eyed, smelly and alone. And every morning we had the same old five foot two elevator operator who would roll his eyes and look away with a disdain that screamed "Losers!" So, on the last day, when we get in the elevator with two cute girls, the guy just arched his eyebrows and mumbled, "Dates? Who knew?" A funny man that elevator guy.

My friend Mitchell Walters was one of the most quick-witted, gravelly-voiced, generous guys, who "borrowed" money from damn near everyone he knew, almost inevitably for something the rest of the world would term degenerate. If you thought you'd see the money again, you're a fool. He delighted in being the first to write jokes about famous people who just died, getting guffaws from the comics and groans from the audience. A couple of them were genius. I particularly laughed at Mitchell one night of a celebrity death when he mimed walking with his right arm hooked back to his waist in a tea cup handle position as he said, "Quick impression. Pallbearer at Karen Carpenter's funeral."

He loved comedy. I truly think everyone who knew him has a story, and I know I'm blessed with several. Knowing Mitchell was a treat.

The Comic Strip in Ft. Lauderdale had an old South Florida house with a pool where the comedians stayed. Hyman Roth lived next door. One "morning" about noon, I rolled out, walked into the kitchen and squinted against the white walls and oppressive sun to see Mitchell, maybe a not so svelte 260, lounging by the pool in a speedo. He wasn't working there, mind you, but as he told me then, "I had two days off, and the ponies are running at Hialeah. I knew you wouldn't mind if I crash on the couch, but my flight was early, and I didn't want to wake you."

Mitchell was a majorly addicted gambler. Horses, dogs, jai alai, and he was a card cheat of the highest order and skill. Most of my sketchy knowledge of reading a Racing Form came from Mitchell.

Somehow, he had broken one of his front teeth, cracked it off horizontally across the middle, He then super glued it back on. Of course, the bottom half was dead, so it was a different color. It stayed that way for months, or longer. So, Mitchell just didn't show his teeth for a while. Maybe over a year later, I was headlining one club in Buffalo, and Mitchell was headlining the other one. It was the middle of dark, slushy winter, and Mitchell called and said, "Vance, let's go have lunch at the mall." So, we're wandering around aimlessly, shooting the shit, and suddenly Mitchell spots one of those photo booths. Turns out that was his main motive all along. I waited outside while the flashes went off in there, then the little strip of pictures comes out. He hands them to me and says, "So what do you think?" He's smiling! He's got these perfect front teeth. I said, "Mitchell, that's great. They look great. I thought you said you couldn't afford to get it fixed." He spreads his hands wide, and in that New York accent, says, "I finally found a dentist who plays poker."

I mentioned Rick Hogan elsewhere in this volume. He was a lawyer who also owned a string of four clubs down in Georgia and South Carolina back in the 1980s. It was a side business with Rick, who was the epitome of the Southern yuppie back then, sporting a sweater around his neck and a genteel Georgia frat boy accent. I always got along with him very well. We were pals. He let me stay at his beach house on Tybee Island when I worked his Savannah room. Once when I was at his club in Columbus, Georgia, he got me an extra ticket, and we went to see his alma mater, Georgia Tech play football over at Auburn. A nice civilized afternoon of football and mixed drinks from a flask. Now that's the Deep South at its best. Thanks again, Rick.

Even though he was a very good man, Rick, like scores of other club owners, occasionally failed to grasp the concept of comedy. A case in point was when Bill Silva was working in Columbus, which was Rick's hometown. I don't even remember what the bit was, and it doesn't matter except to know it had some twisted humor in it. In fact, Bill doesn't recall the bit in question himself. The important part was that after Bill's set, Rick summoned him to the table, pointed to his blonde wife sitting in front of her Crown and Coke, and said one of the unintentionally perfect club owner lines of all times: "I want you to drop that bit because I don't like it, and my wife doesn't understand it."

To be honest, I don't know if his wife was drinking Crown and Coke, but that was a running joke with me and Jimmy Pineapple. When we worked the Southeast together, we spent lots of hours drinking in those fern bars and mimicking the pretty little bow-headed blondes drawling their order, "Crown and Co-oak." And that was before blonde jokes became the rage.

Another great episode took place at Hogan's Columbus, Georgia club. I was booked to middle that week for some reason with Glenn Farrington who went on to become a very successful writer in Hollywood. I don't recall if there was a double booking, but I was happy to do it since Glenn is a super guy. The opener was a fellow who lived in Houston for a time, but never gained total acceptance among the top comics. Let's call him Jeff. Jeff had a first cousin who lived near Columbus, so we didn't see much of him. Now, I should point out from the start that Jeff was a classic example of one of those folks who confused high energy for humor. Nice person, pleasant enough to be around, but not especially funny.

His big closer was something that he insisted on calling improv. What it was in fact was a lame drug bit in which he would take the audience on a make believe road trip while occasionally stopping to let the audience fill in the blank to provide a story turn as important as "I'll put on my jacket. It's ...blank."

"Blue!" They'd shout.

"It's blue," Jeff would say, completing the intricate improvisation.

That's sarcasm, in case you missed it. Real improv, which I enjoy thoroughly, lets the audience make meaningful decisions in the direction of the scene and forces the actors to create. That does not include picking the color of a garment.

The climax of the bit was when he rushed off stage and rubbed his nose in a bowl of powdered sugar. He then rushed back on stage showing the audience that he'd been doing blow as he drove his imaginary bus.

Well, as you can guess, no matter who the other acts on the bill were, the temptation to jack with John's prop bowl of sugar was way too great. We were comedians, for crying out loud. What did he expect us to do? That week the jack-ers just happened to be us. We swapped it for salt one night, moved it a couple times, laced the sugar heavily with black pepper once. By the weekend, he'd completely drop character and come out of his bathroom hallway hiding spot simply cursing Glenn and me. We thought it was hysterical.

Of course, messing with someone like that is only good when they flail about in protest. Jeff's frustration just made us want to do more. And that brings me to that Saturday in March of 1983. I recall the date because Glenn and I were watching the University of Houston and North Carolina State win the games that would lead them to U of H's infamous choke in the title game. Jeff was out on a boat with his cousin.

Now, Jeff had adamantly kept the Do Not Disturb sign on his motel room door all week to keep housekeeping out. He was a big pot smoker and didn't want anybody in there. Come to think of it, he was one of the most high strung pot smokers I've ever known. I think he may have been missing the point from what I've been told. Anyway, that was the impetus for our plan.

Glenn went down to the front desk and said, "I'm one of the comics in room 2 1 7 and I locked my key in room." This works mainly because to a motel putting up comics every week, you are largely an ongoing faceless annoyance, as opposed to real guests. Glenn effortlessly got the key and came back to unlock John's room.

We went in and folded his dirty towels, roughly made his bed, and emptied his trash into a dresser drawer. Then we stuck his bag of pot under the mattress. Finally, we wrote a note that read simply, "I took your pot. What are you going to do, call the police? Hahahaha." And we signed it "the maid".

Then we went back to my room to watch more basketball.

Sure enough, Jeff came back and walked past the open door and window doing his best not to make eye contact with his tormenters. It was almost as if we could count to twenty exactly before the phone rang.

"God damnit! Do you know what the fucking maid did? She came into my room and stole my pot. She even wrote a note. She dared me to tell someone. That fucking bitch. She didn't even take out the trash, she just emptied it into a drawer!"

It was the last sentence that made us break. We both started dying laughing. Jeff failed to see the humor in it at all. But his annoyance was more than offset by the relief in finding that his weed was only under the mattress.

There was a comedy team from Akron, Ohio who pulled off a couple of brilliant practical jokes. One of them involved the old lost key trick, too.

They had been killing time at the mall while they worked in Syracuse one week. The middle act was a guy who might be described as a total queen who'd just gotten the lead in the school play. I don't know if he was gay at all, but his manner was slightly less butch than Divine's.

Once, the same guy was working with Steve Harvey and me in Lexington, Kentucky. He was opening that week, and he would take these, no exaggeration, two-hour baths with the door open and candles and oils and shit. Steve, who was middling for me that week, was beside himself. Every night, Steve would have to hurry through the shower starting at three P.M. in order to be ahead of our opener while there was still hot water. Then he would crack me up by cringing every time he had to walk past the open door.

"Damn it. Close the fucking door. I don't need to see your shit hanging out. I'm trying to get food here." Very funny man, Steve Harvey.

Anyway, back to Syracuse. The comedy duo had a brainstorm while passing a pet store to buy a forty-nine cent mouse and turn him loose in the middle act's room. Well, they got the intended rise, all right; screaming and jumping on the bed like a debutante, no doubt. What they didn't count on was that the poor guy would raise such a stink about being forced to stay in a rodent infested hotel, that the club owner would be called out of bed, have to cancel his contract with the place and move the comics down the street at two in the morning. They kept that little joke under their hats.

One member of the comedy duo was a rather small bald guy and the other was a big, burly heavy man. They were pretty funny guys both on and off-stage. I liked them a lot.

Once they were working in Charleston, South Carolina in a room that had been Rick Hogan's originally. I think Creative Entertainment took it over later. Anyway, they put you up in a house in North Charleston right in the Air Force Base flight path. I had the good fortune to be working there when Reagan invaded Grenada, that brave crusade for American might. It was 24-hour transport take-offs. C-130s trying to gain altitude directly over my bedroom. I'm still trying to catch up on sleep.

Well, the Ohio boys had already gotten to the house on the first day of the gig. About 4:30 in the afternoon, the phone rang. It was the club looking for the other act.

"We haven't seen him."

"Well, he'll be there any minute. He just left the club with the key. Please have him call."

So, they knew that this other comic would be walking through the door at any moment. They quickly stripped down buck naked. When the new guy opened the door, the first thing he saw was the big dude's big bare ass bent over his little comedy partner in front of the fireplace. They both turned toward the door with a straight-faced deer-in-the-headlights look.

The guy never set his bags down; he just closed the door, ran to his car and drove off. It took a lot of convincing by the guys and the club management before he understood it was a joke, albeit a visual that is still tough to shake.

***

There's a terrific road story that I'm afraid I can't say with certainty just who the subject might have been. But it's still worth telling. The very first time I heard it from someone, it was about Jay Leno. In every single subsequent telling, and there were many, it was about John Fox. In fact, Fox loved telling the story about himself. Who wouldn't? On top of that, Leno was never one to chase women as far as I knew. Not at all. He was always a straight arrow. So, enjoy this one for the substance.

It's pretty simple really. A comic picks up a woman at the club. Believe it or not, we liked that. Typically, the comic takes her out for a few more drinks somewhere else. Uses whatever form of charm he can manage to muster, and ultimately prays that he closes the deal.

In this case, they bought a bottle of champagne and headed back to her place. She lived in an apartment complex with several hundred units, very early 80s, all scattered in almost identical three-story buildings, that could have been located in any city in America. Like most of them, visitors scrambled for parking someplace along the street.

Our hero and his date du jour sat on the couch for a brief while, then ambled back to the bedroom. Well, this little vixen wants to be tied up. So, they get good and naked, and he secured her to the bed with ties that she had no doubt used before.

"I want you to dribble the champagne on me and lick it off," she ordered.

Wow!

One tiny problem. The champagne was still in the car. Not to worry, the comic slips back into his clothes and goes out to get it.

You guessed it. And this was a true story, not an old joke. In his boozy state, he can't find the apartment. He spent a solid fifteen minutes wandering through the complex holding a bottle of bubbly and repeating her name in a loud stage whisper to no avail. Finally, thoroughly frustrated by the thought of a naked woman tied to a bed no more than a hundred yards away in some unknown direction, he went back to the car and drove back to his hotel.

Needless to say, he had no phone number and knew only her first name at that point. All day he wondered about little else. That night, as he's hanging around the lobby of the club, the doors open and the woman walked in, a Mona Lisa smile on her face. His heart raced as she came directly for him.

She reached up to his face, ran one long nail gently along his cheek, and said, "Kinky."

I talked about Jay earlier, but I really should stress that he never was the party animal, skirt chaser that most of us were for many years. Jay was just Jay, a straight-forward great guy.

That's why the end to my biggest week of road hijinks had such an ironic ending.

The Punchline in Atlanta was one of the top clubs in the country for many years. None consistently better, really. It was also one hellacious place to party. The guys who ran the joint made sure to hire only the most attractive of waitresses for the most part. Those guys being three Italians from Cleveland. Ron DeNunzio and Dave Montesanto owned it. Chris DiPetta was the manager. While they intimidated some comics, I got along with them wonderfully. My mom's family was a bunch of Italians from Youngstown. I guess I was just used to it.

I loved going to Atlanta for many reasons. The audiences were stellar, the staff was friendly, and the women were gorgeous, plentiful and outgoing. At least that was the case when you were a semi-attractive young comedian in the 1980s.

This was the city where, I think at a nightclub called the Limelight, a very funny L.A. comic, later to be a veteran of many TV sitcoms, bet Ron Robertson that he could walk out of the bathroom with his Johnson out, and nobody would say a thing. He won the bet.

There were some epic times for me at that club in Sandy Springs and the house a couple of blocks away where the comics stayed.

My buddy, Carl Faulkenberry, and I did a week there with the legendary Pat Paulsen who turned out to be one incredibly nice and generous guy. He was doing some comedy clubs then, but mostly he and his wife ran a winery in California. After each show, he would autograph bottles of his wine, which was really good, by the way.

More than once, when the three of us would be enjoying a cocktail at the little Café 290 jazz bar across the parking lot, someone from the audience would come up to tell Pat how funny he was. Without fail, he would give a humble thank you and go on about how Carl and I were the really funny ones, how he was just a guy they used to see on TV. Once, he talked us up to two young women for a good, solid three minutes. Pat Paulsen tried to get us laid. How cool is that?

That same week, Raul Martinez, a comedy friend out of the past from Houston, showed up at the house in a cab. Raul told us how he had been "living" with a girl there in Atlanta, but she had gotten tired of him. Gotten tired of him mooching, perhaps. That would not have been a first.

So, in Atlanta, Raul showed up and spun his sad tale.

"So can I stay here?"

"No. There's not enough room, and it's not our house."

"Riiight. So can you loan me some money?"

"No. We don't have any money."

"Yeah, I know that, man. Can you put a plane ticket on your credit card?"

"No."

"Can I get a ride to the airport?"

That we did.

I was working with Carol Leifer in Atlanta one time, finishing off a beer after the Sunday show while they were still free, when these two guys at the bar motioned me over.

"So, are you going out drinking with us, or what?"

The guys both looked familiar. I couldn't quite place them, but I thought they were likely boyfriends of a couple of the waitresses. Either that or buddies of the owner.

Being the often discriminating drinking companion I am, I said, "Sure. Where we goin'?"

They named a spot up the street and then each stuck out a hand. It turns out they were TV sports anchors, Dan Patrick and Gary Miller, who at that time were working for CNN. They liked my act and thought I sounded like a good guy to hang with. It turned out they were both just incredibly cool guys. We had a blast.

The three of us downed beers and played Pop-a-Shot for hours. It seems that at that time, in the late eighties, that miniature basketball game was all the rage among sports media types. Gary Miller was a pro, let me tell you. He would drop them in with both hands as fast as the balls would roll back to him. It was a thing of beauty. I thought of that several times when he got in trouble for having unfortunate aim in Cleveland's Flats years later.

The coolest part of that night was a fantastic story they told me about one of the Houston sportswriters I knew in passing, and didn't particularly care for. He'd ripped off a couple of my jokes for his column, in fact. It seems during the NBA Finals in Detroit, someone had rented a Pop-a-Shot game for one of the media suites. All of the writer/broadcaster types were boozing it up and shooting tiny hoops.

Well, this writer from Houston shows up with a hooker and announces to the room that he's paying for anyone in the room, but he gets to watch. Gary said that he was drunk enough that he was about to speak up before his producer gently suggested that having a room full of sportswriters watching him receive sexual favors might not be the best thing for his reputation. (That producer should have been there when Gary peed out that nightclub window in Ohio years later.)

While the sponsoring writer took his turn at basketball, a different media guy grabbed the hooker and ducked into the bathroom of the suite. While everyone else guffawed, listening to moaning noises, my acquaintance from Houston pounded the door, screaming at the top of his lungs, "God dammit! I said I get to watch! I'm not paying for this!"

My greatest party week in show biz started the week before Atlanta when I met a truly funny and wonderful guy, Kenny Rogerson from Boston. He was headlining and I was middling at the Punchline in Columbia, SC. A nice little room above a restaurant in trendy Five Points. To put things in perspective, I was about 26 years old, and Kenny was a year or two older. This was before Kenny started scoring his movie roles.

When comics work together for the first time, there is a sort of feeling out process. You're generally friendly, but it makes the week much easier if you enjoy, or at least respect, the other person's act. When Kenny and I first met, there was the usual comedy butt-sniffing. By the time the show was over, I knew we'd get along great. He was hysterical, and he had lots of jokes about partying.

Surprisingly, though, Kenny wasn't drinking. He wanted no part of a party. I remember his exact words, delivered with that Boston accent.

"I quit drinkin' cause I'm a wild fuckin' Indian."

Sure, Ken, blame it on the Indians. Like they haven't suffered enough.

But, that was Tuesday. By Wednesday, a beer or two wouldn't hurt. Friday, one shot won't get anybody in trouble. And finally, Sunday, when South Carolina law required all drinking establishments to close, we were changing our tickets to go party in Atlanta a day or two early. This was a recipe for trouble.

The very first thing Kenny and I saw when we walked into the office at the club was that week's headliner, Kip Adotta, trying to get an advance on his salary for his next booking there - eight months down the road. He had already partied up the several thousand bucks that he was getting paid for that week. Well, that was Atlanta in the eighties.

We stayed for the show. I have always loved Kip's act. Then we hooked up with a couple of other comics and took off for Buckhead, the trendy nightclub area of town. Tim O'Rourke, a very good guy who later played Drew Carey's bartender on that TV series, was driving. Four of us packed into what I think might have been Tim's bitchin' white Ford Escort. Another comedian's chick magnet, to be sure.

The spot we chose was a Mexican restaurant/Irish bar called Carlos McGee's. Needless to say, we were feeling more Irish that night than Mexican. We might have even tried to eat something first, but either way, we were soon at the bar, pounding down shots and beers.

It's sometimes hard to keep track of time in these Atlanta stories because bars there stay open till four in the morning. And we did more than our share of closing them down. That's easier than it sounds when you get off work at midnight, or two on Saturdays. So, with caution I say that not too terribly long after that, Señor Rogerson was standing on the bar screaming personal questions at a CNN camera guy who measured out at no less than six foot six, two sixty-five. Somewhere around the moment when Kenny's impromptu interview turned to the topic of his new friend being a large Black man, the manager of Carlos McGee's told us to get Kenny the hell out of there.

We managed to get him out the door and headed toward the car. Naturally, there was an obligatory pause while Kenny took a whiz on the Corvette parked in front of us, railing loudly the whole time about "rich motherfuckers and their bleached-blonde, fake-tittied girlfriends". The best part was that some guy, with a blonde date, was half way through parallel parking his Porsche on the opposite side of Peachtree when he spotted Ken taking a squirt on the Vette. After a perfect dead pan double take, he pulled back out and decided to try another bar. Priceless timing.

Well, Tim O'Rourke made the mistake of telling Kenny that we were headed home instead of to another bar, as he assumed. When we slowed for the next light, Kenny jumped out of the moving car and went back to Carlos McGee's. This time we let him go. Our attempt at responsibility was over.

Much of the Punchline staff was still there at the bar partying when Ken walked back in through the front doors. I can only imagine the collective rolling of eyes at that point. Meanwhile, now without quite as much potential trouble, we did stop at another bar before we went back to the house.

There was a nice big basement with a TV where everyone hung out, and that's where we were sitting, watching some mindless made for TV concert, when we heard the front door open and, with lots of stomping and banging, Kenny made his entrance. His knight in shining armor was Pam Stone.

People know Pam as a regular on the sit-com, *Coach*. She played the tall, blonde women's basketball coach and love interest of Dobber, one of the dim-witted assistants. But back then, Pam was just an incredibly nice, sweet and genuinely funny waitress at the club in Atlanta. I love her to death.

She had managed to get Kenny into her car and drag him, literally kicking and screaming, back to the comic's house. Along the way she and the other waitresses got a stream of abuse from the "wild Indian".

That night Kenny passed out in front of the TV yelling at Lionel Ritchie. Again, I ain't saying he's wrong. In fact, a steady stream of "Lime-o Ritchie! Lime-o Ritchie! Lime-o Ritchie!" was pretty damn funny.

The next day Ron DeNunzio summoned Kenny to the office and asked him what the hell had happened the night before. He told Ken to tone it down and to apologize to the waitresses. It cost him two dozen nice roses. He asked me later that day who all he needed to apologize to. I told him the cheapest way would be to buy radio time.

One of the greatest party weeks in my career started with Kenny Rogerson almost getting sent home on Monday. And we didn't even start working till Tuesday.

When I say it was the best party week of my career, I mean in quantity, not quality. Bars are open in Atlanta until four, and as I found out, some even later. That week Ron DeNunzio and Chris Dipetta were bound and determined to see that we made good use of each and every available hour. I honestly don't think I slept more than four hours total from Thursday afternoon through Monday morning.

It is a bit of a blur, so bear with me. I know that at some point early in the week Dipetta took me to a kick-ass little Italian place. The food was impeccable. The atmosphere a classy casual. The only drawback was that there was no alcohol license. When we were done,

Chris ordered coffee. Now I don't drink coffee, so I kept declining, and he kept saying, "Get the special coffee."

The special coffee finally showed up. It was Sambuca in a tiny cream pitcher. Now I get it.

That was the night that we later met up with a woman Chris was dating and her semi-cute friend. That led to more partying and drinking, me catching a few winks on the girlfriend's couch while Chris, well, did whatever they were doing upstairs, then breakfast, which oddly occurred at breakfast time.

At this point in the week, Rogerson had hooked up with a stewardess from Eastern Airlines. Neither of those terms is still in existence. She had worked his flight to Columbia the week before and had promised to meet him for the weekend in Atlanta. So, he went into the headliner bedroom and only came out for shows.

Friday at lunch, or was it Saturday, I met up with my buddy from New Orleans, Lance Montalto, who was in town working another room. This part I won't forget. We ended up at Po' Folks, a southern hillbilly themed place. It was a very odd spot to meet a waitress who looked remarkably like what Halle Berry would look like in her prime a few years later. She was phenomenal. And just to prove that I could still sweet talk, I got a date with her for the midnight show on Saturday and some drinks afterwards.

When she showed up, the rest of the guys responded with appropriate dropped jaws. And after the show, the mind-numbing third of the night, we adjourned to some disco further down Roswell Road.

Back at the comedy house, I had just drifted off to sleep, hopeful to miss the sunrise by at least twenty minutes, when the door to my room busted open. It was Ron DeNunzio, the club owner, shrugging his shoulders at me and saying, "Where's the chick?"

"I have no idea. What were you going to do if she was here?"

"I dunno. Let's go get a drink."

"Ron, it's 5:30 in the morning."

Ronnie smiled at me and replied, "I know a place."

Ten minutes later, me and my bed-head were at the bar of an American Legion post downing more cocktails.

I forget most of the other details of that week between then and when the bars closed on Sunday night/Monday morning. It was four o'clock and Ron, Chris and myself found ourselves back at the Punchline with Stephanie, the head waitress and another lovely female staff member. Now that I write this out loud, it dawns on me - there were no ugly ones.

The girls finally cratered about dawn, just before there was some banging on the back door which turned out to be Mr. Kenny Rogerson whose frequent flyer had just left for the airport. So, the four of us were still there pounding scotch when the cleaning crew showed up and started vacuuming. And we were still there at 10 a.m. when Dave Montesanto, the other owner, showed up to do paper-work. He just looked at the sad sight and shook his head.

It was Dave who answered the phone when Jay Leno called from the airport about 11. You see, Jay was the headliner for the following week, this being in the pre-*Tonight Show* days. He had been working another Punchline and was getting to Atlanta early. The plan had been for Chris Dipetta to personally meet him at the airport gate. This was also pre-crazy-security days.

I do wish I could have been there to see the scene that Jay later described. It seems he exited the jetway and stood around looking for Chris. A uniformed driver approached him and said, "Mr. Leno?"

"Yeah?"

"I think I'm supposed to be giving you a ride."

"No, a friend of mine is picking me up. There must be some mistake."

Eventually every single person cleared the gate area except for Jay and the driver. Jay still wasn't convinced.

"Nah. He said he'd be here. He's just late. I'll call the club."

That's when Jay got Dave on the phone. That would be the same Dave who had the presence of mind to call a limo service for a last minute ride from the airport. The conversation went something like this:

"Hey, Dave. Jay Leno. Where the hell is Dipetta?"

"Hello, Jay. We sent a car for you instead."

"Yeah, that's what the guy says. But I just talked to Chris yesterday. He was gonna be here himself."

"Yeah, well, Chris got a little fucked up."

"Fucked up! Fucked up!?!" Jay yelled. "He's got one fucking thing to do all week, and that's pick me up!!"

Jay was much calmer when he got to the club a little after lunchtime. By then we had stopped drinking, and I was on the verge of dropping over dead. Luckily, I had arranged to blow off my flight to Birmingham the next day and ride with Riley Barber who happened to be passing through town. I can't tell you how relieved I was to be rescued from Hotlanta at that moment.

Leno, always upbeat and outgoing, shook hands all around, and then honed in on me.

"Hey, Vance. You don't have to work till tomorrow. Stick around. We can go get a nice dinner and a movie. They have me in a hotel. Stick around, we can stay at the house. I get bored at hotels."

A terrific guy, Jay, but all I wanted to do was sleep. A few hours later, I checked into the hotel in Birmingham and did just that for about 15 straight hours.

———

My first time at Sidesplitters in West Palm Beach I was booked with Dennis Piper aka Dennis Reagan. As it turns out, I knew his brother, Brian, also a comic, from some bookings before. Dennis and I hit it off. He liked to hang out and drink after the shows. He wasn't an insufferable hack. What else did I need to know?

Now when I say West Palm, we were really working well north of there. And the condo that they had us staying in, while a nice place, was almost in Jupiter. Florida, not the planet. Though at the time, they were almost equally developed. Finding a bar there was not easy.

It just so happened that Jupiter was where Burt Reynolds had his ranch. And Burt, being an ex-jock, had thoughtfully opened his own bar there. To be honest, it was a bit too classy for comics to be hanging in, but when it's the closest place to home, you make an exception.

So, we'd been spending our late nights at Burt's bar. It was called some showbizzy type name. Who cares at this point? All we knew is that by introducing ourselves to various people and explaining that we were the comics in town that week, we'd finagled a couple of free beers. The mark of a truly fine establishment.

This was probably Thursday night if I had to guess. I think that because we got

there early enough to find it still crowded, and I recall the next night being a weekend.

With it being Burt's la-te-da showbiz bar, the walls were plastered with the obligatory pictures. Only these were usually autographed to Burt. Some big names, too. Dom DeLuise, even. But right by the front door was an autographed photo of an aging but still impeccable Cary Grant. Great piece of work. And in the place of honor.

The conversation must have waned because Dennis and I started talking about the pictures. After a full evening of cocktails, we thought it was painfully clear that the walls were in need of our autographed pictures. Even if we hadn't technically been hanging with Burt, or even Loni.

So, we came up with the idea to slip one of our pictures, thoughtfully signed of course, into Cary Grant's frame.

First, Dennis slipped over to the door and very stealthily took Cary's picture off the wall and slid it behind the couch by the entrance. It wasn't nailed down. Then, while I distracted the bartender, he slipped out to the car and got one of his 8x10's out of his bag. Brilliant.

He'd just made it back to the bar to borrow a pen when the

manager comes running over screaming at the top of his lungs for us to get our asses out of there. Apparently not so stealthy as we first thought.

We tried our very best to explain the prank we had in mind, but he was convinced that we were simply stealing Mr. Grant's photo. Why he called him Mr. Grant, I have no idea. Poor Cary had been dead for a while. And I doubt if he and Rocco the bar manager were that close to begin with. We again tried to explain the prank. This time we pointed out that if we really planned on taking the picture, we likely wouldn't leave one of ours in its place. Didn't seem to convince our boy.

We were summarily shown the door. Man, I hate that. And I wasn't even done drinking.

Then we started to worry. This goon knew exactly who we were. He didn't have anything criminal on us, but he could call the club. We'd never be booked back in there again. We'd pissed off Burt Reynolds! Did I mention we'd been drinking?

So, thoughtfully heading things off at the pass, we called the club and left a slurred and rambling (just guessing) message on the machine just so we got our story in first. Probably took us two or three calls to get it all in, if I recall.

Needless to say, the phone answering girl was very impressed with the two men of the world they had booked that week after she heard our taped confession the next morning. As they say on the BBC, interview concluded at 1:35 a.m.

Rick Consolo, the owner, called us midday to request we stop by and talk to him. Even mostly sobered up, we were fairly trepidatious when we walked into the club for our conference. Fortunately, Consolo was laughing his ass off. Seems we'd left five panic-filled messages. Believe it or not, I did get booked back there.

I wasn't so lucky at a couple of other Florida clubs. Definitely something about that state, my least favorite in America. Too many tattoos for one thing. South Florida has all the rudeness of New Jersey but with less culture. And no need to even mention the string of political loons like DeSantis, Rubio or that topless dancer wannabee, Katherine Harris.

I had been at another club in West Palm Beach one time with a guy who pretended to be English. He was as American as I was, but he had a nice hook going by being a pseudo soccer hooligan comic. John McDonald, his name was. We got along just swell.

The club was called the Comedy Corner and was booked by my buddy Chris Dipetta out of Atlanta. They had John and I booked in as co-headliners with the idea being that we'd switch off. As the week developed, we found that his rowdy style worked better as the second act. So, every night subsequently, I did about 40 minutes up front and he did 40 minutes to close the show. It was working quite well.

That is until Friday night came along. Second show Friday is almost always the rowdiest of the week because people are the drunkest. They've been up since six or seven in the morning, and by eleven that night, they're just forcing themselves to keep drinking solely because they don't have to go to work the next day. And that Friday night in West Palm was no exception.

There was a group of five couples who were seated in the back of the room. Early twenties with the usual mix of very attractive girls and guys who were desperately trying to impress them. One moron in particular decided that heckling was the way to go.

He hadn't been too bad during my act. I put him down a couple of times, and that was the extent of it. But when John got up, the guy was almost an hour drunker. Not to mention that John's hooligan character used heckler come backs like "Fuck you, you fucking dweeb." Soon they were engaged in a dialogue to the exclusion of the rest of the audience.

The last straw came when this little idiot actually stood on his chair to yell yet another mindless comment at John on stage. The management, quite late but finally, went to escort the kid out. Of course, the rest of the group decided to go, too. Although several of the girls wanted to stay.

As they were leaving, the trouble maker threatened to wait outside and kick John's ass. Jumping into the gutter with him, John walked off stage and headed for the kid. All hell broke loose. The manager, John and three totally uninvolved guys from the crowd started trading punches with the five guys who were being thrown out. One of the girls jumped on John's back, just for good measure. They fell into a potted plant. A bartender and I pulled them apart and got everyone outside. And to his great credit, John McDonald went back to the stage and finished his act.

The upshot of the whole deal was that the next time Dipetta booked me back in West Palm, he called two weeks prior to the date and said that he had to cancel me because they didn't want me back. They told him there was trouble the last time I was there. I explained again what had happened, and that the trouble had nothing to do with me.

"Well, the owner wasn't there so he just banned both of you," Chris answered.

It is beyond me how owning a club can make someone so stupid. I'm sure asking the manager what happened would have been much too difficult.

The Comedy Corner in Dallas was the scene of some great moments. It was a fabulous club for meeting women for one thing. Although it was the one where I asked one of the waitresses out for a drink and, no lie, at the third consecutive club I'd worked, the answer was "Oh I can't, I'm dating Paul Provenza." Reminder that Paul and I had very similar taste.

My buddy, Jerry Dye, headlined there one New Year's Eve and got so hammered that he finished his last set in nothing but purple jockey shorts spraying the audience with a fire extinguisher. I'm sorry I missed that one. But somewhere, there are pictures, my friends. I've seen them.

It's also the place where Franklin Ajaye, a supremely funny man, told people in the middle of his set that he needed to take a leak. He walked off stage, went all the way to the bathrooms in the back of the huge showroom, did just that, and returned to his show. They audience laughed and applauded the whole time. Now that's a good crowd.

But the Corner was the sight of at least two classics for me. Gene McGuire used to be the house emcee there after Bill Engvall moved off. McGuire was a wonderfully sick individual who was a great friend of mine. He is one of my many friends who gave up drinking altogether, but we had some awesome parties before he quit. I can also assure everyone that his impeccable sense of humor remains completely intact.

Anyway, I had finished my show one Sunday night and was out in the front lobby bar there at the Comedy Corner.

Some drunk guy comes up to me and says, "You're a thief."

"Excuse me?"

"I've heard half of your jokes before. You stole every one of those jokes."

Well, I've never stolen a joke in my life, so that is one thing that'll piss me off real quick.

"I wrote everything in my act, pal. And you'd better never say anything about me stealing material again." I got in his face, ready to punch his boozy lights out.

"Well, I've heard it all before."

Gene stepped between us before anything physical could happen and turned to the accusing audience member, calling him by name.

"Larry, you're fucking drunk. You were at the show on Tuesday and saw Mike's whole act."

"Oh yeah." The lightbulb went on. "You're very funny."

It's the first and only time that I was ever accused of stealing jokes from myself.

Gene and I continued to party that night after the club closed. We stayed and hung out with some employees making up different shots behind the bar. I invented one with some fruit juices and brandy and Southern Comfort that was pretty tasty.

That's also the night that I came up with several very twisted celebrity impressions. For years after that, whenever Gene was nearby during my act, he'd yell for Sean Connery pedophile or Gary Cooper at a donkey show.

When funny things happen to comics, it often requires a debriefing. We need to prolong the evening, and have more drinks, just so we can continue laughing and making more jokes about the things that made us laugh in the first place. At some point during the course of that boozy reverie, one of us mentioned our good pal Dan Merryman, a Houston comic who had once been a paramedic. We summarily decided we needed to know what he was up to. Right then.

We called Merryman's house about midnight or twelve-thirty. Or maybe two-thirty. Who knows? By then, we were majorly faced. Not surprisingly, his answering machine picked up. Gene then left the most vile and profanely drunken rambling message ever to scorch that tape, I'm certain.

"You piece of shit," was the opening line. "Where the fuck are you at midnight, you fucking motherfucker? This is McGuire. I'm with Vance. We're calling to talk to you, cocksucker. You..."

We were laughing and having a grand time as we tried to outdo one another in the language department. A phone message version of *The Aristocrats* years ahead of its time.

The next day the phone at the condo woke me up. It was Merryman.

"Hi Mike. This is Dan. Do you remember calling my house last night?"

"Yeah. Sorry about that, man. McGuire and I were verrrry drunk. Sorry if it woke you up."

"No, it didn't wake me up. I didn't hear it. The answering machine is in the den. Right next to the fold out couch. The one where my parents were sleeping."

Now, I knew Dan's parents. They were very sweet Baptist folks from Conroe, TX. Dan just said that his mother made a remark like "that couldn't be Mike Vance because he's such a nice boy." Dan assured her that it wasn't me. But every time I saw her after that, I swear she looked at me funny.

Gene McGuire had another classic. In fact, the whole episode comes from one of the greatest parties of all time. It was in Houston, but since Gene's from Dallas, it's a road story for him. This would be my second bachelor party in late February 1986. This one revolved around the Workshop's employee drink policy – that wonderful anything for a dollar deal. At that time, the place was dark on Mondays, so we decided to open it for a private bachelor party. We started drinking at seven, about thirty comics. The strippers showed up at 12:30. Do the math.

Dante Garza, a very funny Houston comic, was working as a topless bar DJ at the time, so he rounded up two dancers. He selected a very fine looking Black girl as one of them, and for the other, he hired what can only be described as the biggest stripper at the club. A cute girl, maybe, but one who could have benefited by shedding an ell-bee or 35.

Their driver dropped them off, and the first order of business was to sit me on stage and have both women lap dance at once. It was great from what I recall. The better looking one then gave me several more dances that got more and more involved. Meanwhile the chunky one was doing dances for the other guys and cleaning out their wallets as they tipped.

The highlight was when McGuire and Carl Faulkenberry started taking turns lying on their backs in the middle of the club holding bills in their teeth while the big girl danced and squatted over them and picked them up. It was quite impressive.

Needless to say, they were dancers, so they eventually left us all to our own devices and went on their way.

Cut to the next day about noon. The three guys who had driven down from Dallas were finally forced to get out of bed at their hotel and head back home since they had a show to do and a club to run. They had come down in a big old land yacht of a car that belonged to Kevin, the manager. Kevin was a great character, a big, Irish New Yorker.

He had been in the outfield for the game in 1977 when the Yankees won the World Series for the first time in many years. Drunk, go figure, Kevin watched fans along both baselines pour onto the field. His only thought was "I want to do that!" So, Kevin ran down the aisle and vaulted over the railing. The last thing his friends saw was the expression on Kev's face change from exhilarated to "Oh shit". Unlike the little rails along the baselines, the wall Kevin just vaulted over was about twelve feet tall. The friends rushed down to see him mostly unhurt, but splayed across the warning track like Wile E Coyote against a cliff face. When Kevin told that story, he made sure to add that he tore up a piece of Yankee Stadium sod and planted it in his mother's front yard.

Well, this day, the Dallas boys decided that Gene was in the best shape to drive. The other two quickly went back to sleep in the car. Gene had been driving for about an hour, head pounding, every inch of skin in pain. He had particular aching in his face. Finally, after 60 plus minutes, he lifted his sunglasses and looked at himself in the rear view mirror. He had a shiner the size of Rhode Island. I presume that him yelling "Holy Shit!" was what woke the other guys.

Slowly the group memory came back as to why he was sporting

this huge bruise on his face. Naturally being good hosts, we were plying the two dancers with whiskey, not that they showed up sober. I mean they are dancers, for crying out loud. At one point, Ms. Butt had stumbled while hoocheying her coochie over Gene and accidentally stepped in his eye.

Gene McGuire, being a big puss, took the next week off from his job as house emcee at the Comedy Corner. I still think to this day that he missed a golden opportunity to have people ask, "Oh, My God. What happened?"

And all Gene would have had to do is puff up, give that Barney Fife snort, and say, "Stripper stepped in my eye."

Kip Adotta was a funny son of a bitch. And I mean that both ways. Kip made me laugh more than almost anybody I ever had the privilege of working with. He had this very special timing that just slayed me. He was a master joke teller. But Kip also went out of his way to be a dick.

Now I'm saying this while adding that he and I got along wonderfully from the first time we ever met. But Kip loved to see how far he could push people. It was a great game for him.

He once insisted to a club owner that the other comics names not be mentioned in any promo. He even went so far as tell the middle act, my friend Diane Nichols, that she was not allowed to have an intro.

Kip's long-time introduction was a very simple, "Ladies and gentlemen, a nice guy, a funny guy, Kip Adotta." One out of two ain't bad.

So, when Diane handed the emcee a long list of credits, Kip just said no. They argued about it for quite some time before Kip uttered, "Face it, Diane. If you need credits, they don't knooooow you."

. . .

Once Kip was working at the old Pittsburg Comedy Club for Bruno Schirippa. The club was in this old building with a bar out front and along the side of the showroom and the comic's greenroom and offices upstairs. Kip decided that it's too far for him to walk. After the first night, he called Bruno aside and demanded to have a motor home parked in the alley behind the stage. Bruno said, "no". Kip threatened to leave and go home. Bruno said, "okay". Kip replied, "I guess the green room will be fine." He just felt like he had to ask.

He tried the same thing when he and I and Alex Valdez were working together at Bruno's room in San Antonio. Bruno had gone back home to Pittsburgh to get married, leaving this total goddess of a manager, Anna, in charge. Kip, my fellow Italian (Sicilian in his case), and I invited Anna over for dinner before a show. Wow, she was great looking.

After we're done, he called her aside and said in that wonderful cadence, "Anna, last night there was a lot of talking at the tables. I think for the rest of the week, I'll need to make sure that you don't seat parties larger than two together."

Anna just laughed.

And Kip replied, "Well, I had to try."

Alex Valdez, a terrific guy, has been blind since he was a small boy. That week Kip twice rearranged the furniture in the condo while Alex was gone. Just cause he could.

Kip later ended up living with a woman named Linda, a former waitress at the Houston Laff Stop whom I had previously dated. She was a very cool and beautiful person and lots of fun. Not too terribly long after she moved in with him, Kip and I were booked together in one of the Punchlines in Atlanta. On opening night, I walked into the crowded front bar and hear Kip yelling, "Mike Vance, ladies and gentlemen. Mike Vance!" He was standing behind the bar and talking on the phone.

He waves me over and then says in a loud stage voice, "Linda, guess who just walked in. It's Mike Vance."

He insisted that I say hello to her, just hoping that I'd be uncomfortable, no doubt. That was Kip.

With us that week in Atlanta was Terry Mulroy, a very funny guy from Cleveland who was producer of Drew Carey's show for years. This was when Kip was closing with his Wet Dream song, the fish pun number that got tons of airplay. When he first started doing it, he would tour sometimes with two backup singers called "The Bitches". He opened with the song sometimes, preceded only by the words: "I'm Kip Adotta, and theeesssse are my bitches." Sometimes it was his closer.

Well, this week, there were no bitches. So, at the end of one of the shows late in the week, Terry and I borrowed two waitress uniforms, and when Kip started his song, we stepped out from backstage in dresses and singing. Not a pretty sight, I can assure you. We did get a pretty good laugh out of Kip and a great one from the audience. To his undying credit, Adotta finished the song nicely.

Kip told me a terrific story once about another Atlanta incident. He worked there often since the club owners loved partying with him. Kip was a blast to party with.

This one week, he had hooked up with a beautiful attorney there. They spent several days and nights together, until one day she decided they needed to go on a picnic. She had one lunch meeting with clients, then they were off. She told Kip to order drinks on her tab, sit at the end of the table and don't open his mouth.

He was introduced, found a spot at the end of the long table and started downing scotch, or whatever. He said he'd only been awake for an hour, hadn't eaten, and was getting a good buzz fast. All of a sudden, he noticed a very pretty woman alone at another table who kept staring at him. He tried looking away, but every time he glanced over, she was still staring. Finally, he silently and slowly mouthed the words: "Do I know you."

"No," she mouthed back.

Kip spread his palms upward and mouthed, "What do you want."

The lovely woman pointed at him, then shook her finger back and forth, making no noise as she mouthed, "From you? Nothing."

"Then suck my dick!" Kip yelled out loud across the extremely full and extremely fancy restaurant. Needless to say, it made the clients look up.

Without a doubt my favorite Kip Adotta story took place at the Icehouse in Pasadena, California. After the show, Kip was hanging out in a little alcove where the comics congregated. This kid, likely of middle school age, came walking in.

"Mr. Adotta, excuse me, but I wanted to see if I could get your autograph. My mother brought me to the show. I'm your biggest fan."

Kip took the pen and paper and started writing. The kid kept talking.

"I stay up to watch you on the Johnny Carson show whenever you're on there. I know all your jokes, and I do them for my friends at school."

Kip stopped. He very slowly laid the pen down, then the paper, then turned in Jackie Gleason fashion, grabbed the kid by the front of the shirt and lifted him up against the wall. He got right in his face and said in soft, measured tones, "Don't you ever ...do any of my fucking jokes... any fucking place."

Then he turned to the comics in the room and said, "You got to stop this shit while they're young."

That might seem cruel to you, and the kid is probably still in therapy, but I promise that to comics, it's pure genius.

I was not there for this one, but heard the story from Jordan Brady when we were working together one week. Jordan is yet another guy who middled for me on the road then got a television show while I was still working the road. He can join others on the list like Steve Harvey, Mario Joyner, Cedric the Entertainer and I'm sure several others. The best part is that every one of those guys happens to be funny and very cool. Good for them!

Anyway, the story happened once when Jordan was working with another old pal of mine, John Fox. As stated elsewhere in this volume, Fox is one of the all-time biggest partiers in the storied history of stand-up. Case in point - one time I was working at the Laff Spot in Newport Beach. I think Jerry Dye was headlining that night, and Jerry was no slouch when it came to putting them away, either.

One thing about that club is that the acts did about the shortest sets anywhere. The middle act only did 20 minutes. I think it was because they had a bunch of shows throughout the week and a very tight turnaround. That is germane because five minutes into my act, a beer and a shot of tequila showed up. I naturally looked for Jerry. He was in the back of the room shrugging his shoulders with palms uplifted.

I did about three more minutes and another shot showed up. Five minutes later, there was a tray with two shots. I think I ended up doing 22 minutes on stage, fully eight of which were filled by me drinking tequila shots. I walked off toward the back looking to tell Jerry Dye that he'd gone a bit overboard when John Fox suddenly jumped out of a side room with two more shots in his hand.

"Hey, pal!" He was grinning. "I looked in the paper to see who I could go drinking with tonight, and I knew you wouldn't let me down."

He had driven 90 minutes from L.A. to Newport just to party. That's our boy.

. . .

Anyway, Fox and Jordan Brady were working together in some town. Doesn't matter where, you just need to know that the acts shared a condo for the week.

Early in the six-day run, Mr. Fox managed to talk some semi-lovely into coming back to the apartment. In all the post encounter excitement, she left her bra behind. One of impressive size, I'm sure. So, John did the only thing he could. He stashed it in Jordan's luggage.

The next day, Jordan brings this bra back into the living room, laughing. But he told John in no uncertain terms that he is finally living with his girlfriend back in Richmond, and that funny or not, this one will get him in serious trouble. All John Fox heard at that point was "It's on."

Over the course of the next few days, the bra kept showing up in more and more obscure pockets of Jordan's luggage. It took two days for him to find it that last time when John had stuffed it into the pockets of some dirty jeans and then turned them inside out in the dirty clothes pile. This kind of thing went on five or six times.

Finally, it was Monday. The gig was over, and everyone was going their separate ways, which for Jordan meant back to the apartment he shared with his girlfriend. That morning before he caught his flight, Jordan locked the door to his room before he took his shower. Fox was still sleeping one off down the hall. Just to be sure, Jordan emptied every bit of luggage he had and completely repacked. Still, Fox was sleeping and hadn't come out of his room. Jordan heaved a sigh of relief and left town.

Two weeks later, Jordan Brady was off in another state at another gig when the phone rang. It was his girlfriend sounding all sniffling and hurt.

"Jordan is there something you want to tell me?"

After a long pause for thought, as any man would do, Jordan said, "Nooooo. Whhhhhy?"

"Because I went to use your typewriter, and there was..."

Chapter Five

We Really Only Did This to Get Laid

I'm certain that someplace out there is a professional comedian who will yammer on at length about the "art form" and about what joy it is to examine the deep introspective feelings that you tap as you create your unique humor and share the bond of laughter with the audience as they... blah blah blah. But the truth is that most of us started telling jokes because we couldn't dance for shit, and we wanted a way to get laid. I'm not saying we were successful at it, only that we were trying. Back then, we were a bunch of people in our 20s and 30s. The majority of us had very little life experience. Eighty percent of us were single. Like every other 20-something on Earth since the first horny Homo Erectus. In fact, that's how they got their name.

In my personal case, I started writing comedy bits when I was in the sixth grade. I'm not sure I made the entire conscious link just yet, but maybe I was starting to get the drift. Though I wasn't making the girls in Ms. Wetzel's class swoon.

I should stress yet again that in most ways, male comedians are no different than any other males of the same age. We are largely all dogs when we are in our youth. As with any other walk of life, some of us truly enjoy the company of women beyond the physical part and others really adhered to the old joke about the woman who turns into a pizza immediately after sex. I fall clearly into the first category of truly thinking that a nice woman is the best thing God ever made. So much so that in my twenties, I wanted to meet all of them.

The one way that the majority of comedians were very different than the normal male population was in the level of confidence. Most comics were naturally shy when you got them off stage. Some were painfully so. A few were downright neurotic. We had become comedians because we couldn't play an instrument and couldn't hit a curveball. We were the ones who made women laugh, made them stare lovingly into our eyes while telling us how a sense of humor was the most important trait to be found in a man. In fact, they were still laughing at our jokes while they were back home later that night screwing the personal trainer they'd met after our show.

So, keep all that in mind as you consider a few tales of testosterone gone wild. And also remember that it's likely the stories told by UPS drivers are really much, much worse.

Back when Sonny had left as manager of the Comedy Workshop and become manager of the nightclub Celebration, the Houston comics chased most all of his waitresses. Not many of us caught one. I did have a few dates with a particularly pretty little Venezuelan one named Angie. She got mad at me the first, and only, as it turns out, night we spent together because I had the audacity to make her get up so I could drive her back to her car at eleven in the morning. I would have loved to loll around in bed all day, but there were two problems. I had to catch a flight to go work, and we weren't at my place. I was between apartments and sleeping at Andy and Jimmy's. Angie eventually dated Ron Robertson briefly. Presumably he let her sleep later.

The reason I bring up all those waitresses was that they developed a habit of all coming to our show at the Annex on Sunday nights. Never wanting to disappoint, four of us developed a very hokey dance routine. The club manager would play "My Girl" over the sound system, and Jimmy, Ron, Steve McGrew and I would go on stage.

We had these stupid moves and turns that we worked out. After the first chorus, we started stripping. We'd get down to our underwear by the time the song ended, at which point we feigned embarrassment, grabbed up our clothing and bolted for the green room. Eventually we all bought specialty underwear, skimpy little things with hearts, flames or fire hoses on the front. As I said before: I can't imagine why we didn't do better with women.

The concept of dating someone who had previously dated another one of the group was not considered bad. Jimmy and I particularly seemed to end up with lots of crossover. I think we counted up five or six...dozen. But Jimmy had one sterling moment of bad karma when we were working together in Tulsa one time.

Joker's in Tulsa was a fantastic club when it first started, but it went downhill fast due to the mindless greed of the money partner, much like what eventually befell our venture in Oklahoma City. To make things even better, I booked the room. That meant extra income for me, and that I got to work with whomever I wished.

That particular week, I booked Jimmy to open for me. We were both going up in front of our pal, Shirley Hemphill, who had made it big in the sitcom *What's Happening*.

I had first met Shirley in New Orleans several years before. I was booked to do a convention show at the big Hilton on Canal Street. After I was done, I wandered over to the new Clyde's Comedy Corner at Conti and Dauphine. I wanted to check the place out and see if I could get a booking, which I did.

Shirley was headlining there, and a nice and funny local comedian named Ellen DeGeneres was hanging out with her and driving her around town. The three of us ended up going out that night with me crammed into the back of Ellen's VW. Ellen took a liking to me right away because she had a brother named Vance. Not always the fastest on the uptake for these things, I did figure out that I wasn't scoring with either Shirley or Ellen. We had a blast.

Shirley was a trip. She would go on at length about not wanting people to bother her in public, then she would insist on going out to Target to buy something. We would offer to go get it for her, but she wouldn't hear of it. She worked on this tough exterior, but Shirley Hemphill was as sweet a person to her comedian friends as you will find. She bought more decent restaurant meals for struggling comics that she worked with than anyone else I ever met.

That week in Tulsa, Jimmy had met a cute little SMU cheerleader-looking white girl name Tami. Yes, with an "i". Not really my style. Jimmy hoped to ask her out to another show later in the week. We were not thinking about her when Jimmy and I walked to a Wilson's, a big catalogue store, to get batteries for a tape recorder, we met just the sort of dark haired beauty I relished. Her name was Raquel, and she was beyond hot.

We both made complete fools of ourselves trying to ask her out, but in the end, she went for Jimmy. Boy would that come back to bite him on the ass.

At some point, Shirley decided that she needed to take advantage of the fact that both Pineapple and I were good cooks. We planned a big dinner for Sunday afternoon before the show with Shirley springing for the food. Jimmy invited Raquel, and I invited Lynn, the bar manager who become a friend who I marginally dated when I was up there, which was very frequently.

The trouble started when Raquel called Sunday morning to say that she couldn't make it because of some family conflict. So, after Jimmy expressed the appropriate sorrow, he did the next logical thing. He called and invited Tami with an "i". It was a good plan for about two hours. That was when Raquel called back to say that Jimmy had sounded so disappointed that she had told her family she had to leave early. She was in a hurry, but she'd see him in an hour.

I spent most of that hour laughing my ass off. In between, we kept working on the meal, and Jimmy started working on an ulcer. He had TWO dates coming to the townhouse where we were staying. They'd both be hungry, and both be there really soon. And with a guest list that now totaled six, it might be tough to hide.

He tried. After he had begged me to hit on Tami with an "i", Jimmy went upstairs to his room and refused to come down until it was time to plate the food.

Lynn thought that the entire thing was absolutely hysterical, so we all treated it like a big gathering of friends, for the sake of Raquel's and Tami with an "i". Though I got some very odd looks, especially from Tami, I'm not sure that they figured it all out completely during dinner. The only saving grace was that they accepted that Lynn was just the bar manager who we invited to come eat, albeit a bar manager who was prone to start laughing for what the other two women thought was no apparent reason.

During the show, they sat together and laughed at the jokes. Things started to go downhill afterwards when all of us, save Shirley, went around the corner to Pete Mesquite's, the comedian hangout of choice when we worked in Tulsa. That was when it became painfully obvious that Jimmy had two dates. So, he handled it by telling me to keep buying Tami and Raquel drinks on his tab while he jumped into the sound booth and became a guest DJ for a bit. That guest DJ time soon became a few hours. About every other song, at six minute intervals, the club patrons would hear, "Another Jack Daniels to the booth." Since I was twice divorced by that time, Jimmy did dedicate to me, at least five times, All My Exes Live in Texas. Tami with an "i" sadly caught on before closing time, and left. Jimmy did salvage things with Raquel, but oh, how I laughed.

Since we spent so much time on the road, we sometimes got rather bold in asking women out. Or more correctly stated, inviting them to the show. The general theory was that none of us could stand a chance with a woman until she'd seen the set and laughed at the jokes. Most people would say that's pretty sad in its insecurity. Most comics would say, "Nah, it's just the truth."

You have to understand that during the 80s, when comedy was booming on TV, and comedy clubs were just opening in most every town in America, we were celebrities of minor ilk when we'd show up at some place like Columbus, Georgia or Fort Collins, Colorado. One time in Amarillo, the three of us who were working at Jolly's that week went to the mall with club passes and traded them for merchandise at several stores. I recall getting a couple of new shirts and some shorts at a Foot Locker type place. We played it for everything we could. We also thought nothing on Earth was funnier than seeing one of our close friends strike out in spectacular fashion.

Personally, I am quite shy one on one. I rarely got past the part where I invited them to the show, but there were some guys who would never think twice about walking up to some cute girl and expecting them to swoon when they said they were a comedian. Out of the Houston guys, our pal Steve Moore, was hysterical in that regard. When we'd go play college gigs, he would always shave about six or eight years off his age. And he would sit and talk to some woman for hours, whereas many of the rest of us would have long since given up. Moore once brought a John Irving novel to a strip club thinking it would impress the dancers.

He once got literally run out of town because of this nice guy behavior, and that was with a woman he never touched. It didn't help that it was the club owner's girlfriend, to be sure. He had spent a fair amount of time chatting her up after his set at some sleazy place in Lake Charles, Louisiana. Come to think of, just about every venue there ever was in Lake Charles was vaguely sleazy, but this one was the worst of the worst. Fights, stupid and obnoxious patrons and an owner who had fired guys after one show because he didn't like their acts. Granted, the ones I heard about had acts that make me tempted to back the guy up.

The gig was a two-night affair, so Steve had a hotel room. He was there, in bed alone when someone started pounding on his door at three in the morning. It was the club owner who soon had him pressed up against a wall screaming at Steve that he should never have fucked with his girlfriend. Then he added something to the effect of "get your shit and get the fuck out of town now because I'm coming back in 30 minutes, and if you're not gone, I'm gonna fucking kill you!"

Now, Steve Moore had a tendency to over-explain things when he would be better served by shutting up. He even had a bit about that in his act. So that might explain why on the face of the Earth, Steve ran after this thug, hoofing it out into the parking lot in his underwear screaming, "I wasn't with her. Let me explain."

Eventually, reason popped its way into Steve's brain. He packed and drove home to Houston.

There were two other classic moments involving Moore hitting on women. One took place in Odessa, Texas where he, Ron Robertson, Steve Epstein and I had done a show at the UT-Permian Basin. The show went quite well, and we were looking for a bar that would be a nice hang out place afterwards. Driving down the highway back toward Midland, the more civilized of those twin cities, we passed a strip club. Moore was gaga over topless bars, so in we went.

Robertson and I watched a couple of dancers and quickly found more amusement at the pool table. Not that we were hustlers, but during that time period when we were roommates both in Houston and later in L.A., we would occasionally play eight-ball as partners and win a little money. Nothing fancy, five or ten bucks a game at the most, and only in nightclubs, never in pool halls. We weren't that good.

One time we were both in Dallas at the same time, and we ended up at a pool hall. That was the exception. We had gone there just to kill some time in the evening. And I should point out that this was on Greenville Avenue, so it was as yuppie as a billiard place can ever be. We were having a few beers and enjoying ourselves, when some young kid came over to challenge the table. There were plenty of empty ones, but he insisted on playing us. Then he wanted to bet. Like I said, we weren't that great, but this kid just kept losing to both of us and demanding that we keep betting him. Finally, he ran out of money at five bucks a game, so he started betting us drinks. We tried deliberately losing, and he was so bad that we couldn't even make that work.

The sad, sad fact that night was that the drink special was Watermelons, a nasty sweet fruity thing. Ron and I won two pitchers of the shit. That's two more than we wanted, and most assuredly two more than we needed. For guys who couldn't lose, we were throwing up back at the hotel room by 9:30 and nursing excruciating hangovers for the entire day afterward. Winning.

Well, this night at the table in Odessa was similar. Or more to the point, there were some very shitty pool players in this strip bar. We were trying hard to lose by the end because the natives were getting agitated, and we were getting nervous. We'd only won about forty bucks total, but the last game, I made the most obvious scratch you've ever seen, and we headed for the door.

While we'd been playing pool, Eppy had been watching the dancers, and Moore had been seriously hitting on a girl that was off duty. She wasn't working because she was on crutches. Moore probably was commiserating about when his leg got broken, except that he didn't do it skiing. A 250-pound comic fell on his.

We rounded Moore up on our way to the door and quickly

impressed upon him the importance of leaving right then so we didn't all get our collective asses kicked by West Texas rednecks. The four of us went out the front door followed by the limping stripper and one of the biggest damn bouncers on the planet.

Moore was still trying to hit on the dancer, telling her to come meet us at Denny's. Meanwhile, Robertson was making fun of Moore. Just for sport. It was the usual fare, talking about Moore's hair piece mostly. But to this dancer who was impressed by the smooth talking comedian, it was mean. So, she started hitting Ron with her crutch.

For the bouncer who had a head as thick as his biceps, that meant that one of his dancers was unhappy. So, he shoved Ron and said, "Leave the little man alone."

That just made all of us laugh, and Ron, who could get a mouth on him when he had been drinking, said something about Moore being defended by a one-legged stripper.

That got Ron's face pounded into a car hood.

"I said, leave the little man alone!"

Eppy, Moore and I would have loved to explain that we were all together, all friends, but we physically couldn't. Eppy and I were lying on the ground holding our sides while Ron's face was being ground into automotive paint. Finally, Moore managed to choke out the words that made the bouncer let up.

We wiped our eyes. Moore kissed the dancer goodbye, and we went to Denny's. We were drunk and loud enough that when Eppy mentioned ketchup in what we all took to be a normal voice, someone four tables away walked over with it and said, "Here." So we entertained part of Odessa for a second time that night. But...shocker... the dancer never showed up to meet Moore.

My personal favorite among Steve Moore flirting tales is one that sounds amazingly like it was written as a joke, but I was there to watch this one in slow, painful detail. It happened when Moore's favorite lineup for college shows was booked at what was then North-western State in Natchitoches, Louisiana. No lie, we opened for a Three Stooges film in the big auditorium.

After a great show, our student handlers asked us what we wanted to do with the rest of our evening. Duh. Beer. The next thing we knew, they had us in a car headed deep into the North Louisiana woods to some giant metal building. It appeared to be a large night-club, except for the fact that we were about the only people in there. I was afraid for a moment that I'd already seen this in one of those civil rights movies.

They assured us that when the movie let out, this joint would be packed to the gills. Then they gave us the kiss of death- there was no way we could possibly fail to meet women out of this deal.

Sure enough, within half an hour, the place was packed just like they promised. Lots of pretty college girls, and it seemed like all of them had seen our show. One after another, they came up to us and told us how funny we were. Many were embarrassingly effusive. We were like four kids in the proverbial candy store.

Moore tried first by walking up to a real cutie and trying a line that he had presumably been working on for some time.

"Oh my God. Is that your face?"

"Excuse me?"

He realized how stupid that sounded and went into panic mode.

"No, uh, I mean, do you get to take that everywhere you go?"

'Fuck you!"

We laughed until we cried.

Eventually one of the young lovelies bought me a Miller Lite. After talking and laughing for a couple of minutes, she returned to her group of friends, all girls, who were standing all of ten feet away. When I saw her finish her Bud, I bought one and walked over there to her.

"Hi, I bought you another beer." I smiled warmly.

You would have thought I'd handed her a turd. She looked back at me with disgust and said, "That's not my brand."

The guys at the bar, including the geeky looking student who was assigned to be our tour guide, were laughing their respective asses off at me going down in flames. My night of hitting on women was over. I concentrated on beer.

Somehow it was Epstein who ended up in a booth having a seriously productive conversation with some woman. Meanwhile, Moore had spotted a new woman across the bar, and she looked to be right up his alley. He called the bartender over and said that he'd like to buy a drink for that woman.

"Which one?" he asked.

"The cute one in the red."

"She's drinking a hurricane. It's seven dollars."

"Not a problem," Moore said. "Just tell her it's from me."

So, Moore tipped the guy a couple of dollars, and he and the girl waved at each other.

We sat there looking at many women who were way out of our league and laughing at stories. Twice again, Moore motioned for the bartender and sent another tall expensive drink to his targeted woman. He was now tipping four bucks a pop since the guy was working so hard on his behalf, clearly talking him up to Miss Hottie. We urged Moore to go talk to the lady, but he just kept saying that he had a plan.

Finally, when she was ready for yet another drink, likely barely clinging to the stool unless she had the superhuman capacity of the comics, Moore announced that he would deliver this drink to her in person. He paid for it, tipped big and strolled suavely around the big square bar with us watching his every move.

"Thanks so much for the drinks," she cooed.

"Oh, you're very welcome. Say, my buddies and I are going to go grab some breakfast in a few minutes. I'd love it if you'd join us."

"Wow. That's very sweet, but my husband wouldn't like it."

"Your husband?!?"

"Yeah. He's the bartender."

We came unglued. The bartender just gave us a sly smile. What a great night for him. Some other guy had paid for all of his wife's drinks and tipped heavily on top of it.

Not to suffer alone, Moore waited for Eppy to go to the bathroom, then he strolled over to the girl who had been snuggling with him.

"We just wanted to say thanks," Moore told her. "You know, Steve is coming off some really tough times medically, so we appreciate you spending all this time with him. One very important thing that I can't stress enough, use protection, okay. Even though we think it's probably cleared up."

We all enjoyed our breakfast. In a four person booth.

Steve Epstein had some absolute classics in rejection. I remember one time that he, Pineapple and I had met three girls in the audience at the Workshop in Houston. We took them out for drinks, figured out who was with whom, and eventually ended up back at the Comix Annex parking lot saying our goodbyes. Jimmy and I were busy kissing our respective new friends goodbye when all of sudden we heard Eppy loudly yelling.

"Hey. Why no tongue? They're getting tongue. I want tongue!"

Those were among the many, many ladies we never saw again.

Without a doubt the classic story of Epstein in love is one that I found out about when I was roused from a good sleep at about 9 o'clock one morning.

Now, I should insert a commentary here. Show business has always fostered partying that most civilized segments of society would consider outright debauchery. Drugs and alcohol go back to the ancient Greeks and beyond. It's possible that the gossip rags back then were filled with stories of Euripides and his actors getting tossed out of some Korean bathhouse in the shadow of Olympus. Hell, Fatty

Arbuckle and a champagne bottle damn near got Hollywood shut down. And the 1980s and 1990s were a time of particular abandon.

Having said all of that, there were several comics out there, both in Houston and on the road, who did not do drugs. I for one have never tried acid, ecstasy, or many other recreational things on a long list. Hell, I was never even a pot smoker. And I don't have a moment's regret for not having done so, either. One of the reasons was that I always figured that my good buddy Eppy and several others had my portion already covered. In a bow to then popular Herbal Life, whatever that was, Pineapple used to say that Epstein was so into X that he had a bumper sticker on his car that read: "I'm fucked up. Ask me how."

So, when Eppy had been partying up at Bill Hick's apartment at a somewhat fancy downtown high rise called Houston House all night long mixing acid and X on the last night before ecstasy moved onto a higher level of the controlled substance list, he knew which of his buddies would be home in beds when the sun came up. The rest of his buddies were right there at Hicks' place sound asleep on the floor.

So it was that at 9 A.M I answered my phone with a groggy hello. The voice I heard was that familiar Chico Marx accent.

"Hey, Vincetti. Sure. I'm getting married today in a boat on the Southwest Freeway at Hillcroft. You come to the wedding..." And oddly enough, only here did we get to what I considered to be the weird part. "...and dress as a pirate."

Well, you can imagine that I had a few questions. One was concerning the fact that Steve wasn't even dating anyone. Another prominent one had to do with the lack of boats at that particular intersection which was a good solid 25 miles from navigable water. Then there was the issue of dressing as a pirate. For his part, Epstein simply said he was in a hurry, and that he'd see me at the wedding. In retrospect I understand that my many questions were ruining his buzz."

Robertson, Pineapple and I were soon in touch, being the afore-mentioned sober comics. With some more commentary for Epstein to guide us, we decided to meet at Ep's parents' house around noon. We were there, but no Epstein, so we went to a nearby Black-Eyed Pea and had lunch. By the time we swung back by his folks, Eppy was there along with his childhood friend, Craig Zinn. By this time, whatever had knocked everyone else out had simply worn off for Epstein. He gave us the story.

There was an Australian chick named Kay, a cute blonde who happened to also be living with some big guy. Somehow during the partying portion of the evening, at least some of the boys had gone to see some live music at a big rock hall called Fitzgerald's, one where most of us had also performed. There they ran into Kay, a woman for whom Eppy had admittedly had the hots.

Now for this auspicious DEA ecstasy party, Epstein had purchased a few hundred dollars' worth of still legal X. He would be in good shape for some time. Steve Moore had even given Epstein $100 just to buy some extra and put it aside. The happiest boys on Earth were going to go out in style.

Somehow, after the revelers left Fitzgerald's, Epstein decided that, well after one in the morning, he needed to go back. I'm not sure how many of the boys returned, but I do know that when Ep couldn't find Kay, he made the only logical conclusion: She had been abducted by the CIA, and he'd better flush the $500 worth of ecstasy down the toilet in the men's room. Somewhere in Houston sewers there were some incredibly jovial snakes and gators.

In the wee hours of the morning, Epstein showed up at Kay's house and proposed. Amazingly he was not beat up by her boyfriend at that point. The guy obviously had a sense of humor.

Though Kay did not accept the proposal to our knowledge, Eppy proceeded to make plans for the wedding. He showed up at a costume shop exactly when they opened. As the semi-terrified old women that ran the joint watched, he gathered up most every pirate article in the store, told them it was for his wedding later that day, and then whipped out a Rolodex and started calling Robertson, Pineapple and myself from their phone.

When we found the boy after lunch, the only remaining two hits of X were in his parent's freezer wrapped in an envelope with a note in his mother's handwriting that read: "Stevie, do not touch."

To prove that we weren't Mormons or anything, the rest of us started drinking whiskey and then posed for pictures standing in his father's bass boat in the driveway. Needless to say, we were dressed as pirates.

Gary Bun Richardson was the oldest comic among the Houston guys, but it sure didn't stop him from chasing skirts for a time. In fact, Gary Bun went on a tear after he got divorced. At the time he was driving a 240Z. Nice ride, but not big. He spent a month or two living in his car.

To be truthful, I should say that he spent a month or two trying to avoid living in his car. Every night, Gary Bun's goal was to find some woman who would take him home. He figured the getting laid part was great, but the bed was his true goal. And since Gary had been featured as the centerfold in People magazine as a Burt Reynolds look alike, he could get some women. When he didn't succeed, he woke up with striped tan lines across his face thanks to the vents across the back glass of his Z.

He would come into the Workshop Annex with a new story every night, laughing about he had lowered his standards right up until closing time, and still ended up with a stiff neck and back instead of any other appendages. With his signature cowboy hat, every night, he went from the comedy club to one of the C&W discos that were so popular after *Urban Cowboy*.

It was during this time, when Gary Bun was between wives and I was between apartments, that I got a call one night soon after New

Year's at my parents' house where I had been staying. Yes, I know, what a geek.

Gary had a girl for me. I did remember meeting her and her sister at the New Year's Eve show at the Annex. It seems that Gary Bun's quest had led him to meet up with one of them, a cute brunette who worked for the now defunct Houston Post. Her sister mentioned that she thought I was cute. I figured Gary Bun was in an "ask and you shall receive" kind of mood. In reality, it was not so charitable. Since the Houston one was entertaining her out-of-town sister, it was either up to Gary to produce someone for little sis, or it was back to the cargo bay of the Datsun.

I ended up spending a great week or ten days with Kim, who was in town visiting from La Crosse, Wisconsin. She turned out to be not only cute and sexy, but fun and nice. We wrote some letters back and forth after she went back home, but ultimately Wisconsin and Texas are not too geographically compatible.

The best part for Gary Bun was that as long as I hung out with Kim, he got to stay at the sister's apartment.

Gary ultimately got married to a terrific woman named Sherry who was beyond cool. She was much younger than Gary. He had a joke about her being able to help his daughters with their homework. All the comics loved Sherry, which is not something to be said about some of the other wives.

Gary was also working with me in Brownsville when I had the very best luck of my life with women. And gorgeous Hispanic women to boot.

There was a brand new club down there, the first ever in the Rio Grande Valley. They had started booking two comics a night in a co-headline situation at the Raspberry Street Pub on the weekends. Gary and I were there the second week. It was a nice set-up, and the club owners were bending over backwards to make sure we were happy. Little did I know that the newness of comedy would turn us into temporary rock stars. It was great. I got more phone numbers than AT&T.

That Friday night we ended up at a party at someone's house. The string of hot women rubbing up against me seemed endless, and out of all of them, the most beautiful without a doubt was this little darling named Berta. Just purely stunning. I could not believe my luck that she wanted to see me again the next night. The only downside was that she wanted me to call her Bert. That I could not do. No Bert. No Ernie. Girl's names, please.

My mom's family is from the Rio Grande Valley down there on the Mexican border. My parents met when my dad was stationed at Harlingen Army Air Corps Base during World War II. I have several cousins down there, and my folks had friends who still lived there in the 1980s. Among those friends was one of my dad's best buddies, Tommy Monk. Tommy was a cigar chomping ex-sergeant who used to take us fishing out in Laguna Madre when I was a kid. That second night at the club in Brownsville, he came out to see me.

Any guy will tell you that it's a wonderful thing when you show up with a woman so hot that she impresses your friends, but somehow, it's even better when it can impress your dad's friends. I'm not sure why. But it definitely made me happy when Berta walked in the door to the club and Tommy's head turned. When she walked directly toward us, his eyes widened, and by the time she gave me a hello kiss, he was drooling like Homer Simpson.

The oldest of my first cousins came to that first show Saturday, too, bringing a date. After two totally killer shows on Friday, I was feeling pretty solid about Saturday. Gary and I were swapping spots, and, after closing the two shows on Friday, it was my turn to go first on Saturday. It was 45 minutes of what felt to me like tepid death. There was never any rhythm. I never got a roll going. Most unsatisfying, to say the least. Gary, of course, killed. Afterwards, my cousin, my would be date, and everyone else I knew said their goodbyes with nervous laughter and quickly vanished.

To make it worse, half of the people stayed over for the second show!. This time, I went up and was getting huge house laughs from the opening line. After ten minutes of this, I stopped and asked them where the hell they'd been during the first show. They howled. I swear it was almost like the entire audience had played a practical joke on me. They thought tanking my first show in front of my cousin and my dad's Army buddy was just hysterical. Luckily, they yukked it up for another 40 minutes, and the drinks were free.

As noted, I am not necessarily separating young comedians from lawyers, electricians or frat boys in their 20s when I assure you that we were totally, as Carl Faulkenberry used to call it, scanooni loony. We used the comedy club boom to full advantage. But like any other study group, some of us were better than others. And then there were the hot streaks and runs of bad luck.

Back when we were living in the top floor of a duplex in the late 70s and early 80s, Jimmy Pineapple managed to amass a couple of the greatest Stand-up stories ever, and I don't mean they had to do with comedy. I mean that he had a serious string of getting stood up.

Being a devotee of Sinatra and Errol Flynn, Jimmy always valued the romantic touches. He went all out much more so than the rest of us did. He would get dressed up for dates. It was not uncommon for him to bring flowers or candy. And he was doing all of that when he drove out to pick up a cutie that he had met while she was working... at Burger King.

He was trying not to sweat through his sports jacket while he stood on her front porch ringing the doorbell to no avail on a sweltering Gulf Coast afternoon. Just as he was giving up and turning back to his car, she came squealing to a stop at the curb. She jumped out wearing a bikini and covered in coconut smelling suntan oil.

"Oh, hi," she intoned with a remorseful smile. "I'm sorry I can't make it. I'm really sick."

Jimmy just looked at her.

"What are you taking for it? Coppertone?"

She got back in her car and drove off, leaving Pineapple doing the slow burn even amidst the overpowering smell of lotion.

Another time, Jimmy had met a young model. They made plans for an early dinner the next Sunday.

I was hanging around the apartment, no doubt watching some game on TV, when Jimmy came out of his room looking quite snazzy. He stopped to tell me how gorgeous this little vixen was, then left to drive to her house which was in the suburbs a good 30 miles west of where we lived.

I was still watching the game when he slinked back in the door. I didn't think he even had time to drive out to this girl's house, let alone have a date.

It seems that when he got there, the young lady's mother answered the door. Jimmy swore up and down the girl was standing behind the open door the whole time. In a very unconvincing manner, the mom told Jimmy that she was sorry, but her daughter had gotten called to work on an emergency.

This time the boy wasn't silent.

"Emergency? She's a model! She got an emergency modeling job on a Sunday night? What does she model for the fucking fire department?"

Pineapple and I, roommates at two different places, had several times when we ended up on double dates with two girls who also roomed together, or even two sisters. My first wife, back when I was only 19, was the housemate of a girl Jimmy dated. And one of my second wife's younger sisters ended up dating Jimmy. In fact, they lived together for a time many, many years after I ceased having anything to say to the one I married.

It was those two who were at a Super Bowl party when we

embarrassed ourselves big time. I use the term "party" loosely since there were only five of us. It was Jimmy and me and the two women along with our buddy Rob Baker. He had to be there since we were at his apartment.

This was the Super Bowl to which Vince Ferragamo inexplicably led the Rams. I know they got the snot beat out of them by Pittsburgh, but things were likely somewhat fuzzy during the actual game. We were pounding beer, and Jimmy probably had some Jack Daniel's, but the main problem was that Baker had gotten hold of that evil, nasty swill the Scandinavians call Aquavit. Tasteless, bleak bastards.

My date, Meredith, who was merely separated from her high school sweetheart husband, was the only one besides Baker who took a shine to the crap. It's made from caraway seeds, for crying out loud. I'm pretty sure Roundup is tastier and less harmful to your system. The result was that when the game was over, only Jimmy, Kellen and I were in any shape to go to the Annex for the Sunday night show. Meredith passed out at her apartment, unable to answer the phone, and leaving me fearing that something very bad had happened.

For his part, Baker was out cold in his bed. That wouldn't have been a problem, except for the fact that Pineapple left his keys inside that apartment. When I drove him back over there to get his car, it was pouring down rain in that monsoon fashion found only on the Gulf Coast or along the Ganges. So, Jimmy and I got to end the evening standing outside Baker's open window in a downpour screaming for him to wake up. It took over 30 minutes, but we finally got him, and presumably most of his neighbors, to go unlock the door. And let me tell you, seeing him naked was not a high point, either.

The most interesting part of the night also involved making an impression on his neighbors, or at least one of them. Around halftime, when the alcohol had kicked in nice and good, the three guys decided to regale the ladies with a recreation of the "My Girl" strip tease dance that we were doing during those days at the Annex. The best music Rob had was a 45 of Roy Orbison singing 'Pretty Woman". We had that bad boy cranked up full blast, and we were down to our tightie whities when there was a knock at the door.

We all froze while Baker stupidly opened it to reveal his pretty upstairs neighbor with whom he had been trying to get a date. There was, expectedly, a long and uncomfortable pause while she looked at the three guys in their underwear then at the two fully dressed girls on the couch then back at the three guys in their underwear. Then she finally spoke in a quiet little voice.

"Um, could you turn the music down."

"Yeah....sure."

Yep, we were so talented that we could even ruin our friends' chances of getting a date.

Though Pineapple and I dated four or five women after the other of us had already been out with them, the champion of that with me seemed to be Jim Holder. Holder came along later in the Comedy Workshop days. Back when he had hair, it was blonde and disco curly, so he did well with the ladies.

Before I even realized he was around the place, he was already hooked up with this knockout big blonde of a beginner comedienne named Ellie. She was from Wisconsin, and her act needed some help in those days. Then again, so did Holder's. They dated for a while before they broke up. I think it took me all of a day before I asked Jim if he had any problem with me hitting on Ellie. He did not. And I can honestly say that the months I spent with her were a very enjoyable experience.

A year or so later, history repeated itself, and I once again started seeing someone who had previously dated Jim Holder. After that, whenever he showed up with a new date, it became a running joke that I'd ask to meet my future girlfriend, or he'd flat out introduce me as the guy that his date would be with next. Okay, at least it was funny to us, and you know what they say: "If you can just make your friends laugh, ...you'll never go anywhere in this business."

The Workshop had been closed by the time that I was booked with Jim at the relatively new Punchline in Greenville, South Carolina. Those were great days for the Atlanta boys who owned the Punchlines. They had hooked up with partners in most major cities in the Southeast, and the guys that were in with them could get some nice work.

Not long before, I had headlined their brand new club in Charlotte. My week there was only the second week the place was opened. It turned out to be terrific. Nice owner and manager that enjoyed partying after the shows. Good audiences. And a very nice condo that they had for the comics. That's about everything you can want. And did I mention free drinks?

It just so happened that Holder was the opener or middle act for the first week of the Charlotte Punchline, so I had called him to get the lowdown on the place. Top of his list was that they had lots of good looking waitresses, and that he had ended up with one for the entire week. In fact, Jim said, he might even be back in Charlotte to visit this one again soon. I told Jim I would be on the lookout, and that I would see him in a few weeks when we worked together in Greenville.

The first night in Charlotte had a sparse, but good crowd. When we were done, the entire staff went out to a nearby watering hole. We were all having a fine time when a couple whom I had not met arrived to join us. The guy was introduced as the bar manager who had the night off. The girl was introduced as Elizabeth. She was a sultry hot Carolina girl that looked like a young Elizabeth Ashley. A total hottie, but, I assumed, the girlfriend of the bar manager.

We shut the place down. I did manage to get in some good conversation with the pretty Elizabeth, and some harmless flirting, but eventually, I got a ride back to the condo with nobody but the other comic. We hadn't been there long when the phone rang. It was for me.

Who the hell could be calling at 2 in the morning? For that matter, after only one week in business, who the hell had this phone number?

It was Elizabeth. She was sorry that I left and wondered if she might come over.

Hell yes! But out of curiosity, I asked how she got the number of the condo. It seems she was a part time waitress at the club, and was not dating the bar manager at all. That was like a lottery win.

It wasn't until the next day that I discovered that she was the one who had been with Jim Holder the week before. Obviously, a woman who was both sexy and discriminating. We got a big laugh over that when I saw him. That somehow the fates saw to it that I always got his leftovers even when I didn't know it.

But the real punchline of the Punchline story was yet to come.

I got a call in Greenville that week from my close friend, Fred Greenlee. He was working some gig in the neighborhood and wanted to know if he could stop in on Sunday, maybe stay at the condo, hang out for the day, and do a set that night. He had a few days to kill before his next gig which was still in that part of the world.

It didn't take long after Fred arrived and started answering the "what's been going on?" question that Jim and I learned that he had a new love interest. She was a waitress at the club in Charlotte where he had been a couple of weeks before. Speaking together and laughing, Jim and I asked if it was "our" girlfriend there.

Fred could always get very prickly about certain things, and he definitely did not take it well when he pulled the photo out of his wallet, and Jim and I almost wet ourselves rolling around the floor laughing. Finally, Jim pulled out the identical picture from his wallet. I was just a little hurt that Elizabeth never gave me a picture. I mean, clearly she had been ordering them by the dozen.

Chapter Six

Tales of Houston Comics

For better or worse, Houston comics had a reputation for being both very funny and very rowdy. Jim Patterson, one of the prime Houston comics, arrived in Lubbock one time to play a club that had only been open a few weeks. The owner picked him up at the airport, and as they were getting in the car, he turns to Jim and said, "I hate those Houston comics. They keep sending me those damned Houston comics. All those Houston comics are a bunch of assholes."

"Yeah, I know what you mean," Jim said. "I'm from Austin."

The comics who were regulars at the Comedy Workshop Annex in Houston make up most of the best friends I've ever had in life. We may have had a time or two of petty bickering, but we were truly siblings. These are just a few of the people and stories as I recall them. Many more could be told, and many more are better left amongst us. In my book, the core comics from that place are the very best. Most of us watched out for each other, shared lines when it might help the other person's act, and helped get bookings for each other when we could. I love them all and very much miss those who are now gone.

Jim Patterson had one of the classic shallow woman stories, one that I have heard repeated by other comics as being about them. But I trust Jim to be the origin for this one. He was doing an opening act slot in Oklahoma City one week and had been talking to this one woman who had been out to a couple of shows. Things were going well, they went out for drinks, and finally she agreed to go back to the house that they rented for the comics. As they were driving along, her head resting on Jim's shoulder, she said, "I've never done this before."

"You mean go home with someone you just met?"

"No," she said. "I mean fuck the opener."

Jim being a regular guy took no offense and kept driving.

Patterson could always end up with some major wackos when it came to women. He had dated this one who he hadn't seen in months when his phone rang one night at three in the morning. He answered, "Hel-lo.....hello."

"Jim Patterson?"

"Yes"

"Oh, this is Debra. I must have dialed the wrong number. I was trying to get suicide hotline. Well, as long as I have you, when is your next show?"

Still the trooper after all these years, and not having gotten any in weeks, Jim asked her out on a date. He picked her up and one of the first requests she has is that she wants "a Mexican Coke" Okay, I give up, too. She explained that a Mexican Coke tastes completely different and is bottled in Mexico. So, they drove to five stores and restaurants before they finally found a Mexican bottled Coca-Cola at this little taqueria. She took a sip and went, "Oh, that is so good. Man, is that great. Here you have got to taste this." Jim took a swallow, and it tasted exactly like regular Coke.

They stopped at a light on a major six-lane boulevard, and suddenly Debra threw open the car door and took off running across traffic, picked something up, and returned to the car. "Look, a lucky penny!"

Jim replied, "Yeah, it must be lucky cause none of those oncoming cars hit you."

Later that night, after Debra was quite amazed at a magician who was on the bill at the comedy club, ("That must be a trick," she kept saying.) Jim made it back to her house. They went into her bedroom and started doing a little passionate kissing on the bed, when Jim noticed this rank smell and some grunting noise coming from the far side of the bed. He sat up and opened his eyes.

"That's my pet pig," Debra said cheerfully.

This was no cute little Vietnamese potbellied pig; this was like a full-grown sow. Just rooting around and eyeballing Jim on the bed about two feet away. That was the final strike and Jim just shook his head and went home.

Patterson and I once got booked to do a show for the Junior League of Odessa, Texas. A coveted job, I'm certain. Truth be told, they paid us pretty well, and arranged all of our travel without a hitch, something that did not always happen. Then again, they're Junior Leaguers, nothing if not perky and organized.

The only drawback was that they booked a flight for us at some ungodly hour of the morning when comics had barely gotten to sleep. Bleary-eyed, we made it to the airport in Houston (late) and, this being Southwest Airlines, found ourselves some seats near the rear of the plane. Across the aisle from us was none other than Congressman Mickey Leland, the man who followed the famous Barbara Jordan as representative of Houston's majority-Black 18th District. And though it's obvious, I will add this was not the flight that got off course and crashed in Africa.

Jim ordered a Bloody Mary which seemed like such a stellar idea that I joined him. When he had gotten down to just the ice and a paltry few red drops, he accidentally knocked it over on the tray just as the flight attendant was strolling by. She jumped into action, and in a flash, Jim had a brand new full drink at no charge. Well, you can figure that he had another "accident" right as he was finishing that one, and the end result was that I was feeling fine when we landed, and Jim was two and a half, if not three sheets to the wind.

This is one of those stories that I can pinpoint with complete accuracy. It was right before the election in 1988. Even though he had grown up as a Republican, Jim was plenty smart enough to see the glaring error of his ways and had become a full-fledged liberal like the vast majority of the rest of the Houston comics. So, he had nothing but the best intentions when he looked at the Congressman and slurred out, "Mickey Feeland!"

Mickey Leland just gave him a blank stare. Jim was undeterred.

"Are we gonna win on Tuesday?"

Leland's stare turned to ice. "Who's we?"

Oh, but the fun was just beginning for Mickey. We followed him, his lovely wife and an aide through the airport to baggage. Not a long walk in Midland/Odessa. When we got there, a driver was waiting. While we stepped outside to the curb, U.S. Congressman Mickey Leland was getting into an old Impala. I can still picture his jaw dropping open as a uniformed chauffer opened the door to a stretch limo, and the two drunks from the flight stepped inside.

As the driver walked around the car, Jim told me that he needed to hit the bathroom. That's what led to the genius moment when he lowered the power glass to the front and said to the driver, "'Scuse me, but how far is it from here to the airport?"

"Ummm, it's right there, sir."

"Oh yeah. I meant to say hotel, but I'll just go inside and pee here."

The election was definitely on our minds during that trip. Later that night, we caught a cab to some Odessa nightclub. Oddly enough, we were the only two guys in suit and tie. A very cute bartender took a liking to us enough to flash me. A nice perk any way you look at it.

At closing time, I stood out front as Jim stopped everyone coming out and introduced them to their incumbent congressman, Mike Vance. Most all of them promised to vote for me in a few days, and a couple even told me I was doing a terrific job. It's possible I got as many votes in that district as Dukakis. Makes you proud to be an American, doesn't it?

Another one of Jim Patterson's girlfriends was Jeanette Frazier, who did stand-up. She had one notable trait. When it came to dogs, many of the other comics thought she was a raving loon. I should probably explain that. See, I love dogs. Love them all. I have always had dogs since I was born. I think I understand dogs and would never want to live without at least two in my home and life.

Jeanette, though, could be one of these animal-loving nut-logs who have abandoned any shred of logic. She and a friend of hers had an apartment across the courtyard from me in the years when the Workshop was closing. They were nice people in many ways, but Jeanette had Lord knows how many cats living in the place and an occasional dog she would find.

Nice, you say? Yes. Except for the slight fact that these dogs sometimes belonged to other people. Once she was at the grocery store and saw a dog tied to the newspaper rack outside the door. She rescued the thing. Untied it, forgot her shopping, and headed back home with the dog. For hours she dialed the phone number on the poor dog's tag. Finally, a young guy answered.

"I found your dog!" Jeanette said.

"Oh thank, God. He was tied up to a newspaper machine outside the grocery while I ran inside for a loaf of bread, and some woman stole him. I've been frantically looking for him for hours."

She never learned. One time she and Jim were driving down a street in Houston and saw a dog loose in someone's front yard. She screamed for Jim to stop. He slammed on the brakes while she raced up and grabbed the unsuspecting dog and loaded him in the car. This time it didn't take long. She called the phone number and an old lady said, "Yeah, we saw you take him from our front yard. We were looking out the window, but we couldn't get to the door before you drove off."

And those are the good stories. Once she and Epstein were driving through East Texas heading to some one-nighter. There on the side of US 59 was a dog. Imagine that, a loose dog in a rural area.

Jeanette made Eppy stop. She took off down the shoulder of the road chasing this dog. Now, if I was a dog and some stranger jumped from a car and came after me, I'm getting the hell out of there. Horribly, but predictably, the dog ran right out on the highway and got slammed by a car.

Jeanette went berserk. They loaded the dog into the car and drove him to the animal hospital in the next town. The vet got one look and announced the dog was dead. Jeanette was bawling. Weeping and sobbing. Since she was moaning inconsolably, it fell to Eppy to fill out a form so the vet could dispose of the body. He started, talking out loud. "Type of pet...dog. Cause of death...Hit by car. Name....hey, Jeanette, what do you want to name him?"

Speaking of bizarre girlfriends, Epstein has had a few who were brilliant in their eccentricity. One, whose name I forget, was the classic.

She was a petite, somewhat bookish, bohemian looking girl. Dark haired and with the pale skin you would expect from Emily Dickinson. Not Emily in her prime, I mean how Emily would look today. And that is appropriate because the first night I met her she was reciting her own poetry in a bar. The only problem was it wasn't any sort of scheduled poetry recital. It was just her in the middle of a bar.

A group of us had met at the Laff Stop in Houston to hang out, and afterwards we were moving the party down the road about a half mile to a bar named Cecil's. A great place until the black-fingernail, tortured-twenty-something crowd took over. What an annoying bunch of dweebs.

Anyway, Eppy and the date left a bit earlier than I did. I stopped in the restroom on the way out or something. Now, Epstein had bought this car, I guess you'd call it, at a US Post Office auction. A baby blue Pinto with one bucket seat. He tried to duct tape a lawn chair in there for passengers, but never could get it to stick. Every time he hit the brakes hard, the chair would come untaped...you get the picture. So, here I was driving down this busy street on the way to the next stop, and I saw up ahead Eppy's Pinto going about four miles an hour. As I went around, there was his date riding ahead of him on her bicycle. They were on a date.

After I stopped laughing hard enough to drive again, I caught up with them at Cecil's. It was a quiet night. We were enjoying a cold beer and talking when somehow the subject of writing came up. The future ex-girlfriend told us she wrote poems, and without pausing for the slightest acknowledgement, took two steps toward the middle of the room and loudly began reciting this piece about her boyfriend who left her and how she stabs him in the heart in her dreams and how he bleeds and how he begs for mercy as she disfigures his body. Man, that girl was perfect for Epstein. His friends would have been at their house everyday just waiting for the show.

A couple of years later, Miss Poetry married some other lucky guy. She ran into Eppy just a few weeks later.

"Steve! I got married! Guess where we had the wedding?"

"I don't know," Ep answered.

"Just guess. No one else has guessed it. Go ahead, guess."

"In a cave?"

"Yes," she squealed. "I knew you'd understand!"

Jimmy Pineapple's stated goal in finding a wife during those years was similar. He always wanted someone young and pretty and stupid enough to amuse his buddies. We were a very thoughtful bunch in some ways.

I must admit that Jimmy and I were rather big hound dogs in our day. One thing about us is that we were creative and unconventional. That sometimes worked well for us. Other times, not so much. On the plus side of the ledger was a time we had four great seats for an Astros game, but couldn't get dates. That did happen. So, we went downtown to our stomping grounds of La Carafe in hopes of finding someone to go.

There was an office party of some sort upstairs, which we promptly crashed and isolated the two best looking women there. Now, one of the many things Jimmy and I share is an obsession about not missing the first pitch of a ballgame, so after flirting for a very brief time, we handed them the tickets, said we'd love to see them there when they could break away, and we booked it to the Astrodome.

Sure enough, in the second inning, these two lovely ladies showed up. We had a blast. After the game, we decided that we were hungry and somehow arrived at Roy Rogers Roast Beef as being a good plan. I think it was both open and near their apartment.

I should add that traffic leaving the old Dome could be lousy. And they were following us. We knew we had a couple of winners when we stopped at a light on a busy boulevard, and one of the women bolted from the car behind us to pee in someone's bushes. We figured we couldn't go wrong with women like this.

O contraire. I'm pretty sure it was when Jimmy and I each

ordered one of Roy's signature "holster of fries" with our sandwiches. That would have been okay if we hadn't then strapped them to our belts and started doing quick draw dipping in the ketchup.

Miraculously, we still wrangled an invite to the apartment, but it was a couple of quick drinks, a little goodbye kiss and we never saw them again. Unless... hold that thought.

I promised a bad example of our skills, as if that was a good one. We were at the bar of another favorite haunt, Birra Poretti's on West Gray, one night when we spotted two cute women come in and sit at a table in the dining room. Now anybody can order a round of drinks and send them over, but we were comics. We had imagination. So, we sent them a round of dinner salads. Inexpensive was thought number one. And funny and original. We were all smiles and waves when the waiter dropped them off and pointed our way.

If we had waited for thought number two, we might have arrived at the same idea that the two ladies did. They thought we were inferring that they were fat. That earned us a nice large "Fuck you". Really girls, you were cute.

The other story I was thinking about above also happened at Birra's one night. I should mention that when we went there every single night, it had a huge square open bar that allowed you to see the people across the way. One night Jimmy, Fred Greenlee and I were there with an old buddy of Fred's, a radio reporter named Paul Pendergraft. For once we were minding our own business. That is until we noticed three very pretty women on the side of the square to our left. Except this was not a good thing. They were pointing at us and making angry faces. Soon we could hear them using words that you wouldn't expect to hear in public from women like that.

Not used to being animals of prey, animals who would have known to run like hell, we went over to see what the deal was. I swear to you, none of us recognized any of them then, and we don't know who they were to this day. Furthermore, they wouldn't enlighten us except to continue with a string of epithets and an admonishment that "we knew what it was." Obviously at least one of them had a previous problem with at least one of us, but we just didn't know what had happened. Or which one of us did it.

We walked back to our spot at the front door side of the bar, and they kept yelling at us. Soon the security cop came over and told us that we had to leave for the night. I should add here that we knew this cop since we drank at Birra's every single fucking night after the show. We had gotten him free tickets to the Annex. When we pointed this out, he was kind enough to point out in return that these girls were hot. Damn cops.

That night ended with the three of us still arguing over our removal as we were pushed toward Paul's waiting BMW. The girls were outside yelling at us, and Paul drove off with a red-faced Fred Greenlee hanging out the car door yelling back. Damn, I wish I knew who those women were.

Carl Faulkenberry and Jim Patterson moved to Houston in 1981. They had been working together on radio in Corpus Christi, and had made the drive up and back for open mic nights several times. They worked as a comedy team, and were funny. I'm guessing some of the first jokes had been tested on radio.

They met working at small town stations in the heart of Cajun Louisiana, in towns like Opelousas and Mamou. They were also famous for not-so-subtle schemes to duck out of on-air work to either come do an open mic spot or attend a concert. They famously made up the last two innings of a live baseball game when a rain delay almost cost them a spot on the Workshop stage.

One of my favorites of theirs was a tale about Jim being pulled over by small town Louisiana cop with his K-9 partner. Jim, who had been enjoying a bit of an herbal cigarette tried not to panic. It helped when he realized that he knew the cop.

"Hey, Jim. I hope I didn't scare you, cher."

"No, not at all. I wasn't doing anything wrong, was I?"

"Oh, no, cher. I just saw you drive by."

The dog had started to bark an alert at this point.

"Pipe down, dog. Yeah, Jim, I was just wondering if you were going to that dance over in Church Point this Sunday."

Bark, bark, bark, bark.

Jim was sweating bullets.

"Yeah, I hadn't decided. Anyway, good seeing you."

Bow wow wow wow wow.

"Quiet, dog. That's enough."

"Yeah," Jim said, "I got to get going. I told someone I'd meet them."

"No problem. Anyway, how you been? I heard you on the radio this afternoon."

Rrrrroorrr. Bow wow wow. Bark bark bark. bark

"Shut up. I just don't know what's wrong with this dog.

The cop never did figure out why the drug dog was barking, and Jim eventually went on his way to his non-existent meeting.

Cecil's on West Gray was the scene of another classic Epstein moment. A bunch of us were there playing pool. Nice upscale tables with at least some sticks that weren't warped. Different for a bar. While Eppy and I were awaiting our turns, there was a lull in the conversation.

Epstein broke the silence.

"You ever get an itchy ass?"

"Excuse me?" I responded.

"Butt itch! You ever get an itchy ass?"

"No, I can't say as I do." I took a step back, away from Epstein.

"Well, if you do...Listerine!"

"Listerine?"

"Listerine!!"

"Do you drink it, gargle with it?" I asked.

"Hey sure...You rub it on your ass." Epstein was as pleased as if he had just won the Nobel Prize for chemistry.

I had to know. "So Eppy, how many other household products did you rub on your butt before you came up with this one?"

Steve Epstein was absolutely hysterical to hang around because there was no logical reason for what he would do next. We've all heard people described as "having no filter," but Eppy was the only person I've ever met where that statement should have had the word "no" underlined in red.

In one of the most inexplicable moves in nightclub history, Comedy Workshop owners Paul and Sharon Menzel decided to make Steve the manager of the Comix Annex. It did not last long.

The front of the little Annex was solid glass, picture windows from top to bottom. Not terribly long after it opened, they sprung to have a professional come in and artfully cover it with one-way, sunlight barrier film.

As a customer opened the door to the Annex, there was a tiny box office, but Steve, and did many other people working it, chose to sit in the first stool by the windows and skip the claustrophobia of the 4x4 foot ticket booth. It was at that spot, two days after the new expensive window film was installed that the scratched graffiti "Ep-A-Stein" appeared. After at first denying that it was him, Steve somehow kept his job.

Though most comedians perform standing up, the plain wooden barstool is a staple of every comedy stage. It is mostly used as a drink table, but can very often become a prop for bad puns like "my doctor told me to check my stool" to awkward weapons against imaginary foes. Sam Kinison used the one at the Annex for some bit that ended with him hog tying the chair with the microphone cord then jumping on it. With Sam topping 250, the poor stool didn't stand a chance.

Breaking the barstool the second time cost Sam a two week suspension. When he returned, warned by Paul Menzel never to do that again, Sam not only ended his act with the breaking the barstool bit, he tossed a twenty dollar bill on the stage to pay for the damage.

Club manager Epstein, who was stationed at a back table just to watch what Sam did, was overcome with excitement. Yelling something like, "Yeah!" He picked up the wooden club chair in which he'd been sitting and swung it against the wall. An important lesson in physics and material density followed. Bar and restaurant chairs are much harder than sheetrock. The chair went halfway through the wall and got stuck. All decorum was sucked right out of the room. Comics were screaming with laughter. Epstein was mumbling, 'Oh, shit," and audience members were part bewildered, part gleeful and part horrified.

When Paul Menzel walked into the Annex the next afternoon, the chair hanging from the wall was not a big hit. And that was the end of the Epstein as manager era.

Many comics, in Houston and elsewhere had piece of shit cars. Surprise. We were often broke sons of bitches. Tracy Wright had a great line about an old truck he drove being "so slow it got passed up by weather." Not shockingly, a Plymouth land yacht, dubbed the Blue Cab, was one of two comedians' cars that burned up while parked. The other was Jimmy Pineapple's van that turned to toast in a parking lot while he was inside watching a movie.

Lots of us roomed with one another over the years, and one had Jimmy Pineapple and Steve Epstein sharing a house on Colquitt Street not far from the Workshop. At the time, both had pretty sketchy vehicles. I know Jimmy's was an early 60s Chevy that he called the Bossa Nova. Since both cars were already total beaters, the two of them started a game of destruction derby on Houston streets. No matter where they were, if one saw the other one driving through the neighborhood, they'd slam into the other's car.

Often times, this took place in or near the Workshop parking lot. The most frequent location was in front of their rented house. One would be standing in the front yard, chatting with a neighbor when the other would come careening around a corner and smack into their roommate's car parked at the curb. Sometimes, it was a hard enough hit to knock the vehicle onto the sidewalk.

This came up at the subsequent eviction trial. It was can't miss courtroom drama, and Ron Robertson and I journeyed to the courthouse to support, and laugh at, our friends.

Their landlord, an officious man with a brown briefcase, was representing himself. The boys, Jimmy, Eppy and Brad Brown, an actor friend who had previously roomed with me and Jimmy on West Alabama, were represented by a lawyer buddy of ours. His name was Jose Rojo, and he looked exactly like a Latino Ernest Hemingway. Rojo was brilliantly funny, could spin yarns for hours and loved comics. Jimmy, Bill Silva and I had met him first when we were all bartending at La Carafe, the bar not far from Houston's courthouse complex.

We got an inkling about the way things would go when the landlord complained that Jose was 10 minutes late. The judge, not being impressed by anyone who didn't have the sense to hire a lawyer for a trial, pointedly told the guy that Mr. Rojo was a hard-working and distinguished member of the bar. We knew that he certainly looked distinguished when we were all hanging out at the bar.

Jose had a knack for making the most inane things sound totally serious. I had seen it when he handled my first divorce. Carl and Jim had seen it when he was trying to sue a popular radio DJ for stealing one of their bits and turning it into a radio promotion. They were in Jose's office one day when someone called about their important criminal case, to which Jose told his secretary, "I'll have to call him back. I'm busy with Bowling for Pigs."

The trial did not disappoint. Ron and I got gaveled a few times for laughing at the supreme smartassery provided by witnesses Epstein and Pineapple. The biggest laughs came from Jose Rojo's questioning of and objecting to the prim little landlord. The man was outlining a long list of offenses, many of which he had discerned by peeping in the boys' windows. The car ramming played large. Finally, he started down a road to outline their debauchery by quantifying what he had found in their trash bin.

Jose leapt to his feet.

"Wait," he said with slow incredulity. "You went through their garbage?"

The sputtering landlord, and Ron and I laughing again, were about the last sounds in the trial before the judge ruled in favor of the boys. Epstein, ever athletic, promptly jumped over the defense table like it was a tennis net. That earned the final gavel pounding of the day.

For comics who worked at the Comedy Workshop, one of the more memorable guys was Rick Johnson. Not because his act was great, but because he exuded a sleazy, sad, belligerent quality that was impossible to ignore. Like I said, nothing he did on stage was groundbreaking, but neither was it horrible. He had studied drama at University of Houston, and he became a quick regular, and did some regional work on the road. There was a limited market in other parts of the country for a guy who looked and acted remarkably like Yosemite Sam. No lie, I once saw him thrown out of a convenience store.

Rick had various apartments, but he was also voted Most Likely to Crash on your Couch. More than once, audience members called the club two days after they'd been to a show asking how to make Rick leave. One time he walked into the green room, turned proudly to the baseball fans amongst us, and said, "Guess whose floor I slept on last night? Joe Sambito's brother!"

When a person is a caricature, it's easy to always think of them in only that way. After knowing him for several years, Rick told us that he had come from money but was estranged from his family. When he showed up in a one or two year old, full sized BMW one day, he said his mom had bought him the car in exchange for him staying away from her. It gathered a great deal of genuine sympathy from all of the comics.

A few days later, Rick told us that he was headed off on a trip to New York and had some showcases lined up. The story might have worked better if several of the comics had not found him sleeping in his car in the back corner of the parking lot.

The sympathy he had amassed largely evaporated, too, when the cops came and took the shiny new Beamer. It turned out to not be a gift from his mom, at all, but rather a hot car for which Rick had paid about $600.

Bill Hicks was probably the Workshop alum who is best remembered today, especially in Britain where he is revered as a comedy god. When I played over there for five weeks at the Fringe Festival in 2004, U.K. comedians swarmed me to hear stories about Bill. Some London actor was performing a one man show of what he thought Hicks would be talking about if he had lived. Before we left, Bill's mom, a supremely nice lady, called me and asked if I would check out this potential blasphemy and report back to her.

I was there as part of the comedy band I started, the PC Cowboys, so we wore straw cowboy hats everywhere we went. We were obliged to take them off at this show which was about 11 a.m. in a very small venue. I told Mrs. Hicks that the biggest offense of several was that this ghoulish money grab was just plain unfunny. It was, however, plenty radical enough to make my genuine redneck fiddle player damn squirmy.

It's tough for people today to understand that when we were all working at the Annex, those of us who were headlining the national clubs were all equal. Each of us had national television credits and audience members would each have picked someone different as their favorite. The local comedian polls had different winners most every time. Hicks was doing Letterman, others the *Tonight Show*, others were regulars on the top cable networks.

I mentioned earlier that Hicks was a naïve kid when he first started coming around the club in those early weeks. He and I were the only ones still in our teens. The first time I had tried to get into the Comedy Store in Los Angeles, I was turned away for not being old enough. Drinking age in Texas was 18, but it was 21 in California. I heard later that if I had pushed a bit harder, they might have let me do a set, if I left immediately. On my 21st birthday, I had my first spot at the Store's Original Room.

In those days, Ron Robertson had a day job, unlike the rest of us. He had an expense account and money to foot the bill for his close friends. His sales territory was the western half of the United States. That expense account served Ron well, and I often got to tag along and stay in the spare hotel bed. In L.A., it was always the Hyatt on Sunset which was right next to the Comedy Store. We always got a room on the Sunset side which provided an amazing night time view of the city. That's where Robertson, the former baseball player, got his nickname of Longball. The two of us were standing on the hotel balcony, silently sipping a drink and gazing at the city lights when he suddenly spoke into the eucalyptus-scented night, 'If I could have hit the long ball, all this would've been mine."

Entertaining other comedians in the hotel room also became a thing. Another inescapable feature of that stretch of Sunset Boulevard in those days was the hookers. Several of us where in the room enjoying some drinks one night when we started observing the streetwalkers below. Stirred to action by a story I shared of a guy who lived on my dorm floor in college, it was decided that we needed to get Bill laid. A "hey" and a crook of the finger soon got a very street looking lady knocking on our door. Try as we might, Hicks refused. He would soon grow out of that shyness.

Among his Houston friends, one of the best known Bill Hicks stories was his broken leg. There was a singer who was a regular at the Annex named Cindy Olivarez. Today she goes by Julia, and she was a good friend to many of us. She was dating a guy named Lars who was bartending at a little music and drinks place we went called Blythe Spirits. It was a two-story venue in an old house. Lars was a somewhat beefy dude often prone to wearing a kilt.

We learned early on that when Hicks got drunk, or even two or three drinks into an evening, he could turn either surly or profane. Things he thought were funny might cross the line. The night in question, Hicks and Tracy Wright set out to do a night of drinking. They took a cab to the first stop, Blythe Spirits and were hanging at the small downstairs bar. In addition to Julia, Tracy and Bill, the party included Brett Butler, who was a funny woman who had recently moved from Georgia to try her hand at Stand-up full time. It was the old story of friends encouraging her, and in this case, her friends were right. I was there on her first night, and thought she had some real promise. It wasn't long before she was a regular.

There had not yet been much drinking going on, but Bill was making jokes about Julia. More to the point, Bill was explaining in high detail, exactly what he would do to her if she ever wanted to have sex with him. It was a theme Bill used in a few bits on stage, and it proved to be a great laugh getter there. In a group of five, it may have been a mite uncomfortable. At this point, Lori, Tracy's girlfriend at the time, demanded that Tracy go upstairs with her to talk about their "relationship." Oy.

Julia may or may not have gotten annoyed at Hicks, but Lars sure did. When he started telling Bill to mind his tone, Bill's full smartass was unleashed. After the words got more heated, Bill, threw a wad of cash at Lars to cover his two or three beers, and headed for the door.

The rest was pretty simple really. Lars came out from behind the bar and shook Hicks violently, then he slammed him into the jukebox. Bill did not fall well. His foot got caught underneath the machine, and voila, broken leg.

According to the story I heard from Tracy and others, he and Lori ran down stairs when they heard the screaming. They found Bill on the floor with a large man in a kilt sitting on his chest, one arm cocked back to punch Bill in the face. Julia was screaming for Lars to stop, as was Brett Butler who was draped over Lars' back trying to pull him off of Bill. Not that the comics didn't love Brett already, but that incident cemented her as being one of us.

Tracy's first words to the guy at the bottom of the pile, writhing in pain, and a phrase that Bill brought up repeatedly in the years following, were, "Okay, Bill, what'd you do?"

The fun night of drinking and relaxing ended up in the emergency room at Heights Hospital about 90 minutes after it started. And all of us watched Hicks learn to use crutches.

Sam Kinison was the first Workshop regular to reach fame. He did it out of the Comedy Store on Sunset, primarily, but his big break was a spot on Rodney Dangerfield's Young Comedians Special. Rodney and Sam became fast friends. Because his act was consistently dirtier than everyone else's, Mitzi Shore at the Store confined Sam to a midnight spot, and he developed a cult following.

Sam very frequently came back to Houston throughout the rest of life. He would get spots at the Workshop, sometimes in the bigger Cabaret side, but always it was to hang out with friends. Sam and I had an epic evening in Houston well after he was a big star. We ended up at my house about 2:30 a.m., and I promise that did not go over well with my wife at the time. That was probably because when I walked back to our bedroom to tell her I'd brought a friend home, Sam followed me. Kinda creepy. Yep. I will also admit that we might have been a tad loud in the kitchen. Until 4:00. Or 5:00.

When he first came to Houston from Oklahoma, he stated by doing fat jokes that were not funny. Within a couple of weeks, he had switched to using lots of props. He started out wearing a coat and tie. No one quite knew what to make of him. He bombed well more than half the time. Some nights his act bit hard, but there was a feeling that he was looking for a character on stage, as opposed to other new acts looking for material along with the polish. Eventually, Sam found a bad boy persona that worked, and he ran with it. It happened when a prop megaphone broke, and a heckler started really going after him. Sam left the stage and started a totally over the top screaming rant in the guy's face. It killed.

His first regular screaming bit that I recall was when he'd walk into the audience, start singing I'm Mister Lonely to some random guy, advance to stroking the man's hair, then start screaming as he threw the man from his chair to the floor and began to hump him. It got laughs, though an occasional audience guy's ego was sometimes bruised.

From time to time in that first year or two, Sam would leave town for a couple of weeks to go preach with his brothers. They had an evangelist act led by oldest brother, Rich. At first, Sam was ashamed of it, I think. Soon, he opened up more, including showing up with wads or bags or cases of cash which paid for a dozen comics to enjoy late night meals at a wonderful, and long gone, all-night Chinese place called Sun Deluxe. We were regulars there for weeks after Sam preached, and the owners loved us. Or they at least acted that way.

About a year or more into this, Rich Kinison had a preaching show at a church in one of the more joked about Houston suburbs, and Ron Robertson, Steve Epstein and I went to watch. Sam was touted as a guest appearance, and he cautioned us that the people in the congregation would be taking this very seriously. My memory was that we managed to not howl with laughter, but it had its moments. More than anything, we saw firsthand the very direct line between Sam the preacher and the energy and delivery of Sam the comedian.

When Paul Menzel dished out punishment to comedians for various transgressions, or when the short lived comics council laid down the law about violations having to do with jokes that were too close to someone else's, it was generally in the form of a suspension. No stage time for a week, or even two. Given that it was the most sought after stage for several states around, that stung.

There is no doubt that Sam drew more suspensions than any other comic at the club. Between breaking the barstool a few times and him stubbornly sticking with this one bit that the council and/or the Menzels banned, he probably scored as many as half a dozen suspensions.

Unlike other times, though, Sam wanted some mileage out of one suspension. After a week or so making money as a preacher, with some advance warning to several of us, he walked to the convenience store directly across the street, stripped to his tightie whities, climbed onto the concrete base of a parking lot light, and stuck a broomstick behind his hands in a crucifixion pose. Given the plate glass front wall of the Annex, everyone inside the club could see him clearly. It was nothing short of brilliant.

Of course, all the comics went over to commiserate, but the most entertaining reaction came from the motorists who were tooling up and down Shepherd Drive. The Workshop sat on the literal edge of Houston's most prestigious neighborhood, River Oaks. Today, not a house can be had in that large enclave for under five mil. You can imagine what the rich, little blue-haired ladies said when they got home and called the police: "There's an almost naked fat man standing on Shepherd!"

It did not take terribly long for the first of multiple squad cars to show up. The police were already amused, and even more so when Sam explained that it was all tied to the comedy club across the street. Eventually, they persuaded him to leave, but pity the acts who had to go on stage in the middle of all this.

The controversial bit I mentioned above was not the hill to die on, in my opinion, but Sam was obstinate about it. The routine itself is not at all memorable to any of the other Workshop comics save the name. It was the adventures of Baby Jesus and his side kick (N-word) Dog. Sam did Baby Jesus with this baby talk, high voice. There wasn't any reason for the dog beyond him saying the name, as far as I recall. I think that to the majority of the comics, it was a needlessly racist bit, but we were not that worked up over the thing, either. Pushing the boundaries was what comics often did. After Menzel told him not to do it anymore, the next time earned Sam a two-week hiatus. Steve Moore, still recognized by the Menzels as the Artistic Director for the comics, wanted to push it even farther. He was livid that Sam ignored his ruling. Though none of us expected it to stick, Moore wanted Sam banned from the club.

Angry words had been exchanged, and the next night, we all expected fireworks. Carl LaBove, Riley Barber, and Dan Barton were all outside when Sam knocked on the parking lot door to the green room. The rest of us were mostly inside waiting on our spots. We also had the good sense to tell Moore not to go outside. He did not listen.

Not long after the Annex opened in July 1979, the Menzels had a wooden deck built outside the back door, which led to the green room for the comics. Underneath the deck was a curb and what amounted to a drainage channel alongside the building. In tropical Houston, that equated to a registered mosquito habitat, but we were likely so pickled in alcohol that they refused to bite us. That deck was where everyone hung around in good weather. Between it and the smoky green room, the stories swapped were legendary. This deck was where Sam confronted Steve Moore.

None of us on the inside went out after him, but it took less than a minute before one of those outside, I think perhaps Barber, knocked on the door saying Moore needed help. They had grabbed each other's shirt front, Sam twisted him to one side, and the two fell with Sam landing on top of Steve's leg. Bonecrusher Smith lasted longer with Mike Tyson. But bone crusher it was since Moore's leg snapped. An ambulance was called, and now Sam really was in a world of shit with club management.

His answer was to move to Los Angeles. A couple of us had made that attempt already. I moved out there to become a Comedy Store regular in 1980, quickly ran out of money, lived in my car for a couple of weeks and moved back home. Sam's move proved much more successful.

He, Bill Hicks, Riley Barber and Carl LaBove decided to move out together, and there was a quickly planned farewell show to send them off. I was asked to emcee the two shows at the Tower Theatre, a former movie palace that had been converted into a live venue on Westheimer Road. It was in Houston's Montrose neighborhood, as was the Workshop and damn near all of our apartments.

It was a great room with a backstage out of real, old-time show business. It was also a lesson in marketing. There were two shows, and lots of laughs, but maybe only a third of the seats were filled for each of them. It was not the auspicious monetary sendoff they had planned, but the poster of those four guys in prison attire was epic. They all faced the usual hardships of show business poverty when they arrived in the Southland, but it led to fame and success in the end.

Carl LaBove was one of the four guys on that show, and he probably benefitted from the most serendipitous moment I ever saw at a comedy club. When Carl first moved to Houston, he had incredibly high energy going for him on stage but not much more. He got by with audiences more on personality and performance than material. Audiences tended to like him.

Carl came up with an idea for a new closing bit, and he and I were hanging out on the night he debuted it. I was sitting by the big windows in front of the club specifically watching for his new closer.

It was a conceptual thing where he asked the audience if he was "good enough to make it." With his usual super high energy and a sweat going and gestures exaggerated, he begged them for approval. (Carl sweated a ton on stage.) The more they cheered, the more excited he got, until he finally said, "Thanks! I believe in myself! I can do it! I'm going to go out there and make it big!" That was supposed to be his fired up exit from the stage, and instead of heading back to the green room, he walked through the front door all the way to the street, turning back and waving before he threw out his thumb to hitchhike off to stardom. The audience, who could see all this through the giant plate glass floor to ceiling windows, applauded, but the thing is that until they turned back to the stage, it was destined to just peter out.

This debut night, though, he stuck out his thumb, and the second car that happened along screeched to a halt on busy Shepherd Drive. Carl said a couple of quick words then hopped into the back seat, and off they drove. The crowd went wild. I'm sure most of them assumed it was a perfectly timed, well-crafted piece of performance art.

The thing is that it was not. Carl told me before and after that he had no real ending. He was counting on the emcee to switch focus back to the stage. So now, Carl was in a car with total strangers headed south on one of the city's busiest streets. He had to quickly explain that it was a joke, and almost beg to be let out asap. As it was, he ended up walking about 20 blocks back to the club. The bit never worked again after that first night, but what great timing from the universe.

Steve Brasfield was another comic from Houston. Fairly funny, volatile temper occasionally, and always a fun guy to hang out with. He could get mean when he'd been drinking from what I heard.

He walked into a neighbor's apartment and personally turned down their stereo one time. Ballsy move, but one we've all felt like doing. I wouldn't recommend it without Kevlar.

Brasfield and I worked in Bay City, a little town about an hour and a half south of Houston one time, and drank so much free beer at this place that they had to run to the store between shows to buy more.

Like many comics, Steve tended to get long-winded when he'd been drinking. As the headliner who had to follow him, I wasn't too thrilled when he prattled on for about fifty minutes before I hit the stage. Thankfully, the opener, Ray Garcia, a not so big drinker who we had corrupted that night, went short.

To show you how drunk Ray was, we stopped at a convenience store/gas station on the way back for him to use the bathroom, and the man actually bought three corndogs. Scary just thinking about it after all these years.

Brasfield's finest moment may have been when he was doing a little in-town gig for a booker named Marty Schilling. Marty had been in the comedy club business for years. When she started, she was a fun party girl. But somewhere along the line she got touched by some sort of religious fervor. Misguided, I'm sure.

She still had her moments of sweetness, don't get me wrong. I did have a couple of run-ins with her, but nothing serious. Overall, I liked her better than most bookers.

I was scheduled to work one of her rooms one time when I got sick with food poisoning, or pesticide poisoning more likely. I had just eaten a cantaloupe when I started feeling feverish. I subsequently, how to put this delicately, spewed orange all over my apartment. Another cleaning deposit down the tubes.

Well, Marty somehow became convinced that I was faking it to get out of this one night of the week. Her manager told her that I'd mentioned an uncle of mine was in town, so Marty cleverly puts it all together to mean that I was goldbricking so I could go out with my uncle.

First off, my seventy-year-old uncle was likely in bed by the time the show started. Secondly, I had told the manager that I had seen him the night before, and two nights in a row of most relatives is plenty. And third, if I'd wanted out of the show, I'd have come up with something smoother than throwing up fruit.

That notwithstanding, she canceled me for the rest of the week. And canceled another gig I had booked with her. She apparently got over it, because I worked for her long after that. She even called me one Saturday night about nine and asked what I was doing right then. I told her I was off and sitting at home, as it happened. I was flattered to know that when the headliner had gotten shit-faced and was wandering through her showroom knocking stuff over, she thought of me.

But back to Brasfield. See, Marty had decided that the world needs more rules. Never a good plan with comics. But the one which can really piss off lots of them is to limit their drinks. Marty had put in place a two-drink maximum policy for comics until their shows were done. The weird part was that she still charged them for the drinks just like other customers, if I recall.

I had known her long enough to have escaped that rule ever being enforced. I had always had a reputation, deserved I'm sure, for being rebellious. Or a trouble maker depending on whom you asked.

So, Brasfield, ever my brother, was working this same hotel bar gig for Marty out one of the ubiquitous freeways in Houston. Friday/Saturday thing. The first night, he's getting ready to go up in a few minutes and went to the bartender to ask for a beer.

"Can't have one," he was told. "You're already at two."

He bitched a bit and demanded that the bartender ask Marty who's sitting across the room. The poor schmo did just that. And she came over and told Brasfield that he's had enough and to go on up on stage.

Well, two beers are not much to a man of Steve Brasfield's caliber. The next night, he responded in style. Half an hour before the show started, Steve pulled his car up next to the curb, in a red zone right in front of the large picture window that looked from the comedy club out into the parking lot. He pulled a case of Budweiser out of his back seat and plopped it down on the hood. He then proceeded to shotgun beers one after the other until it's his time to go up. He staggered through the exit door, did his 30 minutes, and returned to the hood of his car. A very impressive statement.

Another time I was working for Marty at a room in College Station, a college town as you might guess. It happened to be Good Friday during Spring Break. I kept expecting the date to get cancelled or moved. I called from Houston twice before I made the 95-minute drive to the show. Not just once. Twice. Both times they said, "Oh yeah, we're having a show. Come on up."

You got it. I got there and after waiting 40 minutes past showtime and staring at the six folks who had come for entertainment, they cancelled the show.

The owner said, "I'll tell you what, I'll give you fifty bucks and pick up your room bill."

I answered something along the lines of, "No, I'll tell *you* what. I don't have a room. I'm driving back. So, you'll pay me the whole $225. Especially since I called twice before I left home, and you said to come on up and assured me the show was on."

He got all pissy and stomped off to call Marty. About ten minutes later he came back and said, "Which one of you is Vance?"

I raised my hand.

"Yeah, she said you'd probably insist on getting paid." He pouted.

Yep, I'm unreasonable that way about having my contract honored after I drive to another city. Go figure.

The douche paid me in ones and fives. And I took every single one of them.

. . .

I happened to catch up with Steve Brasfield the week that Pope John Paul II died. He e-mailed me a picture of his dad, an older, even more Texas redneck-looking version of Steve, who lived in Tyler, Texas. It seems that his dad decided at some point that he needed to run for pope.

He had a picture taken of himself in a light purple fleece shirt with a white collar sticking out from underneath. Slapped a cardboard pope hat on his head and grabbed hold of some sort of scepter composed of Easter animals, and he was good to go. He e-mailed the thing to Steve who forwarded one on to me and others, I presume.

As soon as he got some positive feedback in the form of Steve saying that his buddies thought it was a good plan, Steve's dad headed down to the local Kinko's and had flyers made up.

According to Steve, he then put them up at all the bars he frequents. Which turned out to be pretty much all the bars in Tyler. One of the bartenders called him that Saturday afternoon and said, "Harold, we took a poll down here on that pope thing, and you're leading."

Back to Kinko's. This time he had the picture blown up into yard signs that proudly proclaimed "Harold for Pope". It just so happened that weekend was the annual Azalea Trail there in Tyler. So, the signs quickly went up in the yards of all the oil tycoons' homes that were being visited by Junior Leaguers and their whipped husbands who'd paid $40 a ticket.

History will record that the German guy won. But let it be known that Harold Brasfield in Tyler, Texas put up a hell of a fight.

Chapter Seven

Larger Than Life:
Characters from the Comedy World

Not many comics trusted Ollie Joe Prater around their material, but, like him or not, he was one of the all-time great characters on the comedy planet. When I first met him, he weighed close to three hundred pounds. At less than six feet, mind you. Though I didn't see him the last year that he was alive, word on the street was that he got up over 400 easy. In Akron, people told me that when he was picked up for the morning radio interview he had a gallon of water with him to help cleanse the previous night's partying, and he drank it all, a gallon, on the way to the station. When they arrived, he had to be dropped at the back entrance because he didn't have the strength to walk all the way through the front door and down the hall to the studio. Everyone knew that he was on a multi-year party to the death binge, but that seemed to be what he wanted. Or at least what he had resigned himself to.

He had a severe attack of some organ, they were all mad at him I'm sure, while he was working in La Jolla one time. They put him in the hospital and drained something like 60 pounds worth of fluid from his body. Then the next thing he knew, someone was waking him up at seven in the morning at a rehab facility. "Ollie Joe don't wake up at seven in the morning." And he wasn't kidding. He packed up and left. He died one Thanksgiving weekend. I was in Memphis when I heard about it. The body had apparently taken all that Ollie could throw at it. But he died owing a chunk of money to Tom Sobel, one of the biggest agents in the stand-up business. He would have been proud.

I always got along really well with Ollie Joe. Maybe because he never took any of my material. His whole act was either old jokes or stolen. And he was the first one to admit that. But, hey, crowds loved him. Even though he was from Michigan, he had that likeable good old boy slightly out of control persona down to a tee. Crowds across the South especially, just ate him up.

One time Ollie was working Sir Laffs A Lot in Memphis and stayed at the club partying hard with one of the managers until just before sunup. He took off staggering back towards the condo, just about the shittiest condo in the country, by the way. He never made it. Somebody who lived in a house along the one block route from the club woke up to find a 350-pound bearded man passed out in his yard. Being from the South, they were polite enough to wake him and point him towards home. Of course, if they'd been really nice, they'd have let him sleep. Next night, Ollie comes into the club with the biggest grin on his face. He had written a joke. Sure enough, he opened with it. "Had a rough day, guess I woke up on the wrong side of the lawn."

Ollie drank Jack and did lots of cocaine. It got him tossed in jail while working for Rick Hogan or Creative Entertainment or both down in Georgia one time. Just a little drunk and disorderly, but the next night he was in La Grange, Georgia or some such town, and the boss there had to come bail him out and bring him back because they had a big show planned. Ollie was a real draw in Georgia. So, Ollie tells this guy, "I haven't slept, I'm gonna need some coke." Well, that wasn't exactly the guy's forte, but he somehow scrounges up an eighth ounce from somewhere. This was the early eighties, it was every- where. No one knew that it was bad for you, back then.

Ollie was due on stage in front of a packed house any minute by the time the guy returned. Sure enough, Ollie did it all. At once. Just snort and "Let's go." He got on stage and started into his act. It's going great until he starts to feel his nose run. He starts wiping it surrepti- tiously. Now the crowd up front started to let loose a few ooohs and make a few grossed out faces. Ollie kept wiping with his sleeve. The audience was getting more restless. Finally, he looks down and his whole shirt is covered with blood. The audience is beside themselves. Ollie just looks at them and says, "What's the matter? You fuckers never seen anybody party?"

That story appeared in another book written by a non comic that purported to tell all about stand-up comedy. It was a tale of how depraved Ollie and all other comics were. Ollie was never short of faults, but he was also a decent human being, and a fun guy to hang out with if you didn't try to do everything he did. Puritanical preaching from someone who didn't know anything in hell about either him or about comedy notwithstanding.

My great friend Carl got booked in Chicago at Zanie's with him and was more than prepared to hate him on reputation alone. The first night of the week, they get introduced at the club. Ollie sticks his hand out, and Carl just stares at him and says, "I hear you're a big fucking thief." Ollie Joe puts his meaty arm around Carl and says, "Don't worry, little man. You ain't got nothing I need." They hung out the rest of the week. Caught a couple of Cub games and went drinking with Steve Stone, the Cubs announcer. Ollie was not all bad.

. . .

My favorite Ollie Joe Prater story happened in some small to medium sized town. I don't even remember where. I wasn't there for this one, but he showed up for the opening night of a new club. The owner wanted a top club act and Ollie was that. They were so new that the owner hadn't even gotten the comic's lodging all set up yet. So, he planned on Ollie staying at his mom's house.

The hapless owner brought Ollie into the kitchen to meet his poor mom. She had just baked a cake and was finishing putting the icing on, because the next day was her best friend's birthday. She offered nice Mr. Prater something to drink, tea or soda, told him where the clean towels are, and showed him to his room. Ollie showered, went to the club, and surprise, went out drinking afterwards. He came back in the wee hours just hammered. And starved. You guessed it, there's a whole cake on the kitchen table.

Cut to the next morning. The owner's sweet little mother wakes up thinking that she'll go make breakfast for that nice Mr. Prater. She went down stairs, turned on the kitchen light, and there is that same 350-pound man, without a shirt, passed out cold on the floor. The cake was history, a collection of crumbs and icing that stretched across the floor, down the counter and onto Ollie's shirt, which was lying on the floor, too. But you have to hand it to Ollie Joe. He was trying his best to keep things clean. That's why when his shirt got dirty, and he couldn't find another napkin, he used the drapes. Right up until the rod broke. Needless to say, the owner had located other comic's accommodations by that evening.

———

The clubs in New York provided their share of moments over the years. One classic story involves a comic named Ed Bluestone. A wonderfully funny act who was also very dirty. He had a habit of going off on hecklers or even by-standers with a sharp and extremely profane wit. He did some national TV and was notable for his whiny and sing-song delivery that always seemed to go up at the end of sentences.

There were TV executives who loved acts like Ed and Richard Belzer, but were totally limited because the guys were so blue. This was when cable was an infant. One supporter of Ed finally cajoled several of the decision makers at NBC to come to Catch a Rising Star one night and watch Ed Bluestone. He drilled into Ed's skull that the act needed to be clean.

The bosses showed up, and Ed didn't disappoint. He was going through clean material and just killing. Gales of laughter. Then a man in back started to heckle. Ed ignored him. The guy stepped it up. The NBC exec who had put his reputation on the line for Ed just sat there cringing, waiting for the inevitable meltdown.

Finally, Ed lit into the heckler with one witty rejoinder after another. And they were all clean! It was unbelievable. He put the guy in his place without a single curse word, and his tirade was greeted by house applause.

Ed turned to the table of NBC folk, smiled proudly, and said in his predictable cadence, "There. I thought I handled the cocksucker pretty well."

Gilbert Gottfried was another regular at Catch back then. He was an absolutely hysterical genius, but could be a very odd man. Comics would flood the showroom to watch Gilbert. He was a fountain of new material. But then again, he lived with his mother and stayed in his room writing all day.

Ron Robertson booked himself with Gilbert a couple of times. Once he was sound asleep at about four or five in the morning. In San Antonio, I think. Ron awoke with that feeling that someone else was in the room. Sure enough, Gilbert was sitting at the foot of his bed.

"Gilbert, what the hell are you doing?"

A cogent question, I think.

"Ron, when you think about actresses, which ones do you think of?"

"All of them," Ron answered.

"Me, I think of Jane Fonda!" Gilbert exclaimed.

"Fine, now go back to your room."

Comedy was still a relatively small and close-knit community in the 1980s. Most working comics knew each other from the road. If you didn't then you always knew the other guy's best friend.

We used to go to Dangerfield's when we were in New York a few years later. Carl Faulkenberry and Bill Hicks both lived up there in the 80s and were regulars there. Rodney treated us very well when we stopped by, if he was in town. That was another good room to work.

In fact, I should mention that Rodney was always a prince to young comics. He helped out Sam Kinison tremendously. Way back to the very first years of the Workshop, several of us went to one of his concerts at Jones Hall in Houston. Afterwards he welcomed us into his dressing room where he paced back and forth, tugging at a loose bathrobe while he talked about how he didn't like his set.

"You know how it is out there, boys. Sometimes you just want to die."

Dangerfield was not the only name from the pre-comedy club boom who enjoyed interacting with the new guys. Jimmy Pineapple got advice from Catskills super star Henny Youngman one time. Pete Barbutti, one of Johnny Carson's favorite comedy musicians, once told a room full of us "the worst joke to ever tell in front of a woman." And no, I won't repeat it. We adored these guys and loved hearing their stories.

For the Houston comics, it's easy to name a favorite. Slappy

White had been part of a comedy team with Redd Foxx in the 1950s, playing on the segregated Chitlin' Circuit. He was opening act in Vegas for Dinah Washington before most of those casinos were integrated. He had some stories.

The Laff Stop in Houston booked Slappy a couple of times, and the locally based comedians flocked to hang out with him. We howled at his jokes like: 'They put us up in a really nice hotel. Soft bed, and towels so fluffy I can barely get my suitcase shut."

One bon mot from Slappy is still used by the old Workshop comics to this day. In a situation that was expected to be alcohol-free, Slappy said, "I know they don't want us drinking" which he followed up by pulling cold beers out of an ice chest with "...but does anybody here want a sammich?" They are still sammiches to us.

Joe Ancis, one of the icons of stand-up from the 50s, used to hang out at the bar at Dangerfield's. Nobody in the 80's, let alone today, had the slightest idea who he was. But a book about the early days of stand-up comedy was making the rounds. Nice book called The Last Laugh.

One night Tracy Wright and Julia Olivarez were talking about the early days of comedy. It ended up with Julia calling Dangerfield's and talking to Joe Ancis for over half an hour about the old days. It was that easy.

Sometimes I wish I'd made some of those calls. Jimmy Pineapple and I were the two biggest Groucho Marx fans going, having arrived at that determination separately, before we ever met. We both realized that Groucho was the funniest man who ever lived. I stand by that today.

Jimmy, however, got inspired one day back when he was still drinking and such inspirations just popped up out of thin air. At that time in the mid to late 1970s, Jimmy was living in what was called a camp by the locals, a cabin on False River near his hometown of New

Roads, Louisiana. And one afternoon there, he decided to talk to Groucho.

It helps a ton if you know some details about a person. Not surprisingly, the funniest man who ever lived had an unlisted telephone number out in Beverly Hills. So, in those pre-computer and internet days, Jimmy started by calling information in Palm Springs and asking for Susan Marx. That was Harpo's widow. Sure enough, he soon had her on the phone. They talked for quite a while, and by the end of it, Jimmy had Groucho's phone number.

Groucho had suffered a stroke prior to this, if I recall, and wasn't in great shape. He had a younger live-in "girlfriend" who some thought of as a gold-digger. Jimmy was only able to talk with him for a relatively brief time before the woman shooed Groucho away from the phone. But that was more time than I ever spent talking with him.

Not long after, a beautiful 8x10 of Groucho Marx showed up in the mail at Jimmy's camp. It was inscribed "To James, best wishes, Groucho." That priceless piece of history still hangs in a place of honor wherever Jimmy lives.

I did get drunk one night with two old friends of mine and call then Prime Minister Margaret Thatcher. It was with Kathleen and Paul Begala, two high school pals. This was before Paul became an advisor to U.S. Presidents and a national political commentator. But after I'd been his mentor in high school debate and underage beer drinking.

We were at Kathy's apartment and just talking when the usual subject of anti-Christ Ronald Reagan and his trusty sidekick Maggie Thatcher came up. Since it was the middle of the night in the states but already morning in Britain, we decided to call Margaret. But like Jimmy with Groucho, we needed a phone number.

Paul and I got long distance information on the line, back in those days before the internet. It turned out to be an operator in New York with an accent Rosie O'Donnell could envy.

"We need a listing in London, England for a Margaret Thatcher."

"Margaret what?"

"Margaret Thatcher."

"Do you have an address?"

"10 Downing Street."

We could hear the operator writing this down. So, we added more information.

"It might be under her husband, Dennis Thatcher."

Phone etiquette at this time was that the American overseas operator, this undoubtedly lovely New Yorker, had to do the talking when the operator in the other country came on the line. We could hear all of it loud and clear, tough.

"This is the United States operator. I need a listing for a Margaret Thatcher in London at 10 Downing Street."

There was the most beautiful stunned silence on the line as the British operator contemplated just how stupid and uninformed these Americans could really be. So, as we tried not to laugh, our New York ambassadress filled the void.

"It might be under her husband's name, Dennis Thatcher."

We heard a small giggle from across the pond and both busted out laughing. We just couldn't hold it in.

Armed with the number, we let Kathy make the actual call while we listened on the extension. It was a little less formal than calling a huge switchboard like the White House. A woman with that very sexy British accent answered.

"10 Downing."

"I'd like to speak to Margaret Thatcher, please. I'm calling from the United States," Kathy said.

"The Prime Minister is out of town at the moment. May I take a message?"

As Paul and I waved our arms and mouthed "no", she proceeded to leave her name. The call was never returned, as far as I know, but I'm guessing that was the start of FBI files for the three of us.

I know that I risk being accused of nostalgically glossing over the truth with this next statement, but I'll stand by it. Furthermore, I'd expect the vast majority of guys who were there to stand by it, too. I think there was a much greater percentage of nice, easy going and, above all, truly funny people among stand-ups thirty and forty years ago than there are today.

My best guess is that one had to really be drawn to the (for lack of a better phrase) art form of stand-up comedy itself since the possible financial rewards were much smaller. In 1980, the idea of a comic getting a network development package and his or her own show was not yet fathomable. Until *Seinfeld*, a Stand-up comedian's sit-com shots were confined to a one-off as the wacky neighbor. Network executives, without exception, would harrumph and say "Comics can't act."

The biggest chunk of the performers got on stage because they liked telling jokes and getting laughs. We liked writing jokes, honing them to perfection and seeing them blossom into a sure fire thing. Most of us were not dreaming of Broadway or winning an Oscar. We liked dark nightclubs that smelled of stale beer and were filled to capacity with people laughing their asses off. All we wanted was to run off and join the comedy circus.

There were a handful of L.A. acts who were obviously there solely in hopes that a casting agent would stumble into the showroom during their six minutes, actually pay attention, be blown away by their charm and good looks, and ink them to a deal. These people had no act and couldn't write an original joke to save their dog's life. They were actors who saw Stand-up as a potential entrée. The name Jim Carrey leaps to mind. Wonder what ever happened to that dude?

Back about 1980 or 81 when I made my first trip to Hollywood, there were only a relative handful of acts who were getting the regular TV spots. A show called Make Me Laugh was on, featuring several very funny guys who had a nice visual style. Bruce Baum,

Gary Muledeer, Denny Johnston, Vic Dunlop and Bill Kirkenbauer were regulars. The first four were also hellaciously nice guys.

Of those four, I knew Muledeer, champion of the rubber chicken arrow, the least. We hung around because of mutual friends. But you knew immediately with Gary that he was a genuinely funny guy. My favorite thing about him might have been his business cards. He had run across a Baskin-Robins near his place in Studio City and somehow procured boxes of their business cards. He took the time to scratch out each line on the Baskin-Robins cards and replace it with his own information. His name was neatly written in just above 31 flavors.

Gary was also masterful at keeping a straight face while pulling off practical jokes. One of the most subtle involved him and Denny Johnston back in the mid-70s. They had ended up booked on some hotel gig together.

I was never a pot smoker, but apparently it was a much bigger deal to some folks in those post-Vietnam years, namely the police, than it is today. So, after a show, when the two of them went back to Denny's room to smoke a joint, it was with extreme caution. This was a small town, and they sure didn't want to go to jail.

The first thing that occurred to them was that the smoke might go under the door and into the hall. So, they decided to go into the bathroom. They put towels at the bottom of door, sat down on the edge of the bathtub and lit up. After a short while, they heard someone walking down the sidewalk outside the bathroom window. Without saying a word, Denny reached up and turned off the light. He waited a couple of minutes till the footsteps went away, turned it back on, and continued. Gary never said a word.

That is until ten years later. A group of comics was sitting around telling stories about being trashed. All of a sudden Gary, without a trace of a smile, said, "That's nothing, one time in a hotel bathroom, Denny and I smoked some pot so good that I went blind for two minutes."

How cool is that? He waited a full decade between the set-up and the punchline. Of course, the other option was that he actually thought he'd gone blind but was just too cool to mention it. Either way, that is one funny man.

Bruce Baum was another of the Make Me Laugh regulars, and another terrific guy to hang with. One night in Austin we got kicked out of a crowded late night deli before we ever got to eat. Bruce turned to a table of strangers and said in a very loud voice, "I just got back from vacation. Wanna see my slides?" He then executed a perfect hook slide across their polished dining room floor and under someone else's table. We ate someplace else, it was worth the story.

My favorite Bruce Baum story was when he was working in Houston one time, and a group of us went out to play golf at Memorial Park. Bruce was learning the game, so he claimed. His plan was to master one club at a time. He started using only a 3-iron. He played the entire game with that one club. I've seen it with my own eyes on many occasions when he managed to break 130. After a couple of years, he added a 7-iron because, in his words, he wanted to putt better.

This particular round, he had already graduated to the two club "bag". Bruce had put his first shot on the right side of the fairway under a tree. He was hitting off hard pan but had plenty of room to swing. He knocked the ball out, but on his release the 3-iron slipped from his hands and went into the tree. It just hung there about twelve feet or more off the ground. So, Bruce carefully aimed his 7-iron at his three and tossed it up to knock the stuck club loose. It stuck, too. By this time, we were lying on the ground and holding our stomachs with laughter. Bruce smiled, turned to one of us and said, "Silva, let me borrow your four."

Vic Dunlop was also one of the old Make Me Laugh regulars. Vic was a big heavy guy back in those days before a string of health setbacks forced him to lose the weight and start behaving. But through it all he was known for his eyeballs. His regular ones could bulge out and be expressive enough, but Vic wore these fake over-sized eyeballs for his closing bit. He stapled them to special cards and sold them after the shows, too. You'd be with Vic on the road, going out to lunch or a movie, and he'd say, "Okay, but I got to be back by six so I can make some more eyeballs before the show."

It is important to note here that, though it would seem obvious to most thinking folks, there is a pecking order among the comics who are booked at a club during a given week. One of the most important aspects of that being that, if you're staying in a comedy condo, the headliner gets the master bedroom suite and so on down the food chain.

It happened to me once in Atlanta when some snot-nosed kid got there early and unloaded his stuff in the master bedroom with the adjoining bath. He was even wearing a silk bathrobe by the time I got there, like we'd be entertaining some Noel Coward characters forthwith. When I explained that he was in my bedroom, he tried to pull this, I got here first bullshit. After a long day of traveling, I was in no mood to argue. My response was something like: "I'm gonna call the club and get you fired, but first, I think I'm going to kick your ass." He moved.

Well, Vic was booked into a club, and by the time he had arrived at the apartment, the young opener had staked a claim to the master suite. A very similar argument took place, but this time the opener, who turned out to be Billy Elmer, a very good guy who stayed in the business, wasn't budging. He apparently thought that Vic was trying to pull some sort of trick on him, and he refused to be gullible.

The first time that Vic heard Billy taking a shower back there in the master bath, he hauled the television out of the living room and the refrigerator out of the kitchen and hooked both of them up in the other bedroom.

Billy came out to get a snack and watch TV and found empty spaces. He immediately knocked on Vic's locked door. When Vic answered, Elmer saw that he was watching TV and eating things out of the fridge. It took a few minutes, but Senor Dunlop had made his point. He got the master bedroom.

Ron Robertson was on a bill in Oklahoma City one time with Vic headlining and Steve Epstein in the middle. That's a booking that you knew is going to be fun even before you got there.

As it happened, this was a couple of weeks after David Sayh and I had rescued the stray dog I mentioned earlier. She was super sweet. Some kind of schnauzer looking thing. Maybe not what I would have picked at the pound, but a nice little girl who needed a place to stay warm and safe during this Oklahoma winter. So, we adopted her and made her the condo dog. We bought food and gave her the run of the two-story townhouse where we stayed. At the end of the week, we left written instructions for the next comics on how much to feed her and reminded them to give her fresh water.

When Vic, Ron and Eppy checked in, they had an instant pet. It made life on the road even better.

Now out of all the things about Epstein, top of the list has to be that he is great to fuck with. You just can't help but pick on him because you know that you can either a] get him to do something really stupid, b] fool him for at least a little while or c] both. Not surprisingly, Ron and Vic had been jacking with him all week. That includes them busting into his room when he had brought a girl back, only to find her clutching her purse to her chest and completely clothed, including her coat, while Eppy danced at the foot of the bed in his tightie-whities.

So, when the condo dog had an accident on the floor, it smelled like nothing but opportunity to Ron and Vic. So to speak.

One of the boys snuck very quietly upstairs, went into Eppy's room and placed the turd in the middle of the book that Steve had been reading. Possibly due to a deathly fear of bookmarks, Eppy had simply left the book open to his place and laid it on top of a tallboy dresser.

The next morning, Vic and Ron were jerked from their sleep by blood curdling screams from down the hall, screams that would have worked just fine for the horse's head scene in the Godfather. It was Epstein screaming, "The dog shit in my book! God damn it! The dog shit in my book! You sons of bitches, how did you get the dog to stand on the dresser and shit in my book?"

The piece de resistance took place on the last night of the week. Eppy had gone upstairs early while Vic and Ron sat downstairs watching TV into the early morning hours. Suddenly they heard a huge crash come from the little fenced patio outside. They jumped up and pulled open the sliding glass door. There was Epstein in his underwear picking himself up from the snowy concrete.

"Hey, sure. I thought I heard you guys coming into my room to fuck with me, so I jumped out the window."

Chapter Eight

Sure, That's Embarrassing,
But It's a Great Story

L et's face it, if comedians had any true self-respect, they would never have gone into that line of work in the first place. We wanted to have unbridled fun and to be able to drink while we got paid. Getting the fun and gratification of knowing that something you created and delivered made a lot of people laugh was only a bonus.

What that means is that there are a buttload of stories that would be mortifying to normal people, but comics look at them more as "Sure that's embarrassing, but it's a great story." I've never come close to meeting any class of people who were quicker to tell a story at their own expense. In other words, to a comedian, humiliation means very little if you get a joke out it.

. . .

There are so many places to start with this category, and so many of them involve things I did. You know, the old "I'm not proud of it, but..."

One that comes to mind right away is the time that the woman who answered phones at the Workshop called me one afternoon to say that I had a package up there. When I arrived, everyone who worked in the office was quite amused. Some girl had stopped by to drop off a brown grocery sack with my name on it. She said I had been to a hot tub party at her place the night before, along with Andy Huggins and Jimmy Pineapple, and that I had forgotten a few things at her place.

Needless to say, by the time I got there the staff had already opened the bag to find my shirt, underwear, watch and shoes. Hey, I didn't have a bathing suit, okay? I suppose you can do the math to figure out what I wore home.

I will strongly say that all of my circle of friends was always aware of the drinking and driving thing. We loved to imbibe, but we always tried to be careful. None of us ever had a problem with letting the other guy drive or taking cabs. Sometimes that worked to a fault, as in the time that D. C. Malone, a very talented musical comedian and accomplished drinking companion, got back to the hotel where they used to house the comics at the Houston Laff Stop only to figure out the next day that he had car keys but no car.

There were a few clubs that provided an old car for the comics to drive around town. D.C. had taken the big white Ford that the Stop furnished when he went out on a tear after the show. Somewhere along the line, he judged himself too drunk to drive, so he left the thing and started riding with someone else... for the next three hours of partying. The only trouble was that when the other comedians came knocking on his door the next day looking for the car keys, D.C. couldn't recall where he'd left the car that went with them. No clue at all. Hell, D.C. wasn't even sure what audience members he'd gone out partying with. It took them two days before they found it. Hey, Houston has a lot of bars.

That same vehicle was the one that was involved in a fantastic tale about Jerry Dye and Alex Valdez. They finished a show at the Stop and moved the party down the street to a bar named Cecil's which used to be a nice place back in the early 90s. Jerry proceeded to get knee walking, to the point that when they left, he tossed the keys to Alex even though they were only three blocks from the hotel.

It was parallel parked at the curb right in front of the joint. Alex got in and threw it in reverse with his foot on the brake.

"How far to the car behind me?"

"About eight feet," Jerry answered.

Alex backed up a few feet, put it in drive and cut his wheel.

"How far to the one in front of me?"

"About twelve fe... Wait a minute, God damn it! You're blind."

True enough, Alex had been totally blind since he was about eight years old. They took a cab.

Only twice that I can think of have any of my friends gotten in trouble for drinking and driving. Of course, that's twice too many. But considering that through luck, neither one of them managed to drive more than about a hundred yards, it turned out as best as can be expected under the circumstance of poor choice. One of them, in fact didn't even make it out of the parking lot.

There was a bar down the Pacific Coast Highway near where I used to live in Marina del Rey called Brennan's. A California-ized version of an Irish pub. Not being able to find much of anything resembling a real bar anywhere in the general Los Angeles area, a group of us used to drink there.

This was the place where a small group, four maybe, including Andy Huggins, Jimmy Pineapple and Ronnie Kenney, were celebrating St. Patrick's Day one year. They were sitting at a table, minding their own business, swapping stories and spending large amounts of money on Jack Daniel's. The manager, who knew them well, walked over at one point and put his hand on their shoulders. He thanked them profusely for all their business and told them in the most heart-felt manner how much he looked forward to seeing them tomorrow. He explained how it was closing time, and he personally walked them to the door and shook their hands on the way out.

The boys piled into Ron's car and drove back to his apartment in Santa Monica. Along the way, they stopped at Fat Burger to grab some sandwiches. When they got home, Ronnie turned on the TV just in time to see Carson doing his monologue.

That's right. They were loud and obnoxious enough in their conversation to get thrown out of an Irish bar on St Patrick's Day before 10 p.m.

So that's the place that Jimmy and Andy had been drinking one night when they decided to leave. True to form, Jimmy knew he couldn't drive so Andy volunteered. There were two slight problems with that scenario. First, they were in the marked Comedy Store car. Jimmy had a job driving for Mitzi Shore during the day, running errands around town and chauffeuring her bratty middle school kid, Paulie, wherever he wanted to go after school. Yes, driving Paulie Shore over to play with Smokey Robinson's kids, for example.

The second problem was that Andy not only didn't have a current driver's license, he truly didn't know how to drive. He never even made it out of the parking lot for all intents and purposes. As he ran over the curb, he got pulled over immediately. To be fair, Andrew is not the most athletic person I've ever known in his best moments, and as he himself described it, his walking the line test largely resembled the big plastic feet the Arthur Murray Dance School might use to teach the foxtrot.

Andy went to jail, and Jimmy pulled the car back into a parking space and slept it off. The only amusing part of the story was when Andy's roommate, John Pate, got home and played back the answering machine. The first call was Jimmy's voice, crackling, popping, slurring and screaming something about you've got to find Andy. The second call was more of the same. And the third one was Andy saying, "Officer, I got an answering machine. Do I get another call?"

For the record, the answer was no.

A buddy of ours named Don was truly trying to do the right thing. He was working somewhere down in Orange County where he happened to meet a very attractive woman at the show. What's more, she thought Don was cute. No accounting for taste, as they say. They went around the corner to a bar then Don drove them a few blocks to her place. Soon they were in the bedroom where he hoped, not too soon, he would be sleeping soundly.

They were blissfully occupied when Donny vaguely heard the front door to the apartment opening.

"Oh, shit! That's my husband!"

"Husband!?!?!"

Yes, a small detail that the shapely lovely had neglected to mention.

Staggering into action, Don scooped up his clothes from the floor and jumped out the window into the bushes. Behind him he heard the husband screaming a nice string of obscenities as he climbed out the window after him. Clad only in his underwear, Don jumped into his car and pulled out onto the Pacific Coast Highway.... About 200 yards in front of a cop.

You can imagine that as he tried to drive and pull his pants on at the same time, he might have crossed into the other lane.

Let's fast forward to the trial. Don, son of a former cop, no less, was standing before the judge as his honor read from the arrest report.

"Now, sir, it says here that you were leaning against the front of your vehicle wearing nothing but your underwear. Is that true?"

"Yes, your honor. I believe that is true."

"And furthermore, it says that had to lean against the car because you had one pant leg hanging from your ankle."

"Yes, your honor. I think that was the case."

"And it also says that you told the arresting officer: 'I'm sorry I fucked your wife'".

"Well, that could have happened, your honor."

Our buddy Don has been sober more than 30 years.

My good buddy, Carl Faulkenberry has a couple of doozies. After one of the many road trips we booked to allow ourselves to go to baseball Spring Training, we ended up in Charleston, South Carolina. The club, and the three bedroom house they put us up in there, were technically in North Charleston, a suburban military community that managed to bypass all semblance of the wonderful charm of the real city. The major industry was an Air Force base.

That was also the place where I had met a very hot, slinky lady at a little club we sometimes went to downtown. We were talking at the bar, and it turned out that she knew the club and had seen shows there. Eventually I invited her back to the house, explaining that they put us up in North Charleston, at which point she said, "So are you staying in one of the front bedrooms or in the bigger one down where the hall turns?"

One of the coolest things about that club was that on one of the weeknights the huge dance club next door had male dancer night. No men except the dancers were allowed in until 10 p.m. Why is that cool? Because the comedy club was adjoined to the dance club by a common service bar area, and our show ended at 9:40 or so. In other words, when the male strippers were done making 300 drunk women very horny, the comics got a twenty-minute head start on any other guy in town. Come to think of it, I don't think that ever paid off for us once.

Carl's classic moment came the same weekend our buddy, Dick Rea, the Indianapolis sports caster, had come down to hang out. He had driven his new Celica down there because he wanted to see how it rode on a long trip. The three of us had been out someplace, probably a bar and then Waffle House, if I know South Carolina. By the time we pulled up in the driveway, all three of us were in serious need of a place to pee. I mean serious.

Dick put it into park, and he and I bolted from the front seats and raced into the house to the first two bathrooms down the hall. Carl, who was sitting in back, got hung up in the seat belt attached to the passenger front bucket like he was Steve McQueen trying to get to Switzerland. By the time he broke free, we were long since out of sight.

Now here's the embarrassing part, though he was in the driveway of our house, he somehow thought that we had gone to some party that was taking place three houses down and across the street. So, he headed over there.

He strolled past a knot of guys standing around on the driveway drinking beer, never breaking stride, but nodding a hello. He then went into the lower part of the split level and started knocking on what looked like a bathroom door loudly whispering, "Home boy. Home boy." That would have meant me.

Eventually a very frightened looking woman came out of the bathroom, gave Carl the big eye, and Carl went in there to take his turn.

By the time he finished peeing and opened the door, that cadre of guys had formed a muscular semi-circle in the hallway and were menacingly asking just who the hell he was.

Meanwhile in the correct house, Dick and I were feeling worlds better and had begun to realize that our buddy was missing. We walked out front to look for him just in time to see Carl sprint out of someone's garage a quarter block away and bolt past us heading for Lord knows where, yelling, "Get inside!"

For sheer visuals, I'm not sure anyone can top Faulkenberry's embarrassing moment after he had picked up a girl in Corpus Christi, Texas and got her back up to his hotel room.

The High Tide Comedy Club there happened to be in the nicest bayfront hotel in town. Each of the guest rooms had a balcony that afforded a right-angled view of the water. Because we were the comics, when the hotel was full, we got put on the third floor facing the street and above the loading docks. Fewer esthetics for us, you understand.

It was a nice night, and my buddy and the young lady opened the balcony door and began messing around in the romantic salt air breeze.

The next thing Carl knew was that his head was pounding with a hangover which was certainly not being helped by an entire high school band pounding out "The Washington Post March" under his window. Damn that is loud, he thought.

Slowly he began to grasp a few other items: He was now alone. The bright Saturday morning sunshine was hitting him full force. The annual Buccaneer Days parade was passing just under his hotel room. And most importantly, he had passed out in a chair on the balcony with no pants.

Yep, the third-floor vantage point might have cut down on the view for us, but it sure enhanced the view for all those parade watching kids who were wondering "Mommy, what's that man doing?"

There was this comic named Roy who loved to party, and loved chasing any women he could find. I'm talking completely indiscriminate choices of women. At least turned out to not even be a woman. As far as he could see, there was no shame in sight. Roy was about ten or fifteen years older than most of us, but still.

I was working with him in Georgia one week when he started hanging around with this older, as in Medicare-eligible, widow who had been to the show the first night. She was back the next night, and the next. Each time, Roy was laughing it up with her after the show, headed to some fancy watering hole. By night two, we had discovered from the manager that the woman owned a chain of jewelry stores. When we brought it up, he denied any ulterior motive, assuring us that she was just a nice old lady.

We got the last laugh, though. When the other comic and I got back to the condo on Saturday night, there was Roy sitting dejectedly on the couch watching bad TV.

"What's wrong? Your lady friend dump you?"

"Fuck yeah, she did," Roy told us. "I've been sleeping with her all week, and she broke it off. I woulda bet money I was gonna get a Rolex."

Roy had a knack for questionable behavior with unintended hilarious results. He was working the old Comedy Showcase in Houston one time and was hanging out in the green room soon after the first show had begun. He was alone in there when he noticed this perfectly straight line of white powder, nearly twelve inches long, on a table against the wall.

In true Elmer Fudd cartoon fashion, he looked right then looked left, said a small prayer of thanks to the 1980s party gods, and snorted the whole thing.

The next sound the audience heard was a blood-curdling scream from the back of the house. It seems the club had been doing some light repair work that afternoon, including cutting some drywall that they temporarily had stacked in the green room. When they tidied up before the show, there was a nice straight line left. Yes, you guessed it. Roy had just snorted a foot of sheetrock dust.

My favorite Roy story happened before the comics, save one, had ever met him. Roy used to be a firefighter up in the Dallas-Fort Worth Metroplex, and it just so happened that back in the mid-70s, one of our future comedian pals lived in the same giant apartment complex.

The way the story goes is that about 200 young single people were lounging by the gigantic pool one summer afternoon, broiling in suntan oil and trying to look cool. Suddenly a ground floor apartment door flew open, and out came a completely naked Roy, all 6'4" of him, holding a flaming love seat over his head. Not far behind him was a similarly naked woman. Needless to say, it was a visual that stopped everyone poolside in their tracks.

Apparently, Roy and the young lady had paused their rolling around to smoke a joint, and had dropped the lit doobie between the couch cushions. Then they couldn't figure out how to get it out. Soon there was smoldering, then smoke, then actual flames. The best part of his firefighter training that sprung to mind was that there was a huge swimming pool relatively nearby.

So, big, naked Roy jogged out of his apartment with the burning furniture and tossed it into the pool. He stood there for a brief moment eyeballing his handiwork, nodded to himself with satisfaction, then he and the naked woman walked back into his place and shut the door without ever saying a word.

Rob Haney is a very funny comedian from Ohio. I am not certain if there has ever been anyone in history who looked the part of a nice, slightly bumbling white guy from the Midwest more than Rob did. That persona allowed him to get away with things on stage that would have made the more conservative in the audience squirm if they heard it from a New Yorker.

Every comedian has certain bits from other comics that will crack them up every time. Rob had a classic bit of questionable taste in his act that still makes me laugh. Here was this nice young man from Dayton talking about vaginal odor. His question was how a guy goes about politely telling a woman about it.

"You can't just send them flowers and a note, can you?" Rob asked

"Roses are red.

"Violets are blue.

"Flowers smell sweet,

"But your pussy, Whooo!"

One time Rob and I did a week together in Rochester, New York. That was the week that the airlines completely lost my luggage and gave me a whopping $75 to replace my wardrobe. I wore the same discount jeans, sweatshirt and tennis windbreaker for six days.

At some point during that week, I told Rob just how much I loved that joke, and he told me the idea for it oddly came from a real experience that one of his childhood friends shared.

It seems that back during college, this friend of his and a girl he knew had carried on a long time unrealized love thing. They had always been friends, had felt a mutual attraction, but had never gotten together because one or both of them always seemed to be involved with someone else.

Then suddenly one day, out of the clear blue, the guy was at work when he got a random call from his office's front desk. A woman had left him a message. It was the girl from college. She was in that town on business and had looked up her old pal on a lark. They were both single, and since it was to be her last night in town, they planned a late dinner at a nice restaurant.

After dinner and wine, they ended up at the man's apartment. The kissing grew more passionate, clothing came off, and this woman from his past was even more lovely than he recalled. Suddenly, as he was tenderly kissing her smooth belly, he felt this terrible nausea. In mid act, he had to run to the bathroom and throw up.

Imagine you're this woman. A guy you've dreamt of, unrequited, for years just neared your nether regions, and it made him throw up. She started sobbing uncontrollably, and while the poor fellow was puking his guts out, trying his very best to say "Wait", she got dressed and bolted from the apartment in tears.

It seems that the guy had a violent allergy to shellfish, and even though it wasn't in the description on the menu, the sauce on his fish contained enough crab or something to set him off. What a terribly helpless feeling that must have been.

The happy ending is that he did get her to listen the next day long enough to understand and forgive, and hey, his old pal Rob got a great bit out of it.

There is one story, that was much more embarrassing for the non-comic involved. I think I heard Larry Amoros tell this story, but I'm not certain. It could have been someone else, so don't quote me. Larry was one of, if not the first gay comic to come out. And he was very damn funny.

The story is that after a show in some big East Coast city, another gay comic went out and got drunk with a naïve young guy. The next morning the guy wakes up naked in bed with the comedian.

He lies there silent for a while, then sheepishly asks, "Did I commit a homosexual act?"

"No. Peter Allen is a homosexual act. You just took it up the ass."

I worked with Jeff Gerbino in Austin one time. Gerbino was a Minneapolis comic who could pass as a poster child for words like caustic and cynical. My cousin, who was about 15 at the time, rode with me from Houston to Austin so she could visit some friends. She walked up to the hotel room with me until her friend's mom got there to pick her up. Gerbino was loitering in the hallway. It seemed his room was right across the way. The week started with him leering at my little cousin and making wise cracks.

"Cousin, eh? Good to see you, Vance."

So, keep that personality in mind when I say that Jeff Gerbino is exactly the last person I wanted to see when this other thing came down.

Later that week, a group of us from the Comedy Workshop went out to the Cedar Door, a very cool bar which had physically been moved, building and all, from its original location on 12th Street down to a new spot on 1st Street. My good pals, Tom and Alice, were among those present. Tom Robinson I had known since early Houston days at La Carafe. He was one of the group that had been in drama at University of Houston along with the Quaids, Robert Wuhl, both Epsteins, Fred Greenlee, Riley Barber and others. In fact, I had put in the good word for him to get him the job as the club manager in Austin. Alice was the head waitress and his live-in girl-friend. Hanging out with Tom and Alice was always a laid back blast.

They told me later that much hilarity ensued at their table as they watched me make a pitch to score with this overweight, very average looking girl. They swore up and down that I couldn't have been trying any harder if I was hitting on a young Raquel Welch. According to my buddies, who did not once try to stop me, I must add, I was giving it my best shot.

I also have strong memories of comedian Mike Nilsson and me trying to sneak out of an apartment in Syracuse one morning after we had made the same mistake with a couple of chunky roommates. We would have made it, too, if Nilsson hadn't insisted on getting his shoes.

To my everlasting chagrin, I closed the deal that night in Austin, and she and I went back to the hotel, a two block walk away. At some point during the next couple of hours, my eyesight returned. When the fire alarm went off in our high-rise Sheraton, I knew full well who I was with.

Yes, the alarm woke us up, but it was Gerbino pounding on my door yelling, "Hey, Vance. This is for real. There's a fire on a floor below us. You need to come on now."

As I told him to save himself, and that I'd be right behind him as soon as could find my pants, a myriad of ideas flashed through my head. Top of the list being would this woman buy it if I suggested that she stay here while I go downstairs to see if it's a real fire.

Instead, we headed to the evacuation point in the street outside the front lobby. She was wearing only the complimentary hotel robe. Eeesh. Thankfully there was a large number of folks, so I herded her off to one side while constantly praying that Jeff Gerbino wouldn't see us.

No such luck, of course. He sauntered up, opened his mouth to speak, took a look at the semi-clothed woman holding onto my arm and bent over double laughing. Eventually, in my memory, he dropped to his knees and was pounding the pavement.

She got a terribly hurt look on her face for a moment, then she glanced at me.

I shrugged. "Some people just react differently to tragedy."

Romie Angelich was a young lady who came around the Austin Workshop in its very earliest days to do open mic. I thought she was pretty funny right from the start. And as it turned out, she was also super cool.

Once while working on the road, she met Peter Moor, a comedian and actor in Chicago whom she later married. When I'd work up there, I always made it a point to meet up with them and hang out, since they were both just top notch people. We went to Cubs games and hit some cool bars, usually little dives. To show you how cool Romie was, she met and became pals with Cy Young winner Rick

Sutcliffe just while walking across a street in Wrigleyville one time. He would see her months later and say, "Hey. Romie!" She has also had some nice success as a writer. In other words, you couldn't say anything bad about her.

So, it was that after a night on the town, Romie, Pete, another comic and I ended up back at their place for a night cap. As we shared great conversation, I was sitting on a little couch, playing catch with their dog. It was a wonderfully pleasant evening, and Romie went to the kitchen to get us all another beer.

In one of those perfect Stooges moments, the dog ran around the back of the couch, and I turned and fired a tennis ball... right into Romie's eye. I'm talking the high cheese that almost knocked her down.

Now, most people would have been horrified to have just done that to their hostess and friend. And I was. But for some reason, I could only express my emotional turmoil by laughing. Not a little. I mean hysterical guffaws. And each time I would look at her husband's incredulous expression as he wondered why I was laughing uncontrollably even as I kept choking out the words "I'm so sorry", it got worse.

For her part, Romie was holding her eye, cleaning up spilled beer and looking pretty perplexed herself. I was still hooting as, sensing this would be a good time to leave, we walked out the door and to the car.

The saddest part is that though it was one time in my life I can truly say I was totally embarrassed, I still can't explain why I reacted by howling till my sides hurt. No, let me correct that. The saddest part is that as I'm sitting here typing this story, I'm laughing my ass off.

Jef Brannan was a really funny road comic who had a reputation for being one of the biggest partiers doing clubs. Given what everyone else did on the road in the 80s, that's saying something. He was working a week at one of the Charlotte clubs with Dicky Palmer, a hysterical guy from South Georgia/North Florida who was one of the easiest dudes to hang out with in the history of hanging.

Jef had a rent car for the week, likely some non-descript Chrysler or Buick four-door, and they drove it to a nearby bar after the show. Perhaps it was more of a club, really since it shared a parking lot with a mall. After a few drinks, the duo decided they were ready to move on down the road to another stop.

As they were getting into the car, Dicky said to Jef, "Hey, is that your coat in the back seat?"

"No."

"Hmm."

They drove to the next bar. Charlotte had a good local comedy scene by the mid-1980s. Ronnie Bullard, one of those North Carolina comics of note, was ripping it up hustling pool. Life was good. At least until Charlie Viracola, another funny local act, came racing through the door in a total panic.

Apparently, some rental cars shared interchangeable keys. Jef and Dicky had inadvertently stolen a car that looked very similar to theirs. Oh, shit! On top of that, they'd had a couple of drinks beyond the point where they needed to be interacting with legal jeopardy.

After a quick brainstorming session, Charlie drove the hot wheels with Jef and Dicky in it back to the original parking lot. They could see flashing lights from two blocks away. It looked like the final scene in Die Hard. They slowly eased the rental into a parking place at a far corner of the lot, wiped down the steering wheel, and skulked over to their actual rental, which oddly enough, was parked even closer to the door than the one they left in. The escape was safely made, and so was a great road story.

It's a story that I heard from Jef Brannan that I think is the best way to end this chapter since it sums up the sad demise of the rip-roaring

1980s comedy club golden era. Aside from the influx of owners who didn't care about comedy, the replacement of paying customers with free tickets, the erosion of owners' respect for their performers and the egregious cuts in pay for headliners, there was one other thing I have not mentioned until now. Some of the guys who came in to work for these cheap wages were just unfunny. They were boring off stage. As much as anything else, that could make a week drag on like time in a Russian gulag.

Brannan was stuck with a couple of those deadbeats one week, in what town it doesn't really matter. Suffice it to say it used to be a gig comics would look forward to. They were young guys whose acts and lives seemed rather devoid of personality. Neither of them wanted to go out for meals, let alone go drinking after the shows. To make matters totally unbearable, one of them would wake up early and go running. The nerve.

Like many of the true road warriors would have reacted, Jef took this as a personal challenge. He was lucky enough to make friends with a young woman in town, or he may have known her already. In either case, the two of them made sure that they had plenty of fun late at night in the condo. And when I say late at night, I mean the exact time that comedians are expected to be winding down after getting off work sometime between 11 p.m. and 1:30 a.m. As I repeatedly had to tell my first wife, people who get off work at 5 p.m. don't go to bed at 6.

The straight arrow middle act, who may have seen this late night noise as a detriment to his daytime door knocking to discuss the gospel, or whatever like-minded fun sponges do of a morning, had already called the club management to complain that the headliner was having too good a time.

One afternoon late in the week, Jef and his girl, possibly following some day drinking, came home giggling and headed straight to his room. The middle act heard especially exaggerated carnal noises before Jef started calling the guy's name and asking him to come in there.

Finally, undoubtedly after much puritanical eye-rolling, the middle act opened Jef's door to find both Jef and the woman sitting on top of the covers, totally naked except for cardboard Tony the Tiger masks.

The naked woman looked straight at the middle act and said, "He's greeeeaaaaaatttt!"

Chapter Nine

Hell Gigs

O ne of the favorite pastimes for comics is to compare worst gig stories. Never good gig stories. There is a joke that has made the rounds for years that goes like this:

Two comics are talking.

One says, "Hey, did you hear Bill had a spot on the *Tonight Show*. Absolutely killed."

"No, I didn't know anything about that," answers his buddy.

"Yeah, he got a development deal from NBC, too."

"No kidding. News to me."

"I also heard he died a truly horrible death doing a one-nighter in Clarksville, Tennessee," says the first comic.

His buddy grins really big, "Yeah, that's what I hear."

So with that in mind...

. . .

Probably my worst took place on a trip to British Columbia while I was living in Los Angeles. That would make it in November 1983, I think. There was a guy named Neil something who booked a little tour of B.C. You started in Vancouver, then spent the rest of the week hopping small prop planes between resort towns. The key word here was November. Sure, they were lake resorts in the summer, but by November, no lie, over fifty percent of the towns were unemployed. They woke up, put on plaid and drank till they passed out.

My trip started in high fashion. Because I was working in Canada, I had to go to a special Customs area to pick up my work permit. One comic who thought he could bypass this had been deported from Canada, which I never thought was possible. They're the most polite people breathing. Off my flight it turned out that only two people had to go to the work desk- me and Ella Fitzgerald. If I recall, she was working a bigger venue than I was that night. I asked where she was playing, and she told me the Vancouver Civic Centre. She asked about my gig, and I answered Nanook's House of Suds. She turned out to be an incredibly nice lady. She asked questions about me and my career as if she truly cared. Lots of class. Though she did not take me up on my offer to buy her a Molson's after her show.

My ride was there once I got my paperwork, and I made it to the hotel and on to the little bar where I was working. It really didn't look like much more than a neighborhood place with a small dance floor and a game room. The manager assured me there would be a crowd by show time, the show being more precisely...me.

Go figure, he lied. I did 45 minutes to a mostly empty room, though to be fair, occasionally one of the loud drunk guys playing table hockey in the game room would poke his head in and laugh at a joke.

As they say, no harm, no foul. It turned out that I'd had one of the better sets of any of the comics who'd worked there. And the rest of the night I drank courtesy of the hockey playing group who were a bunch of guys about my age.

Once we'd bonded, one of them felt comfortable enough to ask me a personal question.

"Okay, I've always wondered, your American money, how do you tell it apart, eh? I mean, they're all green."

"Well," I said, trying to be diplomatic. "They have different numbers on them."

This Canadian tour might be all right, I was telling myself as I boarded a small plane to fly to Kelowna, B.C. the next morning. It was the kind of aircraft where the pilot personally supervises the boarding so he can ask each passenger how much they weigh.

I never minded flying, but am not too crazy about those tiny planes where you can't Stand-up straight or they balance the passengers and buy gas according to how heavy people are. As my friend Gary Richardson used to say, "Here's my credit card. Fill that motherfucker up!"

A short hop later, I deplaned in a grey slushy "resort" town. The tour had changed the week before when Kamloops, B.C. was dropped and an extra night in Kelowna added. It seems the patron's highlight of the comedy show in Kamloops, and I do mean every single show without fail, was when the crowd dumped a pitcher of beer onto the comic's head from the balcony. Surprised that didn't last.

The venue in Kelowna was a very nice hotel called the Capri. The manager there was a super guy. He had put the tour together. He even had me over to the house for dinner and introduced me to a very pretty young woman who I was told was one of fewer than ten female Mounties in all of Canada at the time. I couldn't tell you if that's true, but she got her man. Insert your own joke here.

The show that night was packed. A couple of hundred people at least. Maybe 70% of them were ringing the dance floor where the mic was set up, itching to see some comedy. The rest stood near the bar partying loudly. From start to finish it was a battle to be heard over the din from those not there for the comedy show. But picking on some of the crowd members was a big hit, and I don't think I had to buy a drink the rest of the night.

I was walking out of the bathroom at one point when I saw this hulking mountain man headed right for me. Jet black hair covered his whole body. He had one of those beards that started just below his eyelashes. Like a sheepdog, he had to part his facial hair to see out. He wore a heavy leather jacket and ripped jeans. His stare was intent and menacing, and I imagined that somewhere beneath the hirsute face was a Clint Eastwood sneer. I glanced for the nearest exit.

The guy swaggered up to me, stuck out his hand, and in a high-pitched North Boston accent said, "I really appreciated the intelligence of your humor. It didn't reach for the lowest common denominator like so many of the acts who seem to be sent up here."

It turned out that this mountain man had dropped out of Harvard his junior year and taken his Harley across Canada. He lived there now doing odd jobs and writing. Pretty cool fellow. And an endorsement for my show that I never quite expected.

The day of the hell gig started off easy enough. I had lunch with the Mountie and hung around the hotel. There truly wasn't much to do there during the winter. Anyway, the hotel manager and his wife, whose names sadly escape me, picked me up in the late afternoon for the drive to Penticton, B.C., the site of that night's show.

Penticton is located at the opposite end of Lake Okanagan from Kelowna. As we drove through the darkness missing the magnificent vistas, my host told me the story of the Canadian version of the Loch Ness Monster, a prehistoric serpent that was apparently good for business.

When that yarn had been spun, there was a lull in the conversation. He filled it.

"Did I mention that this was a strip club, eh?"

"No, you didn't."

"Oh, it's a nice one, though. I think this will really work out. It's much better than the other places we've tried there."

"How many other places have you tried?"

"Aww, I'd say six or seven. But this should be the one. It's got a really nice Italian restaurant."

"How big is Penticton?"

"Oh, it's pretty good size. Must be eleven, twelve thousand."

Well, I was hooked. The first six strip clubs didn't work out. And wouldn't that stripper to townsperson ratio be rather high, by the way. What really made me shudder was that I was going to be forced to find out what passed for Italian food in the wilds of British Columbia. My mother's entire family were spinning in their graves, no doubt.

When we arrived at Slack Alice's, I was given a quick look at the show room. Some skinny person who appeared to be a woman was dancing on stage. The place was packed. Two hundred surly flannel wearing men each slumped over their own individual pitcher of beer were trying to focus on the dancer.

The owner patted my back, "Don't worry. This is the happy hour crowd."

What happened next I still find tough to believe. I had one of the best northern Italian meals I've ever eaten in my life. It was clear that I had found a chef who was in the Royal witness protection service. Everything was perfect. I was starting to think I may have misjudged this joint.

To reach the five foot high stage, you had to walk down a spiral staircase. It was the only way, I was told. So, I walked down an upstairs hallway past a series of small rooms with cots and into the green room. My intro came next.

"We've sent the girls home, eh."

The crowd reacted. "Boo! Piss off!"

"But we have a comedian."

"Boo! Piss off!"

"I can't remember his name, but he's from Los Angeles."

I sauntered down the spiral staircase and down the long runway toward the microphone amid the chorus of half-hearted boos. Boozy boos, I guess you'd call them since I was certain they wanted to be louder.

Just as I got to the mic stand, I heard a loud noise from the back corner of the room. It sounded like something very large pounding on metal. It was a bartender ramming an Eskimo's head into the exit door. Finally, he kicked the door open and tossed the dazed local out into the snow. He then turned to me and gave me a nice Oliver Hardy smile and nod. That must be the equivalent of throwing out the ceremonial first pitch at Slack Alice's, I commented.

I made it about nine minutes into the act. Mixing my material with old jokes. The scene had calmed down, and over half the folks were listening and laughing. The other half were soundly sleeping over their individual pitchers of warm beer.

Suddenly the front door opened, and the Eskimo came in with a pool cue. Small trickle of blood still dripping from his scalp. He took a lunging swing at a passing waiter, missed, but cut a perfect swath through the lower of two trays full of freshly poured beer glasses. Suds and glass exploded in a twenty foot arc. He then picked up a wooden chair and broke it over the waiter's back before he bolted to the street.

I kid you not, the entire bar jumped up and chased him out. It was a live version of Boondock Saints.

I had gone from 200 people to seven people. Six of whom were passed out cold. The seventh one sat at the back bar wearing an entire bear, eating a live salmon on a stick and leering at me with a certain "this river don't go to Aintry" grin.

I busted out laughing. What else was there to do? Then I slinked back up the spiral staircase and made my way past the hooker cubicles, down to the back of the room where the owner stood. He looked at me deadpan for a moment then said, "Rough go, eh? It'll be better next show."

"Next show?! Are you nuts?" I pointed to the bleeding waiter who was struggling to his feet. "There's not going to be a next show."

It turns out that I did a second show. I did lots of impressions and character voices, and it went very well. The policemen even stayed for some of it after they had finished their questioning. They had shown up in the nick of time and rescued the Eskimo from the mob which was poking him with sticks as he hid under a parked car.

Oh yeah, and since I had initially complained about the previously unmentioned second show, they cut my pay. Even though I did the thing anyway. Slimy club owners transcend all national borders.

For a long time, I kept a Slack Alice's t-shirt as a souvenir. Wish I had another one.

As I was first writing this story down over 20 years ago, I did a web search on Slack Alice's just for the heck of it. They were still in business, had an appropriately racy website that included a story about them from a mere two weeks before my search about a drunk patron stabbing two employees. Someone there was quoted as saying, "Although there've been other stabbing incidents, we haven't had one involving an employee in almost 20 years." That would put it about the same time I played there.

Update number two: Slack's burned down around the start of 2012, allegedly the last strip club and potential bordello in Penticton. Shortly after the blaze, a local historian called it "the end of an era". On behalf of comedians everywhere, thank God.

I guess if you work long enough, you're bound to find yourself in some hell gig situations. But I can't help wonder if I've picked up someone else's share, too. For example, no lie, I was booked in Waco the night after David Koresh's compound burned. I did my show while Dan Rather and the CBS news staff had dinner in, and watched my set from, an open balcony over the stage. By the way, Vicki Mabry was kind of cute in person.

Number two on the shit parade, after Penticton, is probably a private show I did for the 75th anniversary of the Volunteer Fire Department of Hannibal, New York, a small town way up by Lake Ontario. Bruno, the owner of Wise Guys in Syracuse, had scored me $500 to run up there on an off night at his club. Sweeten up the week, Brun. Way to go.

The event was booked into some hall in Oswego, the county seat located right on the lake. I'm guessing Hannibal proper didn't have a building big enough to hold the 300 folks they were expecting at this shindig. I mean, one without hay in it.

The first thing you have to do at these private gigs is hunt down the client contact. Sometimes you've met them, sometimes you haven't. This night it took a few minutes before they located the VFD treasurer, a Don Knotts looking guy with a nervous giggle- like he was always tap dancing so the other fireman wouldn't beat the crap out of him.

The minute he showed me the stage, I knew that I was in for a less than stellar evening. The large stage in this ancient cavern of an auditorium was a good solid forty yards away from the closest audient. Forty yards. It was a dance floor for when the band played following my act. Checking out the collection of musty double knit sport coats mingling around the room, I could only imagine the fine rug cutting I was going to miss out on.

Oh, and there was one other detail. There were no stage lights except what the band brought. I would be pretty much in the dark almost half a football field from the front row. Fried pies have had more light on them.

The front row was the real prize of the set up. Since it was the 75th anniversary celebration, they had placed all the original volunteers up front. Or technically, I should say, all the original volunteers and their full time health care professionals. I shit you not, three of these gentlemen were hooked up to IVs. One must have arrived in an ambulance since he was in a bathrobe, semi-reclined in a portable bed with a uniformed nurse next to him. Either that or he was upstate New York's answer to Hugh Hefner.

I talked them into letting me work on the dance floor. The mic cord allowed me to get about fifteen yards closer, though still in the dark. Comedy needs to be intimate. Period. And at this lame ass set-up, that was the best I could do.

Long ago I learned that in some bad situations, you need to start simple. Over the years, I've developed several silly little lines relating to being at these private functions. They break the ice. In Oswego, none of those got even a smile. I tried an old joke. Blank stares. I wondered if this was an English-speaking crowd. I went into several of my regular bits. Nada.

Finally, some voice from the middle of the crowd yelled out, "Ask Larry about his truck."

Not to say no to any idea at this point, I said, "So, Larry, what happened to your truck?"

Huge, thunderous house laughs and applause.

"I wrecked it."

"You wrecked it?" I repeated.

Even bigger house laughs and applause.

Now, I got you, I told myself. I continued the little interview. I do lots of talking to the crowd anyway, so this was a piece of cake. Larry told the very simple story of how he had backed into a tree. I suggested there might have been alcohol involved. He denied it, whereupon I pointed out that it was even sadder that he was that bad a driver sober. The whole time, the place was going crazy. People were pounding their tables and wiping their eyes.

So convinced that I finally had them warmed up, I segued back into material. Total silence, except perhaps for a cricket in one corner of the barn. I tried a big Ronald Reagan bit that I used to do then, filled with impressions from the Andy Griffith Show. Not a noise.

"So, Larry, what else have you done?"

I ended up going about ten minutes long simply because I was

trying to get a good house laugh to leave on. It was a dismal experience. After I was done, all I wanted to do was get my money and get
the hell back to Syracuse. That of course meant that I had to find Don
Knotts again. Before I got the chance to go looking, the head guy of the
department came over with his attractive seventeen year old daughter
in tow. He shook my hand and gave me a transparently fake "good job"
which he immediately followed up with a "they're a tough crowd." He
suggested that I sit in a chair by the exit door while he finds Barney.

For what must have been the longest ten minutes in history, I
fidgeted by the front door while people gave me a variety of looks.
The band was still setting up, so me in a chair was the only other
viewing option. I felt like a zoo animal in time out. Nobody dared
approach me, mind you, except for one. The high school girl kept
staring at me with a dreamy expression. Finally, she came over and
started making small talk. I kept inching away. I mean, this wasn't
Georgia, but they had enough nearby water to do their own version of
Deliverance. Seeing his daughter over there must have done the trick,
cause the two honchos were soon on hand.

While they leaned over the check-in table, a small knot of people
started to gather around us. With more than a dozen pairs of eyes
watching, the treasurer nervously counted out fifties. One at a time.
Fifty. One hundred. One fifty. After each one he'd look up at me like
a cabbie giving change. It was as if he expected me to stop him at
some point and say, "You know, that's enough."

He kept going slower. Finally, after three fifty, he looked up and
said, "We cashed a savings bond for this."

Uh-huh. Keep counting, junior.

I was shaking hands and saying thanks at the instant the last
Grant hit my palm. I fairly sprinted to the door, fired up the rent car
and took off toward the south. It might have been my imagination
about the truckload of guys following me to the city limits, but let's
just say I made damn good time.

Good Stand-ups made a fair amount of money doing private parties. Back in the day, a comedian was almost a standard part of company Christmas celebrations. Sometimes they went swimmingly. Often, they were designed for the act to fail. In spite of telling the party planner the two or three must-have ingredients for a good comedy set, you'd show up to find yourself working a banquet without a good microphone, or on a dark dance floor. I've been introduced with, "The buffet line is now open, and here's your comedian."

Most common among the stacked decks, though, is a miscommunication or bad judgment about material. Your company party contact will tell you that the boss is a good sport and loves to be made fun of. Don't believe them.

Then there is the level of cleanliness. I cannot begin to list the number of times I or a comic I know was told "PG is fine" only to discover that the crowd is mostly 80-year Church of Christ deacons. Such was the situation that Jack Mayberry, Steve Moore, Steve Epstein, Ron Robertson and I found when we did a mega-show for fifteen or so high school bands at Astroworld.

They had us on a stage at one end of a very large outdoor pavilion, and yes, many famous people have said, "There is no comedy outdoors." The marching bands from around Texas and the Southwest were grouped together with their band chaperones. We sensed trouble from the get go. Since we were each doing an equal amount of time, we arranged the order in what we thought would be the cleanest acts first. It turns out that it totally did not matter.

One of Jack Mayberry's most famous bits at the time was about the pointlessness of people cursing at you from their car in traffic. Nobody can understand what you're saying. Nobody can read lips while driving. His punchline was that there was one word everyone could tell. "Asshole. That guy just called me an asshole. Asshole goes through glass."

As soon as he dared utter the word, the sound of scraping chairs drowned out the rest of the joke. Pucker-faced chaperones were yelling, "Hillsboro, up" 'West Valley, up."

Moore dared utter the word breast, not relating to fried chicken, and four Christian schools plodded out. Surely many of those kids could have used the instruction.

When an entire marching band is being ordered from a room, it's not one or two kids leaving. It's a solid hundred of them getting up and walking out en masse. Marching loudly from the audience like storm troopers with impeccable foot timing.

Every one of us managed to walk at least one band, and it became a game back at the comic's table to predict which bit was going to get those chairs a-scraping. By the time "closer" By the end, there was exactly one band left under a pavilion designed to hold 2000 people. Our work there was done.

The last thing you want to do after a hell gig is have any further contact with the people who hired you, but sometimes it can't be helped. Like that getting paid thing, for example. There are no guarantees that every set is going to be stellar. And some of these private gigs can be set up where it's damn near impossible.

I had a Christmas party a year or two ago where the woman hiring me insisted on meeting beforehand to discuss things. My time is valuable, at least to me, so I tried to just go over things on the phone like I do with every single other one of the thousands of clients I have had over the years. But she was offering lunch near my house at an Italian restaurant I liked, so what the hell.

We had totally finished the discussion before we ordered. She asked if I wanted a hand-held mic or a clip on. I told her hand held with a cord that allowed me to move a little. She asked if there was anything else.

"Not really," I said. "Just make sure that they can see me and hear me."

That's a very standard answer for me.

These folks were paying top dollar for me and renting an entire side of the then brand new Reliant Stadium suite level for the party venue. We're talking some bucks here.

Sure enough, when I showed up there on the night of the gig, they had a podium with a fixed mic. And it was set up behind a four-foot wide column that blocked over half the crowd from seeing me. That is not my fault. I ended up doing the show next to the DJ's system with a two-foot long mic cord. I had to hold it in my right hand the whole time.

That one turned out okay. Dozens of nice people took the time to thank me for a funny job well done. But the woman who was coordinating it all treated me like I had let her down by not using the podium behind the pillar. Sometimes these parties are the biggest thing that the secretary does all year. So, they can get a little high strung. Or half in the bag.

As my pal, Buck Stonebroke, always said, "What they don't pay us, they're just gonna blow on balloons."

Gary Bun Richardson had the ultimate in no escape hell gigs. Back in the very early days of the Comedy Workshop, when the oil economy was kicking ass in Houston, he scored a corporate gig in Puerto Rico. It was one of the first such private shows any of us had ever gotten. The deal was that they would fly Gary and his wife down to San Juan, he does the show, and they pay him plus let him hang out for a few days on their dime. I've had a few of those, and they are sweet. My entire band got four days in Cancun when we were doing a half hour show for a corporate sales force retreat.

The trouble for Gary started when he found out that half of the audience had Spanish as a first language. Gary spoke no Spanish at all. Secondly, they had the room set up with Gary at a podium. Comics hate podiums. You can't do a good stand-up routine behind a podium any more than you could standing behind a dresser. No furniture, please. Anyway, the podium was bad enough, but the head table was up on a high riser behind it. In other words, the bosses of the company would be sitting behind Gary looking down on the audience. It was playing the Mayday parade with the Politburo looking over your shoulder.

After he saw the room, they led him into a broom closet behind the stage. That's where he'd be waiting and dreading the challenging set up of the room. To make sure he was comfortable, they'd iced down some beer for him in there. Enjoy yourself and they'll come get you when they're ready.

The beer was very thoughtful, but the fact that there was no access to a restroom was not. Gary himself didn't figure this out until it became an issue, of course. So, to add to the discomforting situation, he had to take a whiz in a mop bucket. I'll bet those hotel floors had a special sparkle to them the next day.

Finally, after some 45 minutes of waiting in the closet, they brought him out and introduced him. Now, Bun was never a particularly clean act, and that was even more true in those early days. But the guy who hired him was adamant that the jokes would not be a problem. You can see this coming, right?

Gary hit the podium and started his act. The audience, or at least the English speaking portion of it, was trying to laugh at the routines. However, over Gary's shoulder sat all the company bosses, and they were frowning at the risqué humor. Consequently, the crowd followed suit. They clammed up on him. And since Bun, like all of us then, was not overly used to rough sets outside the friendly confines of the home club, it turned into one big ass downward spiral of alleged comedy.

Okay, so the set was bad enough. But the kicker was that Gary and his wife were now stuck at this island resort for another three days, running up a tab on the company which hired him. At first, he said that he tried to keep a low profile and shrink away from the glares he was getting from any one of the few hundred folks who'd watched him bite it. But as the silent treatment kept up, Gary rallied. By the end of the trip, he was hanging at the pool bar damn near

24/7, making sure to order up another big rum punch whenever he spotted one of the top dogs.

———

Everyone with a screen has seen Will Smith slapping Chris Rock over a joke at the Academy Awards. Any road comedian from the 1980s could happily share a tale of some drunk coming on stage and the act having to defend themselves with a microphone stand or whatever else was at hand. There are plenty of those stories. All the Hollywood media needed to do was ask us.

In the late 1970s, Fred Greenlee, who had learned his stage craft in a popular local band, found a music venue willing to do a comedy night. It was a busy club in a small strip center on Chimney Rock Road in southwest Houston. The name of the place was Kawliga's, and it was a country & western place that did the proverbial land office business. Shows there were known to be rowdy, but if you could handle that, they loved you.

Houston at the time was in the midst of a huge oil boom. Seemingly the entire Midwest had moved to the Gulf Coast for employment. That was especially true of those fleeing auto industry contraction. I had a stupid joke in my act then: "Why are people from Michigan like hemorrhoids? If they come down then go back up, they're not too bad, but if they come down and stay, they're a real pain in the ass."

It was the kind of thing guaranteed to win over a crowd like Kawliga's.

When I told it that night, there was a huge house laugh. It also prompted a giant of a man in the center of the audience to Stand-up. He was about six foot six. He was wearing tight Wrangler jeans, a pearl snap shirt, a tooled belt with a dinner plate-sized silver buckle, and a grey felt cowboy hat with one of those feather bands that looked like an owl's ass had exploded on your forehead.

"I'm from Michigan," he said loudly.

I didn't miss a beat.

"That would explain why you got taken so badly at the country & western store."

The place exploded with laughter. As I was savoring the response, looking around the room, I saw something out of the corner of my eye coming straight at my head from behind the bright stage lights. Purely out of reflex, I ducked slightly to the left and stuck up my right hand. I caught an empty longneck bottle, head high, on the fly.

The audience made a variety of loud noises, most of them wildly approving. The big dude stared at me for about two seconds and quietly sat down. In his drunken mind, he was figuring that anyone who could pull off that kind of ninja shit was not to be trifled with. I was physically shaking for the next couple of minutes, but I finished my set. I probably had another 20 minutes to go. No one in management ever said word one to the bottle thrower, let alone toss him out. I finished to a giant ovation, and when I walked off the stage toward the bar, the club boss was standing at the bottom of the steps to shake my hand.

"Man, when you caught that bottle! That's the funniest damn thing I ever saw."

Ten years went by, and I was working the club in Corpus Christi. Good show. It was stage with a drink rail where the people closest to you were right next to the stage, using a sort of shelf as their table. To my right was an older man and two younger women. When the show was over, he motioned me over and bought me a drink to sit down with them.

We were visiting nicely, shooting the shit, when he said, "You know, you said you're from Houston. I used to own a nightclub there."

"Oh, really? What was it?"

"Little place on Chimney Rock called Kawliga's."

I couldn't believe it. Part of me clicked back to that near injury, and I started excitedly, and maybe a tad indignantly, recounting the story. Before I was halfway through, he cut me off.

"Wait, that was you? Holy shit! When you caught that bottle, that was the funniest damn thing I ever saw."

Bill Silva, Bill Hicks, and Ron Shock had a doozy of a time at the worst of several rooms that came and went in Lake Charles, Louisiana. It was the two-nighter I mentioned earlier where the club owner threatened to kill Steve Moore. It was a survival gig. You just wanted to get your money and go.

I should mention two things here. First, that a good comedian's idea of a bad set is probably quite different than an audience's idea of how things went. We are our own worst critics. What you think is very entertaining might have been a rank disappointment for us. I remember coming off stage at the Annex one night in the early 80s. I had four or five new jokes that I was trying out. Only one of them made me happy. The others had laid there like soggy pudding. As I was getting a drink at the bar, shaking my head to myself, a new regular, Conrad Lawrence, came up to me and said, "Great set." I instinctively answered, "Fuck you." Then I saw his face. What I took to be a snarky comment on the failure of my new jokes had been a genuine compliment from someone who didn't know my act inside and out. I apologized profusely. He and I became lifelong friends, and nineteen-year old me gained an important lesson.

The second thing is that bad sets, like every other difficulty in life, is where you learn the most. A killer show is incredible fun. I would come off stage with notably more energy than I took onto it. Everything the audience gives you comes right inside of you until you're floating on clouds after a killer show. But as far as learning anything, a good set doesn't teach you jack shit. It's those bad sets where you figure out what jokes you can count on. My example used to be that the laughs were like playing a piano with no sustain pedal. They don't carry from one to another. You have to work hard for each one. The jokes that get laughs every time in those situations, well, those are your best jokes.

So, there is something to be gained from an off night. Then there are the gigs where you only want your money and to see the joint in your rearview mirror. The only thing those offer is a story. Ron Shock told a wonderfully embellished version of this story, but this is the straight dope.

Hicks, Silva and Shock arrived at the Lake Charles room to find it standing room only. Packed to the rafters. They could also tell from the outset that these people were already shit-faced, rowdy and out of control. And the show didn't start for another half hour. They were booked to do equal time, and Silva and Shock started jockeying to go on first. They were both savvy enough to know that things were likely only going to get worse. Finally, they tossed a coin, and Silva became the opening act and emcee. As they were standing in the back of the room, stewing in dread, Bill asked a waitress if it was always like this. She smiled knowingly, lifted her untucked shirt to show a hand gun, and said, "Don't worry, honey, I got you covered."

Silva stepped onto the spot in the middle of the dance floor that qualified as a stage and started his act. The decibel level dropped from jet plane to turbo prop. Much of it was directed at him. He managed to make it about 20 minutes out of his expected 30 before he brought up Ron Shock. Shock lasted nine. With his slow, story-telling delivery, that may have been only one bit. Silva brought up Hicks. Nothing was working. The noise and heckling continued unabated. Some of the yelling had devolved into simple shouts of "Shut up and get off the stage."

Even Hicks' put downs of the hecklers were not winning people over. About 10 or 12 minutes into his act, an enormous Cajun stood up and walked out onto the dance floor. He was the size of man who can cause his own eclipse. Stopping about three feet from Bill, he said, "Show's over." Then he pulled out a knife that probably looked to Bill like a samurai sword, picked up the mic cord, kinked it double, and cut it in two. Without another word, he returned to his table. The first night show was over.

The manager explained to the three comics that this was one of their regulars, and as long as he didn't start breaking furniture, they left him alone.

All the next day, the guys were trepidatious about that night's repeat performance. To make things better, Shock and Hicks decided to drop acid. Since Bill Silva had never tried it, they gave him only half a tab. While Silva recalls little effect, he remembers Hicks enjoying the most vivid Ms. Pac-man games of his life in the hotel lobby. He was animated and talking to the game to the point that it totally unnerved the random dude he was playing.

Finally, it was show time. Fearing the worst, the three chemically altered comedians stepped inside the big club. It was virtually empty. Whereas the first night had well more than 200 screaming, surly patrons, the second night offered up about 20 quiet people scattered about the lounge. Doing their full time was no issue, though getting laughs certainly was.

Knowing how the first night had gone, all three of them had checked out of their hotel rooms before the show. They were not going to stay in Lake Charles any longer than necessary. The plan was to drive the two and half hours home immediately after the final joke. The trouble with that plan reared its head as soon as Silva went to collect their pay. The booking agent had promised the club owner a joke contest after the second show, and the owner was damned well expecting for that to happen. So, Silva, who had driven Hicks, was obliged to stay and run this thing.

The jokes were exactly what was expected. Vile, racist and terribly unfunny. And they kept coming. After a solid half hour of this fresh hell, Silva walked over to the other two guys and said, 'Okay. The guy finally gave me all our money. I'm going to bring up this next guy, and you both meet me by that back exit door. We're going to run to our cars and get the fuck out of here."

That's exactly what they did. A little drug induced paranoia was making them look over their shoulders the whole way. They ran across the gravel lot, reached their vehicles expecting the club door to bust open and people to come pouring out after them any moment a la some Charlie Daniels song. That's when they found that Shock had locked his keys inside his truck. It took 20 minutes to get the door open with one of Silva's coat hangers, but they did it. If they learned any valuable lesson, it may have been don't play Lake Charles.

———

Sometimes just what happened in getting to gigs should have been a tip off. T. Sean Shannon and I were headed to Abilene, Texas one time. We'd just passed through the Metroplex when we started to look for a place to pee. Suddenly, just as we both had to go really badly, the landscape had turned completely desolate. Finally, as the bladder threat level turned to red, we spotted a state rest area. I whipped the car into a spot, and we hustled to urinals for what was likely to be a lengthy spell. No sooner did we feel that first relief than a loud voice said, "Howdy. How are y'all?"

On the other side of a three-foot tall partition from T. Sean was a big, middle-aged dude dropping a deuce. There was no stall, just this tiny wall. Apparently, the state architects thought openness was the safe way to go. Presumably, these were the same architects who designed Texas prison cells.

This guy sitting on the hopper was just as comfortable with the arrangement as could be.

'Where y'all coming from?"

Loud straining noises.

We had both been waiting to pee for 70 miles. We weren't going anywhere quickly. Fortunately, we finished before he did, so we never got to exchange numbers.

.   .   .

Steve Epstein had car trouble in Arkansas one time and had to catch a ride to a one-nighter in the back of a fish truck. He showed up in Russellville or some similar town reeking like day old amberjack. The show must go on. If there were any visually impaired folks in the crowd, they probably wondered why their headliner didn't come with slaw and hush puppies.

All of us who worked the road during those years, especially as more unscrupulous club owners jumped on the comedy bandwagon at the end of the decade, experienced trouble getting paid after a gig. Comics very quickly learned to never take a check, always cash your check back at the bar. There are several stories of guys and gals leaving a gig with over $100 in ones. Some even got paid in rolls of quarters.

Leaving with a check was just asking for it, particularly at one-nighters where the stakes for the club owner was relatively low. Some clubs got reputations quickly. Other clubs were known to cash checks for comedians they liked while other acts found things to be more of a crap shoot. There was a fantastic room in downtown Beaumont, Texas for a time, but as the owner developed more and more of a cocaine habit, getting your check cashed grew more dicey. Eventually, the owner just vanished.

Ron Crick and I were the first comics booked into the San Antonio Comedy Club after my good pal Bruno Schirippa sold the place and moved to Syracuse. The new owner loved comedy. He also loved strip clubs. In fact, he owned a couple of them. When Ron and I arrived, one of the first things we learned was his disappointment that the Texas Alcoholic Beverage Commission has turned down his application to change the name of the joint to Big Pecker's Comedy Club. He had a logo with a giant rooster and everything.

After the first night's show, he took Ron and I out to a fancy restaurant for a late meal. As we were about halfway through, a friend of his showed up and invited himself to join us. The dude was

Colombian, and it quickly became evident through his conversation that there was a good chance this "importer with his own plane" may have cartel connections. He started buying us bottle after bottle of Dom Perignon. He offered to take us flying, which we very, very politely declined. We were focused on not pissing off the South American guy in the shiny suit jacket.

When it came time to get paid, the new owner pled ignorance of the ins and outs of the comedy business. He said he had deposited all his cash after the big Saturday shows and didn't have enough on hand to pay both of us. So, we each left with about two-thirds in cash and a check for an additional $500 or so. Monday was a bank holiday, or we would have worked this out before leaving town. By Tuesday, I was on the East Coast someplace when I heard from my bank that the check had bounced. Phone calls to the club were not being returned.

Lucky for me, I had an old school friend in San Antonio, and she had had a baby less than two years earlier. She was happy to help. On Wednesday, when the club opened, she showed up in person to pick up my money per the messages I'd been leaving. The owner tried to tell her it was already taken care of, but she told him she had spoken to me only 15 minutes before. Then he brusquely told her, "it would be a while." She said she could wait. She sat down in the office and turned whatever switch there is on a one and a half year old. Instantly, the little guy was bouncing off the walls, squealing with fun, and scraping paperwork off desks and shelves onto the floor. After less than eight minutes with the toddler terrorist, my friend walked out with my $500 in cash.

Weeklong gigs were very used to handing out advances to comics early in the week. If you were out on the road for weeks at a time, you paid your bills by mail with checks or money orders. There was no online bill pay in the 1980s, and very few nationally available banks. After you mailed off your money, you were frequently tap city. I had trouble with Stanford & Sons in Kansas City from day one because they refused to give advances even after a performer had completed multiple shows for them. Consequently, I only worked there one or two times. There were too many better choices, like the Funny Bones chain.

Another pitfall was that the sketchier of the clubs could close without warning. It was the nightclub business, after all. These places were not exactly Sears Roebuck. Okay, poor example. By my count at one time, I had been part of the opening week lineup at seven comedy venues and the closing week lineup at six. The worst were the gigs like Bill Silva and Steve McGrew had in Tallahassee one time when, after several positive reassurance phone calls to booking agents, they showed up to find the club locked and bereft of furniture and booze. Silva called me to break the news since I was the following week's headliner.

My favorite club-closing week, and the closing story of this volume of Stand-up stories, was at Clyde's Comedy Corner's third location in New Orleans.

Clyde had three clubs in New Orleans, and they got successively worse. The first was in the French Quarter at Conti and Dauphine. The building now houses a great all-night bar and restaurant, and I'm not certain what is in the upstairs space where that little comedy room was. Those crowds were great. When that deal went sour, Clyde moved out to Fat City, suburban Jefferson Parish's attempt at getting a bigger share of the tourism dollars. It had a heyday in the 70s. Clyde's room was there in the 80s.

His third place was right on Bourbon Street, directly across from the Royal Sonesta Hotel. As party locations went, there was likely none better in all of America. But comedy clubs require a certain attention span. Unlike daiquiris to go, bare tits and vomit, a good attention span is in short supply on Bourbon Street.

Like most of the Vieux Carre bars, the third Clyde's was in what had been built as a fancy Creole home in the early 19th century. It oozed charm from every damp, mildewy pore. As you entered the front door, there was a long bar on your left. Through doors on your right was the comedy showroom with the stage in front and big windows open to the chaos of Bourbon Street to the audience's backs. If you walked straight through the bar, you entered a courtyard which was where a live band played until 3 a.m.

Immediately to the left of Clyde's was a female impersonator bar named the Gunga Din. It was a boozy drag show. We never forgot it was there since they had a loud barker on the sidewalk out front. Throughout your comedy show, you heard this guy shouting, "Check it out. Check it out. Boys who want to be girls. Girls who want to be boys." Just to add one crowning piece, there was an air conditioner that never stopped blowing on the back of the comedian's head. By the end of you set, your hair had become a visor.

The first signs that the club was in trouble came when my co-headliner and I, my great friend Lance Montalto, noticed that Clyde himself was no place to be seen. Certain things in New Orleans have been a little mobbed up for more than a century, so it was not completely surprising to see a couple of goodfellas coming around every night asking about the owner and saying they needed the cigarette machine money. Lance, a native of Metairie, had previously introduced me a couple of times to a guy he grew up with named Moose. It was the way things were.

Lance and I did see Clyde one night. As the last show was ending, he came by to take us drinking. That was always fun. While we were walking through the Quarter, Clyde looked at us and said, "What size shoes y'all wear? I got some good ones that fell off a boat at the dock."

One other thing to mention about Clyde's III was the accommodations. Lance, being local, was staying at his place. I stayed upstairs at the club. I had a bedroom that was straight out of To Catch a Thief. It was this gorgeous and humongous room, overlooking Bourbon with its private balcony. Totally furnished in lavish antiques, even if they were a tad down at the heels. The downside is that the bathroom was outside on a part of the building overlooking the open air patio. You walked along an open second floor gallery to get to it, and when you did, you damn sure wore shoes. Originally, it had been part of the slave quarters, perhaps. And it was debatable whether it had been cleaned since Emancipation.

One night that week, I came back to the club after a night of post-show drinking to find a six-year-old kid asleep in my bedroom. One of the club waitresses didn't have a sitter, so she dumped him in my room. It took me half an hour to find his mom so I could get him out of there and go to sleep. That sleep was fleeting, by the way. The band in the courtyard stopped at 3 a.m. And just when you had some good REM going about 6 a.m., the garbage trucks rumbled under the front balcony to clean Bourbon Street.

In spite of all these things, though, we had a grand time. New Orleans never disappoints, and Lance Montalto, with whom I'd worked many times, was one of my favorite guys to hang out with. We had booked this week together just for that reason.

The shows were up and down, and there were two every night. One night, time for the second show rolled around, and there was no one in the room. As in zero people. The manager looked at Lance and said, "Okay. Time to go up." Lance said no, that he was not doing a set for an empty room.

"You want to get paid, you get your ass on stage. They'll see you through the window and come in."

Lance did 45 minutes to me and the bartender, just shooting the breeze and telling old tales. As he was closing, two guys walked in. They were Bob and Chris who were in town from Minneapolis for a convention. I did about half an hour of just talking to them. With less than 15 to go on the night, another six people came in. I still remember Bob and Chris.

Between shows on Saturday night, the manager called Lance and me aside. He told us that the club was closing for good that night after the band finished their last set. We were slated to work Sunday, and he was going to pay us for that, but there would be no Sunday show. I used the bar phone to call Southwest Airlines and change my flight to one on Sunday morning, then I booked with the French Quarter airport shuttle to pick me up about 8 a.m. The manager thanked us, and told me to just lock the front door to the club with my key, then drop it back through the mail slot. Lance and I did the final show at Clyde's then partook of the Quarter for a few more hours.

The next morning, way too early, my little travel alarm went off. I rushed through one last scary shower, grabbed my suitcase and headed downstairs through the quiet, odiferous nightclub. As I went to push open the ancient front door, I could barely get it to budge. A homeless dude was passed out cold and wedged tight against it. My shuttle would be there in less than five minutes. I pushed and shoved, and finally moved him enough so I could squeeze through the door. Then I had one final flash of brilliance. I stepped back behind the front bar and grabbed a full, unopened bottle of bourbon. As I stepped over him, I handed it to this guy on the stoop. He looked up at me, groggy. The morning surely had me backlit to the point that his story might have included something about the angel that descended to give him a fifth of Jim Beam. Then I caught my shuttle and headed for the next gig.

Also by Mike Vance

Oilers Anonymous

The PC Cowboys Book

Houston's Sporting Life: 1900 -1950

Houston Baseball: The Early Years, 1861 – 1961

Murder & Mayhem in Houston (with John Nova Lomax)

Zeke Gets Glasses: A Jungleburgh Children's Book (with John Swasey)

Mud & Money: A Timeline of Houston History

Getting Away With Bloody Murder

Brenham

About the Author

Mike Vance started as a professional comedian at age 17 in Houston and Austin and made his living on stage for over 25 years. Along the way he headlined shows in almost every state and five countries, was featured on multiple national television shows, sold scripts for TV, opened for dozens of top music acts and had his own shows on Houston-area radio and TV. Vance also accepted thousands of free drinks in highly sketchy and suitably dark bars, taverns and lounges.

Learn more than you want to know at:
www.mikevancewriter.com

www.ingramcontent.com/pod-product-compliance
Lightning Source LLC
Chambersburg PA
CBHW020441130626
46549CB00001B/244